THE DESIRE FOR METAPHYSICS:
SELECTED PAPERS ON KARL JASPERS

RONNY MIRON

THE DESIRE FOR METAPHYSICS: SELECTED PAPERS ON KARL JASPERS

RONNY MIRON

First published in 2014 in Champaign, Illinois, USA
by Common Ground Publishing LLC
as part of the New Directions in the Humanities book series

Copyright © Ronny Miron 2014

All rights reserved. Apart from fair dealing for the purposes of study, research, criticism or review as permitted under the applicable copyright legislation, no part of this book may be reproduced by any process without written permission from the publisher.

Library of Congress Cataloging-in-Publication Data

Miron, Ronny.
 The desire for metaphysics : selected papers on Karl Jaspers / Ronny Miron.
  pages cm
 Includes bibliographical references.
 ISBN 978-1-61229-372-1 (pbk : alk. paper) -- ISBN 978-1-61229-373-8 (pdf)
 1. Jaspers, Karl, 1883-1969. 2. Metaphysics. I. Title.

B3279.J34M57 2014
193--dc23

2013045320

Cover image credit: "Desire for Metaphysics", Lukáš Weishäupl

To Ben A. Hecht

Table of Contents

Foreword xii

The Desire for Metaphysics 1
    Introduction 1
    The Object of the Desire for Metaphysics 7
    The Articles 11
    Afterword 15

The Covenant between Philosophy and Revelation: David Hartman's Thought in the View of Karl Jaspers' Philosophy 17
    Two Perceptions of Deity: Ontological and Universal 18
    Two Types of Believers: Prophet and Sage 22
    The Perception of Judaism as a Covenant 31

From Psychiatry to Philosophy: The Concept of Self in Karl Jaspers 51
    Mental Illness as an Expression of the Individual's World 52
    Selfhood in "Worldviews" 56
    Selfhood in the Face of Immanence 58
    The "Foundering" of Selfhood and the Transition to the Discussion of Being and Transcendence 67
    Conclusion 71
    References 72

From Opposition to Reciprocity: Karl Jaspers on Science, Philosophy, and What Lies between Them 77
    Abstract 77
    Foreword 77
    Discussion 81
    Summary 93

Transcendence and Dissatisfaction in Jaspers' Idea of the Self 95
    Abstract 95
    Preface 95
    The Self of the Mentally Ill Person 98
    The Self of the Normal Person 104
    The Worldly Self 106
    Summary 112

Towards Reality: The Development of the Philosophical Attitude to Reality in The thought of Karl Jaspers 114
    The Internal Reality of the Subjective Being 116
    The Reality in Which Existence Takes Place 119
    Reality as Being 124
    Reality as a 'Cipher' of Transcendence 128
    Conclusion 132

Was Jaspers Really a Kantian? **133**
    Preface 133
    Jaspers' Elementary Understanding: Kant as Transcendental Idealist 136
    Objectivity and Subjectivity: Jaspers versus Kant 137
    The Explicit Departure: Jaspers' Answer to Kant 141
    Postscript and Summary 149
    Jaspers' books and their abbreviations in this article 152
    Secondary literature 153

Between Freedom and Necessity: The Conception of Guilt in Jaspers' Thought **156**
    The Question of Guilt from the Viewpoint of Selfhood 157
    Guilt from the Collective's Viewpoint 164
    Guilt from a Metaphysical Viewpoint 173
    Conclusion 180

The Guilt Which We Are: An Ontological Approach to Jaspers' Idea of Guilt **184**
    Abstract 184
    Introduction 184
    The Experience of Individual Guilt 187
    The Collective Stage—The Group's Guilt 192
    The Metaphysical Stage—Guilt as a "Boundary Situation" 197
    Conclusion 202
    References 203

Original Publications **205**

Acknowledgements

First and foremost, I wish to thank Common Ground Publishing and the series editor, Ian Nelk, for publishing this book and for their professional accompaniment during its production. I also thank the editors of the periodicals where the articles were first published for their generous consent to have the articles republished in this collection. My special thanks to Ruth Ludlam for her devoted and meticulous work in translating the articles that were originally published in Hebrew. The translation of the articles was financed by the Center for Continental Thought and Culture at Bar-Ilan University, and I would like to thank the manager of the Center's fund, Prof. Avi Sagi, for supporting the financing of the translation and encouraging the publication of this collection. My thanks go to the readers of my research on Karl Jaspers over the years, whose comments and questions stimulated my thought and opened it to new horizons. Among these, I would particularly like to thank my students Dr. Miri Mahabad-Kuttin, Hila Naot, and Irit Wolfgor for reading the introduction and making useful comments. Last but not least, my children, Shira, Noa, Itamar, and Neta, who were born and raised into my studies of the desire for metaphysics. I would like to thank the Czech artist, Lukáš Weishäupl, for his generosity in allowing me to use his artwork on the cover. In honor of this collection's publication, he has named the piece "Desire for Metaphysics".

Foreword

Karl Jaspers (1883-1969), an existentialist contemporary with Heidegger, was born in Oldenburg, a German town near the North Sea, where his ancestors had lived for generations. At the age of eighteen he started studying law at Heidelberg University. As part of his studies he was required to take a few lectures in philosophy, which he reported disappointed him because they lacked instructions for self-development. Jaspers was not interested in his law studies, either, since they seemed to him to involve quibbling that was not based on a real perception of reality. Following these experiences, he decided to study medicine and specialize in psychiatry. He completed these studies in 1909. After finishing his studies, he started publishing his first works in psychiatry, until he decided to leave this field too. In 1916 he was appointed professor of psychology at Heidelberg, and in 1920 he was appointed professor of philosophy thanks to his publications, particularly *Psychology of Worldviews* (1919), despite never having studied philosophy formally. His great philosophical works were written during the 1930s, but in 1938 the Nazi regime banned the publication of his works due to his opinions and his loyalty to his Jewish wife, Gertrud Mayer. Jaspers remained in Germany during World War II, but his books were only published after it was over. He returned to teaching in Heidelberg after the American forces occupied the city, but in 1948 he accepted the invitation of Basel University in Switzerland to serve as professor of philosophy there, and left Germany.

This collection examines the desire for metaphysics through a study of various thematic issues discussed in his philosophy or arising from contact with it. The introduction, written especially for this collection, presents a personal view of the fundamental nature of the desire for metaphysics and notes Jaspers' unique contribution to its elucidation. The articles appearing in this collection have been published in various places, and three were originally written in Hebrew and have been translated especially for this collection. The gathering of the various articles here is intended to present the reader with a systematic, in-depth treatment of a wide range of philosophical issues that are not usually discussed in relation to each other. The collection of articles introduces the reader to the great diversity and wealth of Jaspers' writings, along with fundamental structures and principles that recur in handling the different issues. The articles also conduct a critical dialogue with the research literature written about Jaspers in his time and up to the present. I hope that at a time of renewed interest in continental philosophy, this collection will enrich the approaches of researchers of existentialist thought and stimulate the thought of intellectuals, even those not familiar with Jaspers' work and the extensive research literature written about it, which has not all been translated from the original German.

The Desire for Metaphysics

Introduction

The Desire for Metaphysics

What is the desire for metaphysics? Is it like all desires, possessing the typical intentional structure of a subject direction at an object and thus exceeding his own boundaries? A positive answer to this question would lead to a tautology, since both the desire and the metaphysics denote the person's going beyond himself. However, I argue that the desire for metaphysics is greater than any other human desire, due to the nature of metaphysics itself, thanks to which it cannot simply be considered as an object like all other objects. Metaphysics is not just a worldview regarding the things that exist in the world, human nature, the essence of human consciousness, and so on. The metaphysics to which human desire is directed denotes the *evident and all-embracing consciousness regarding the existence of an abstract and profound level in the world of existing things that is simultaneously responsible for their formation and for the fact that they can never be exhausted by their manifestations*. This insight is established as consciousness of the dimension of a gap or distance between things themselves and the human experience as such, which can never unravel the complexity permeating the world of existing things.

Indeed, a certain dimension of desire is present in every intentional relationship, meaning wherever subjects aim at objects existing beyond them. In the end, subjects are not indifferent to the objects of their reference, and the special interest a person shows in something will not usually be formed as an object for him. But in the desire for metaphysics the two components of the reference are the most inclusive possible—at the subject's pole, the individual's selfhood is positioned as a complex beyond which stands Being with its immanent and transcendent aspects. Placing selfhood and Being side by side in the desire for metaphysics creates increased seething and tension that threatened to devour the intentional structure precisely because the inclusiveness of the participating subject and object is inherent to viewing them as a whole. Therefore, the positive actualization of the desire for metaphysics constantly involves a special effort to maintain within it the basic duality at the basis of human experience as such. Only to the extent that this duality is preserved can the subject experiencing it stand in face of the abstract layer permeating the world of existing things. The desire for metaphysics denotes the effort to maintain the distance separating the subject and the object involved in it; an effort thanks to which it is possible to experience the gap dwelling in the world of existing things between the things themselves and their manifestations.

In no place in Karl Jaspers' monumental work does the desire for metaphysics appear as an explicit theme for philosophical clarification. Nor do his writings teach us directly about the moment of its birth, the conditions for its formation, or the nature of the world that enables it. However, I believe that his work is not merely one of the grandest philosophical products of the desire for metaphysics, but that a deep study of his writings can grant the reader a lesson and training in nurturing this desire. First and foremost, Jaspers presents a wide and general view of the self and of Being, as in his retrospective essay "Regarding My Philosophy":

The philosophical mediation is an execution (*Vollzug*) where I reach the *experience* and *myself*. This is no calm thought where I deal with an object without involvement. Philosophizing is the praxis of my own thinking source in which the full essence of the human is realized in individual people. The peak of the praxis is the internal action (*inneres Handeln*) through which I become what I am. [This action] is *making the experience discoverable (Offerbarwerden), it is the activity of the selfhood (Selbstein) which is at the same time experienced as passivity in the turning into the given to yourself* (*Sichgeschenktwerden*) (Report, 341).[1]

The two described components of the philosophical practice, self and Being, are the forces that ignite the desire for metaphysics and at the same time the contents that fills it. This means that this desire on the one hand permeates the occurrence in which the individual constitutes his selfhood and is given to himself, and on the other hand the various manifestations of Being itself joint together, thus making it discoverable. The self-formation of the individual and the discovery of Being are simultaneous in the desire for metaphysics, which lives within the network of relations between them, and they are preserved distinctly in the same work that has an internal and external dimension. The self is constituted as a reality in the world and as an internal experience within the individual's consciousness and experience and Being becomes discoverable and manifests in the world. However, since the desire and the metaphysics themselves denote the mode of going beyond, this desire can never be identified with the self striving to experience it, nor with the object entity to which it is directed. It is actually the dense network of relations woven between the self and the entity in the desire for metaphysics that frustrates its idealistic identification with selfhood on the one hand and the constituting of a realistic position that would lead selfhood behind on the other hand. As a result, it is impossible to achieve an inclusive understanding of the desire for metaphysics. Jaspers states that certainty in philosophy is a process of confessing that the entire essence of the person participates in it, and that "Philosophical thought must always spring from free

---

[1] For further discussion, see his two essays in Karl Jaspers, *Rechenschaft und Ausblick, Reden und Aufsätze*. Munich: Piper, 1958: "Uber meine Philosophie" (1941), pp. 333-365; "Mein Weg zur Philosophie" (1951), pp. 323-332.

creation. Every man must accomplish it for himself'.[2] Therefore, the desire for metaphysics will always remain connected to the self experiencing it, and will never be capable of granting him a general and objective ontological picture of the Being to which it is directed.

However, the self and the Being are not givens of the desire for metaphysics. Real desire does not assume a safe ground and has no guarantees. Indeed, such desire is an expression of recognition that what exists is not satisfying and cannot grant guarantees, and thus it strives to lead to what is beyond it and has yet to reveal itself as a reality. Moreover, more than any other desire, the desire for metaphysics denoted by its very nature the ultimate power and daring in exceeding givenness as such. But since the realization of the metaphysical desire involves maintaining the distance between subject and object and containing the tension threatening to devour the subject through the object of its desire, the self and the world involved in the experience of the desire for metaphysics are at the same time the achievement of this desire itself. In other words, the desire for metaphysics takes the self and the world far beyond their givenness. As a result, the self-experiences an internal reality that permeates the layers of phenomenal givenness of things and the world itself is revealed as containing an abstraction thanks to which it cannot be exhausted in its manifestations. But since the desire for metaphysics depends upon maintaining the gap between the subject and the object, its positive realization also denotes the struggle for the framework of givenness itself. The fate of the desire for metaphysics is to discover that it does not possess even the same original givenness that was experienced as unsatisfying and as something that must therefore be exceeded.

The paradox revealed in the experience of metaphysics is that the human experience to go beyond reveals that what exists is not itself a guaranteed reality. This paradox fundamentally and extensively undermines human existence as such. But the desire for metaphysics is not exhausted by this. The deeper it goes, the more it leads to the first transpiring as the last, meaning that the givenness of the subject and of Being, which were first considered as the starting point for the desire for metaphysics are revealed as its achievement. This does not mean that the primary givenness denotes a self-deception by the object, or that the manifestation of Being is illusory. Indeed, these continue to exist, but the desire to metaphysics yearns to constitute a different self and world, and the individual's involvement in them revealed them to be transcendent.

The Subject Desiring Metaphysics

One of the most important milestones in Jaspers' mature philosophy of Existenz, enfolding the central aspects of the human experience of the desire for metaphysics, is phrased in the perception of Existenz as the "origin" (*ursprung*):

> Existenz is not a target, but an *origin* of the philosophizing within which it perceives itself. The origin is not the beginning through which I [could] always search for additional beginnings… but *Being as a*

---

[2] Karl Jaspers, *Way to Wisdom: An Introduction to Philosophy*, trans. Ralph Manheim, New Haven, 1951, 9.

freedom I transcend to *when I reach myself in the philosophizing from the unknown*. The helplessness of the philosophizing that is in doubt regarding the origin is the expression of the helplessness of my selfhood, the reality of the philosophizing at the beginning of the impetus of this selfhood. The *perception* of Existenz is thus a premise of the philosophizing that at first is only a desire for significance and for a support, which is turned away empty-handed to the doubt and despair regarding its very possibility and then appears as unperceived certainty that clarifies itself in the philosophizing. (Jaspers, Ph2, 5).

First and foremost, the perception of Existenz as the origin positions the status of the self as a firm foundation of the desire for metaphysics. Existenz as the origin denotes a potent subjectivity that can be understood through observing it without the enforcing mediation of external factors (Ph1, 1). Existenz's freedom denotes its ability to rise above the external factual givenness that surrounds it in favor of realizing its possibilities, whose meaning and value are determined only in relation to itself,[3] to the extent that Existenz is described as living "in the world, without becoming knowable (*erkennbar*) as a world-Being (*Weltsein*)" (Ph1, 17).[4] On this point, Jaspers responds to the ultimate wish of the modern human being,

---

[3] I have discussed the meaning of freedom in Jaspers' philosophy in my monograph, Ronny Miron, *Karl Jaspers: From Selfhood to Being*, Value Inquiry Book Series, Rodopi, 2012, 91-94 (henceforth: Miron, Monograph, 2012). On this issue, see also: Elisabeth Young-Bruehl, *Freedom and Karl Jaspers' Philosophy*. New Haven: Yale University Press, 1981, 64-65, 105-106. On the concepts of freedom in existentialist thought, see James Collins, *The Existentialists*. Chicago: H. Regnery, 1968, 77-87; Austin Marsden Farrer, *The Freedom of the Will*. New York: Charles Scribner's Sons, 1960; Hazel Estella Barnes, *An Existentialist Ethics*. New York: Alfred Knopf, 1967; Reymond Diane Barsoum, *Existentialism and the Philosophical Tradition*. New Jersey: Prentice Hall, 1991, 440-504; Robert Goodwin Olson, *An Introduction to Existentialism*. New York: Dover, 1962, 100-161.

[4] In this context, see Bollnow's interpretation of Jaspers' existentialist philosophy as an attempt to reveal man's "last internal core". See Otto Friedrich Bollnow, *Existenzphilosophie*. Stuttgart: W. Kohlhammer, [1942] 1960, 24. In his opinion, Jaspers' opposition to the ontologization of the concept of Existenz through consciousness, and to the very possibility of its being understood as a category capable of objective knowledge, was intended to protest the dimension of freedom that serves as a central pillar in the perception of Existenz. See Bollnow, "Existenzerhellung und philosophische Anthropologie," *Bulletin für deutsche Philosophie*, 12:2, (1938–1939), 136-139. Bollnow criticizes this approach as extreme relativism (Bollnow, 1942, 11), from which arises an image of the person as internality lacking content (Bollnow, 1942, 27). A similar position was also expressed by Lenz (Joseph Lenz, *Der moderne deutsche und französische Existentialismus*. Trier: Paulinus Verlag, 1951, 32, 14 ff.) and Imle (F. Imle, "Jaspers als Existenzphilosoph," *Philosophisches Jahrbuch der Görresgesellschaft*, 50, (1937), 78–93, 86). William Barrett stressed the irrational dimension in existentialist philosophy, in particular regarding the philosophy of Heidegger, Kierkegaard, Nietzsche, and Sartre (his references to Jaspers were marginal). This interpretation exists in the literature written about Jaspers, with various levels of decisiveness. See: Kurt Salamun, *Karl Jaspers*. Munich: Beck, 1985, 46; Fritz Heinemann, *Existenzphilosophie—lebendig oder tot?* Stuttgart: Kohlhammer, 1954, 30 ff.; Fritz-Joachim Von Rinteln, *Beyond Existentialism*. London: Allen and Unwin, 1961, 204.

which he phrases as follows: "to be from the source of my selfhood" (Ph2, 6), and in this spirit he described it in the first person as follows: "I hear the demand from my possible Existenz: to detach myself from the world into which I am in danger of sinking" (Ph2, 3). This means that realizing the modern person's wish to be his own source involves "pulling Existenz from the world's reality", as a result of which it "does not understand the other, but itself" (Ph2, 6). Existenz's crystallization as a solipsistic being is thus an inseparable part of its perception as the origin.[5] In other words, precisely because Existenz is examined in relation to itself, it is considered its own origin.

The solipsism of the Existenz is even increased with the removal of the aspects of the beginning and the target from the idea of the origin—the beginning is rejected as it embodies an expectation for a future process of change that Existenz will undergo, making it not holistic, while its understanding as a target is removed as it contradicts its being seen as primary. The perception of Existenz as an origin grants it a deliberately pivotal position, in which its self-totatlization as a present and real being occurs. The pivotal position is typical of the attempt of the metaphysical desire. Just as Existenz "finds itself in the world" (Ph1, 17), so too does the person desiring metaphysics find himself already in his desiring, without knowing the origin that caused it. This means that a given situation can ignite the desire for metaphysics, i.e., serve as its beginning, but it can have "other beginnings", different from the one from which this experience grew. This is the freedom equivalent to what Jaspers called the "not knowledge" that surrounds the being of Existenz, without which the desire for metaphysics would be derived from a particular state of affairs, and thus enforce itself upon those who encounter it. At the same time, the person desiring metaphysics does not know and cannot know the end of his desire, which is not aimed at a target, but which occurs as a distinctly primary experience.

Thus the desire for metaphysics transpires as responding to Jaspers' basic demand for "unconditionality" (*Unbedingtheit*) originating in the person's innermost internality (*Way*, 57) and is experienced as certainty and self-affirmation (Ph2, 344).[6] The unconditional is characterized as "its own purpose" (*Selbstzweck*), meaning an activity whose purpose is exhausted in itself (Ph2, 293), or alternatively "precedes any aim, it is that which determines all aims. Accordingly it is not an object of our will but its source" (*Way*, 55). So the unconditional as such expressed our freedom, despite the fact that choosing the unconditional in itself expresses our recognition that there is no other way but it (*Way*, 56-57). This is in contrast to conditioned actions, meaning those that serve defined purposes that exist beyond them (*Zweckhandeln*) (Ph2, 294). The statement that the unconditional as a source of activity is not a matter of consciousness and cannot be represented as "existence in the world" continues

---

[5] The solipsistic perception of the self-played a very significant role in Jaspers' philosophy of Existenz, which sought to exhaust the discussion of the individual within the boundaries of his self-consciousness. However, this perception encountered serious difficulties, as a result of which Jaspers expanded the scope of the discussion of it to include relations to various modes of otherness—other Existenzes, objectivity, Being, and transcendence. This issue is extensively discussed in my book. See Miron, Monograph, 2012, 103-168

[6] Jaspers discussed the issue of unconditionality extensively, and linked it with many aspects of his thought. See Ph2, 292-335.

the idea that Existenz cannot be known as a world being (Ph1, 17). Jaspers explains that when a person can state the reasons and targets of his action he remains within the area of the finite, and the conditional and real historical occurrences do not prove it when he exists beyond them, but only when the person lives from something that cannot be explained by object knowledge does he live from the unconditional (*Way*, 57). The aspect of the central location of the desire for metaphysics also echoes in the context of the discussion of the unconditional as an experience the person reaches in a non-gradual way (*Way*, 58) but as an original becoming "existing in every new moment through recurrent rebirth from the source" (*Way*, 58), and as such it encounters the primacy of the Existenz experiencing the desire for metaphysics.

However, there exists in the perception of Existenz as an origin another aspect dealing with the experience of helplessness, doubt, and despair, which also partake of the experience of desire for metaphysics. Jaspers details this point elsewhere, when he explains: "Placing itself absolutely on itself alone is for Existenz *the truth of its independence of the reality of time, but this turns into despair for it*. It [Existenz] knows itself that by standing completely by itself it must sink into a vacuum" (Ph3, 4). Thus it transpires that the in same self-totalization that occurs in the perception of Existenz as an origin lacking both beginning and end it is also gnawed by doubt and despair that threaten to turn away the freedom that enabled the self-search for meaning and value in existence. We can use Jaspers' words to phrase the problem as follows: "Whatever can be objectivized from within me is valid due to my empirical individuality", but as the elucidation of Existenz "*achieves space for me, but does not shape a substance through the expressions of a Being capable of objective perception*" (Ph2, 5). This means that placing Existenz as the pivot did not lead it to achieve a view of objectivity or the reality that as such transcend the boundaries of its individuality.

Against this background, Jaspers coined the unique philosophical concept "foundering" (*Scheitern*), marking a radical turning point in the development of his philosophy that moved the balance of the philosophizing from selfhood to Being.[7] This turning point is based on a new self-consciousness of Existenz, phrased as follows: "where I myself really exist, I do not exist only as myself" (Ph3, 220), and in greater detail later:

> True selfhood cannot hold itself through itself alone; it can lead to its absence for itself [but] it wants not to force itself to this. As it succeeds

---

[7] In my monograph about Jaspers, the central argument is that his thought developed around two axes of philosophizing: one directed at selfhood and dominant in his early writings, but then the discussion of Being occupied Jaspers' focus, though without completely pushing aside his early interest in selfhood. The "foundering" is discussed in this book as a milestone in shifting the balance from selfhood to Being. See Miron, Monograph, 2012, 174-184. Other interpreters of Jaspers have discussed his concept of foundering. See in particular: Johannes Thyssen, "The Concept of 'Foundering' in Jaspers' Philosophy." In *The Philosophy of Karl Jaspers*. Paul Arthur Schilpp (ed.). New York: Tudor, 1957, pp. 297–335. See also: Salamun, 64-67, 146-158; Von Rinteln, 240 ff.; Johannes Pfeiffer, *Existenzphilosophie, Eine Einführung in Heidegger und Jaspers*. Leipzig: Felix Meiner, 1952, 41 ff.

at this more decisively, so are better clarified the boundaries where it is denied. It becomes poised for its other, [for] transcendence, when it founders in the wish for its self-sufficiency. ...*I can founder as me myself...* (Ph3, 221).

The statement that "foundering is the ultimate" (Ph3, 220), and in characterizing the unconditional in terms of eternity (*Way*, 58) contains the positive facet embodied in them, dealing with their relation to transcendence. Thus, just as Existenz's experience of the unconditional is "a leap into another dimension" (*Way*, 57) and transpires as directed at transcendence (*Psychology*, 308), or alternatively "itself feels transcendence" (Ph2, 361), so it learns from its experience of the "foundering":

> To the extent that it should become real out of itself, i*t realizes that what is coming toward it fills it*. It is no longer itself if it happens that it remains outside; it faces itself, as if it is given to itself. *It verifies its possibility only if it knows itself as based on transcendence* (Ph3, 4).

The two unique experiences of the "unconditional" and the "foundering", the insufficiency of existential freedom leads to constituting a relation toward transcendence. Thus the idea of the "origin", at the basis of the explication of the subject's disposition in desiring metaphysics receives its full meaning: Existenz is the "origin", being a necessary primordiality like no other. The strong anchor of the desire for metaphysics in selfhood cannot enable a generalization about it, but it will always remain embedded in the individuality and freedom of those who have experienced it. However, the "origin" is only worthy of its name if it is of something that is not it itself. The desire for metaphysics therefore assumes the achievement of self-consciousness that has matured to understand its own lack of sufficiency, and as a result wishes to constitute an unconditional relation to transcendence as a reality above and beyond it.

The Object of the Desire for Metaphysics

The transformation occurring in a selfhood that experiences the desire for metaphysics breaches the boundaries of self-consciousness and introduces into its world the presence of difference and otherness. The consciousness of the world's reality and objectivity in general, which Jaspers termed "not I" (*Nichtich*) (Ph1, 63), was part of the process of crystallizing the existential selfhood. However, the desire for metaphysics cannot rely on negative, unqualified relations. Against the background of the despair and dissatisfaction with an existence exhausted within the selfhood's boundaries of reference, Jaspers follows Existenz's motion of transcending toward the reality beyond it. Jaspers' important discovery in this context is that the entry of transcendence into the space of existential consciousness changes the fundamental understanding of immanent reality as a whole, and it is now perceived as a symbol or cipher (*Chiffre*) of transcendence.[8]

---

[8] Jaspers usually used the terms symbol and cipher as synonyms. On this see also: Aloys Klein, *Glaube und Mythos, Eine kritische, religionsphilosophisch–theologische*

This understanding leaves behind it everything that "must be doubted before the *uninterpretable foundering*" in favor of an observation dealing with "the origin of the life that experiences... Being" (Ph3, 234). This means that the perception of immanence as a cipher of transcendence realizes the constructive possibility arising from the foundering; it makes the insufficiency, the doubt, and the despair encountered by the existential consciousness into a starting point for a more encompassing and complete understanding of the entity and of transcendence. Jaspers explains the necessity of the perception of immanence as a cipher of transcendence as follows:

> Everything must be capable of becoming a cipher. Were there no cipher [there would be] no transcendence....
>
> *The very fact that there is a cipher is identical for us to there being transcendence* ... Instead of asking why there is existence, the question appears before us why there is a cipher. The answer to this: for existential consciousness it is the only form where transcendence rises, *a sign that for Existenz transcendence is hidden, but had not disappeared* (Ph3, 205-206).[9]

The perception of immanence as a cipher of transcendence has two main implications—one relating to the Existenz experiencing the desire for metaphysics and the other to the object of this desire, meaning Being and transcendence.

From Existenz's viewpoint, the perception of immanence as a cipher of transcendence causes an immanentization of transcendence, or alternatively indicates the presence of transcendence within the human world. On the one hand, Existenz's handling of the gap between experiencing the presence of a transcendent dimension in existence and the limitations of representing this presence in consciousness is responsible for transcendence not sinking into complete otherness for Existenz (Ph3, 137), but accompanying and enriching human existence in the world. On the other hand, transcendence's otherness serves as a barrier to Existenz's sinking into the despair and emptiness that are the products of the tautological space of self-reference. In this respect, the existential experience of constituting a relation to transcendence fortifies the existence of

---

Untersuchung des Mythos–Begriffs bei Karl Jaspers. Munich: F. Schöningh, 1973, 88; Thyssen, 31; Kurt Hoffman, "The Basic Concept of Jaspers' Philosophy." In *The Philosophy of Karl Jaspers*. Paul Arthur Schilpp (ed.). New York: Tudor, 1957, 95–113, 108. The concept of cipher first appears in Jaspers' *Psychology of Worldviews*, and is later discussed in other works, and even had a whole essay devoted to it, *Chiffren der Transzendenz*. Munich: Piper, 1970. But the most extensive in-depth treatment is found it the third volume of the *Philosophy* trilogy (*Metaphysics*). See in particular: Ph3, 129-167.

[9] The issue of the necessity of the concept of cipher in Jaspers' metaphysical position has been discussed by several of his interpreters. Thyssen explains cipher as "semi-objectivity" that enables transcendence to be represented in finite reality without turning it into an object. See Thyssen, 309. Tilliette interpreted the ciphers as "sparking lights" for Existenz, thanks to which it does not revolve around itself. Xavier Tilliette, "Sinn, Wert und Grenze der Chiffernlehre: Reflexionen über die Metaphysik von Karl Jaspers." In *Karl Jaspers in der Diskussion*. Hans Saner, (ed.). Munich: Piper, 1973, 390–404, 391.

Existenz as such, as Jaspers states explicitly: "only immanent transcendence grants Existenz weight in the world" (Ph1, 35).

It is important to clarify that the perception of immanence as a cipher of transcendence does not involve denying the world's reality or even denying the empirical dimensions of reality, which continue to exist alongside it. As Jaspers put it, the perception of ciphers "is simultaneously *across the width of any objectivity*" (Ph3, 137), or "taking place simultaneously across the width of reality in a depth dimension where man must sink himself but from which he cannot emerge without immediately losing it [this reality] completely" (Ph3, 146). The deep affirmation of the world embodied in the perception of immanence as a cipher does not enable the ciphers to be viewed as internality that has no external expression in reality.[10] Indeed, the ciphers "exist in […] like an unignorable depth" (Ph3, 170) in the person's historical reality.[11] In this spirit, Jaspers states that "ciphers are not new objects, but newly filled objects" (*Truth*, 1043), and elsewhere adds:

> Sinking into symbols is not a mythical sinking, which in the lack of objectivity of transcendence enters a union lacking any objects and thus is also uncommunicative. In fact, *in hearing the language of the symbol, the phenomenon of transcendence is articulated for Existenz in the split existing between object and subject* in the medium of clear consciousness (Ph3, 16).

These words indicate that precisely the immanence appearing in consciousness as a split between object and subject, to which the action of consciousness grants clarity and a degree of communicativeness, has weight in Existenz's acquaintance with transcendence.[12] The necessity of consciousness for the perception of immanence as a cipher of transcendence affirms that metaphysical consciousness is anchored in the same immanence accessible to the tools of consciousness. Unlike what Jaspers called "mythical sinking", the action of consciousness occurs according to clear rules that are not derived from the needs or personality of the owner of the consciousness. Indeed, the viewpoint seeing immanence as a cipher of transcendence exceeds the boundaries of objectivity and grants it, as we have seen, a much wider meaning than the one formal knowledge gave it. As he put it, "The clarification through the symbol walks a path that is above objectivity" (Ph3, 17). However, Jaspers stressed that he same consciousness with which the person "participates impersonally," enabling "unambiguous understanding," is the basis of our trust in order, and "dread takes us if its collapse appears real" (Ph3, 184). It seems that consciousness, as an extra-existential anchor of Being, stabilizes the desire for metaphysics by tying it to the immanent reality in which the person lives and acts. Accordingly, the metaphysical consciousness that is constituted

---

[10] See also: Ph3, 139, 151.

[11] Compare: *Truth*, 1032, 1034.

[12] Olson proposed a different interpretation of the perception of ciphers, stating that the source of the split between objectivity and subjectivity does not necessarily stem from objective consciousness but from an ontological element, i.e., the unified being of transcendence. See: Alan M. Olson, *Transcendence and Hermeneutics: An Interpretation of the Philosophy of Karl Jaspers*. The Hague and Boston: M. Nijhoff, 1979, 122 ff.

through this desire does not involve a "total transformation" of existence and of the consciousness in which the person lives, but its entire depth stems from its ability to expose hidden aspects embodied in immanence, as both reality and consciousness.[13]

At the same time, the perception of immanence as a cipher of transcendence recognizes the presence of a fundamental and unconditional metaphysical dimension in the reality in which people live and act, thanks to which the understanding of immanent reality cannot be exhausted within the boundaries of human consciousness alone. In other words, the perception of immanence as a cipher of transcendence indicates the metaphysical surplus of immanence over its manifestations. In this framework, objectivity is perceived as "contain[ing] the transcendence revealed in it" (*Truth*, 1031-1032), or alternatively is termed "metaphysical objectivity" (Ph2, 341). Jaspers characterizes reality in this context as "unity without identity" (Ph3, 138)—the unity refers to the ontological level where the ciphers bear the meaning of transcendence, while the epistemological facet is expressed in the absence of identity or the gap between consciousness of the reality restricted to the immanent dimensions and reality itself, containing a transcendent presence.[14] The definition of the cipher as "Being which *transcendence* brings to presence without [it] having to turn Being into object-Being" and as "a gift from the source of Being" (Ph3, 137) assumes that transcendence itself possesses a force that drives it to be revealed in immanence. The transcendence embodied in reality in the shape of ciphers (Ph3, 230) appears as an element *a priori* to immanence, thanks to which immanence becomes a medium in which transcendence is revealed. The argument that "in penetrating the world we fall into transcendence" (*Truth*, 1031) as a "prototype" (*Truth*, 1038, 1044) reflects the perception of transcendence as prior in presence to immanence. In this respect, the very presence of transcendence does not depend on being revealed through the viewpoint of the cipher. Indeed, the perception of ciphers appears as "responding" to the already existing reality of transcendence (*Truth*, 1044). In other words, the cipher's viewpoint is *a posteriori*, and is enabled only thanks to the *a priori* presence of transcendence, characterized by the power that motivates it to realize its immanence. Even if the ciphers of transcendence "exist directly only for those for whom it is transparent" (Ph3, 146), i.e., for the Existenz directed at them, transcendence itself "is not in a relation." (ibid.), meaning it is not a speculative matter and is not dependent upon the constituting of consciousness towards them.

---

[13] For further discussion, see Waardenburg's argument that the creation of symbols always passes through some existential crisis, and thanks to the symbolic expression internal and external reality become tolerable. See Jacques Waardenburg, "Symbolic Aspects of Myth." In *Myth, Symbol, and Reality*. Alan M. Olson (ed.). Notre Dame: University of Notre Dame Press, 1980, 41–68, 45 ff.

[14] The origin of the metaphysical perception of immanence is in the criticism of the positivistic worldview that identified Being with the empirical and the finite (Ph3, 137-140). This criticism was apparent already in Jaspers' early writings dealing with psychopathology. Jaspers called the positivism that dominated this science "prejudice" and "mythologies of the brain" (*Psychopathology*, 8). See also Miron, Monograph, 2012, 27-32.

The two described implications of the perception of immanence as a cipher of transcendent are mutually dependent. On the one hand, the subject desiring metaphysics requires an *a priori* and independent metaphysical reality without which his desire would be in vain. On the other hand, reality as a cipher of transcendence requires the subject to decode it through his desire for it, otherwise reality would appear entirely immanent. However, the mutual dependence described does not remove the gap between the desirer and the object of his desire. Quite the opposite. Jaspers' fundamental requirement to maintain the tension originating in the split between subject and object (Ph2, 336-344) becomes a primordial duality that is critical for the desire for metaphysics. Moreover, the persistence of the gap between selfhood and Being is the ultimate indication of the metaphysical nature of the objet itself, thanks to which the desire for metaphysics is not like any other desire.

The Articles

The desire for metaphysics, as the ultimate impetus of philosophical engagement, is present in the depth of each of the articles in this collection. However, this presence does not infuse unity and similarity on the articles. Quite the opposite, the articles are so different that the connection between them is sometimes unclear. However, I argue that precisely the variance apparent in them reveals a fundamental thing about the desire for metaphysics: it does not have an ultimate or typical expression, but each time different facets of it are revealed from which it appears as a self-standing whole. Precisely because the desire for metaphysics is holistic, it can never be exhausted in particular contents, and is still always revealed in the commitment to the particular experience in which it appears. Therefore, just as the desire for metaphysics reveals each time a different facet of selfhood and of the entity to which it is directed, so also any interpretation of a philosophical work is a new interpretation, revealing a new facet of it. Now it transpires that the gap separating the subject desiring metaphysics and the object of his desire is not merely formal, meaning defining this desire in itself. This gap leaves its mark also in the interpretation that seeks to follow the desire for metaphysics in the written philosophical work. In the end, the variance among the articles not only affirms my desire for metaphysics, which ignited the thought that led to their writing, but also supports the original gap that characterized the desire for metaphysics as such.

My monograph, *Karl Jaspers—From Selfhood to Being* (Rodopi, 2012), centered on the elucidation of the processes of the crystallization of metaphysical consciousness in Jaspers' writings.[15] The discussion in this book traces Jaspers' writing from his early steps as a young psychiatrist until his maturity as an existential philosopher, in contrast to most of his interpreters who usually ignored his early writings on psychiatry and psychology. The critical viewpoint was guided by a dual methodology: genealogical and thematic. The former, examining

---

[15] The book is mostly based upon a doctoral dissertation written under the supervision of Prof. Avi Sagi, submitted in Bar-Ilan University in 2001. The book was first published in Hebrew (Bar-Ilan University Press, Ramat Gan, 2006), and later translated into English by Ruth Ludlam and published in 2012 by Rodopi.

the development of Jaspers' ideas in the order of their appearance in his writings and in relation to the context in which they appeared, sought to deal with his work's lack of system and the deliberate avoidance of general conceptualizations. The latter, laid out alongside the genealogical study and relying upon it as a starting point, sought to achieve a comprehensive understanding of the two basic issues in his writings: selfhood and Being.[16] Through these two paths, I sought to trace Jaspers' attempt to grant meaning to the human search for self-understanding by examining his wide-reaching work in itself, and through studying the complicated interrelations between its parts. Along with revealing the difficulties and frustrations entailed in this search, the book examines Jaspers' attempts to deal with them through constituting a philosophical relation to the Being existing beyond the individual—other people, the world, and transcendence. In the end, the monograph exposed the unity of the world from which he created—first as a psychiatrist and then as a philosopher.

The general title *The Desire for Metaphysics* for the collection indicates that the articles gathered here deal with the desire for metaphysics as such. This means that while the articles deal with Jaspers' works, their horizon extends beyond his writings. Indeed, the realization of this reflection required me to give up the uniform understanding of his philosophical work, which I had earlier achieved in the monograph. The dual methodology that guided me in the monograph is still apparent in almost all of the articles. But the need to balance the two observations acted as a mutual restriction on both of them—every step in the genealogical development had to be crystallized as a thematic insight, and in parallel the thematic formation was tied to the development framework in its background. Moreover, this framework imposed restrictions upon the dialogue with the research literature, which was used in the book only to the degree that it contributed to the development of these two observations—the genealogical and the thematic. The discussion in the articles is largely free of all this. Each of them is the fruit of a unique experience of the desire for metaphysics, and reveals a different and complete reflection of it, although the status of the thematic observation is dominant in the articles, while the genealogical observation only enters the discussion to the extent that it helps with the thematic crystallization. This is also true regarding the dialogue with the research literature in the articles, which was also liberated from the restriction of balancing the two observations in favor of elucidating the main theme around which the articles are formed.

Furthermore, the title *The Desire for Metaphysics* was given to the articles in this collection retroactively, as a sort of main title of which the articles' titles are subtitles. The choice of this title is a reflexive account after a significant time had passed since the articles were written, and after I had turned to new philosophical horizons. Of course, one can ask what the new title contributes, since the articles here appear in their original order of first publication.[17] Moreover, my

---

[16] For more on the dual methodology in the monograph, see Miron, Monograph, 2012, 14-17.

[17] In principle, the articles appear in the same phrasing in which they were originally published, apart from minor corrections due to errors in the published version. All the German sources cited in the articles are translated by me, except for the few places where it has been indicated otherwise. The English versions of the articles originally published in Hebrew omit comments referring to the Hebrew text. Additionally, in all the articles the

fundamental commitment to metaphysical clarification is an overt and explicit aspect not only in the early monograph about Jaspers, but also in other studies, and in this respect the new title does not denote a new awareness. However, these considerations are rejected in light of understanding the power of reflection to change both its object and its subject. This means that the very placing of the title *The Desire for Metaphysics* above these articles grants them new meaning, even though their original phrasing remains mostly unchanged. Below I shall point to a central aspect, though not the only one, of the contribution of each of the articles to my understanding of the nature of the desire for metaphysics—both that realized in Jaspers' work as a uniform whole to which the monograph was devoted, and that afforded me by returning to his writings when I wrote the articles. Of course, just as each of the articles reflects my personal experience of the desire for metaphysics, they also invite the readers to experience it themselves and to discover new facets of this desire. Despite the variance between the articles, they are all based on the same desire for metaphysics, and each of them has a holistic nature that makes it self-standing.

"The Covenant between Philosophy and Revelation: David Hartman's Thought in the View of Karl Jaspers' Philosophy" (Miron, 2004a)

The article deals with the connections between the philosophical theology of David Hartman (1931-2013) and Jaspers' existentialist perceptions. The article reveals operatively the indispensability of two elements of the desire for metaphysics—the gap between the subject and the object of his desire and the tension this gap entails. It also shows the depth of the experience of the unconditional, from which no particular understanding of the person or of reality is derived. Moreover, the article is unique compared to others in the collection in revealing the vast hermeneutic value embodied in Jaspers' ideas for elucidating another philosophical perception that shares the desire for metaphysics originating in the person's finite being. Jaspers' ideas not only help understand some unclear general statements in Hartman, but also fill with contents some gaps existing it his thought. The article naturally reveals the realization of Jaspers' vision regarding communication between different philosophies and people that share the desire for metaphysics.

"From Psychiatry to Philosophy: The Idea of the Self in Karl Jaspers' Philosophy" (Miron, 2004b)

The article follows the main milestones in the development of Karl Jaspers' perception of selfhood from his early days as a psychiatrist to his philosophical writings. This article grants first and foremost a detailed genealogical understanding of the subjective pole in Jaspers' metaphysical desire. In this context, the solipsistic dimension of the search for selfhood is revealed, along with the inevitable dead end this search encountered in the absence of an otherness surrounding it and separate from it. This article also establishes the basic argument that the desire for metaphysics is born from a self-search, and

---

bibliographical references to my publications that were being prepared at the time of original publication have been updated in full.

shows the loyalty of this desire to its origin in selfhood, which is persistently apparent in the various manifestations of this desire, which Jaspers called "the desire to observe my soul and find its real reality" (*Psychopathology*1, 12).

"From Opposition to Reciprocity: Karl Jaspers on Science, Philosophy, and what Lies between Them" (Miron, 2004c)

The article follows Jaspers' movement from an early perception viewing science and philosophy as opposed to each other, which contributed to Jaspers' decision to leave psychopathology in favor of philosophical creation, toward the more mature perception he crystallized as a philosopher, identifying dimensions of mutuality between the two areas. The fact that the "reconciliation" between science and philosophy occurred in his mature philosophical writings, where Jaspers' treatment of metaphysics was overt and explicit, reveals the power of the desire for metaphysics to contain difference and to identify the deep shared element connecting what appears as different and even contrasting.

"Transcendence and Dissatisfaction in Jaspers' Idea of the Self" (Miron, 2005)

The article deals with nature and the forces that motivate the search for self in Jaspers' writings. The contribution of this article to the elucidation of the desire for metaphysics is overt and clear, since it traces the fundamental path of the desire for metaphysics, originating in the experience of dissatisfaction and eventually leading to the constituting of a relation to transcendence.

"Towards Reality: The Development of the Philosophical Attitude to Reality in Karl Jaspers' Thought" (Miron, 2006a)

The article deals with the perception of reality external to the self in Jaspers' writings, and could be considered as dealing with the objective pole of the desire for metaphysics. The discussion is focused first on locating and analyzing the aspects in Jaspers' early perception of self that prevented a discussion of external reality, and then turns to expose the factors that enabled the explicit discussion of reality within his perception of Being. The article affirms the principle that the desire for metaphysics originates not in a solid givenness that enables it, but itself involves the achievement of the givenness of its two essential elements—selfhood and Being.

"Was Jaspers really Kantian?" (Miron, 2006b)

The article proposes a critical view of what seems to be an accepted claim in the research literature, that Jaspers' work was Kantian in its meanings and intentions. The article follows the fundamental way that the meeting with ideas from the history of philosophy nurtured Jaspers' philosophical search, while not dictating its contents and structures. The desire for metaphysics transpires against this background as selective and accurate in relation to the contents that can fill it, including contents that bear metaphysical meaning. In this respect, the article stresses the dominance and peculiarity of the search for selfhood that is active in the desire for metaphysics.

"Between Freedom and Necessity: The Conception of Guilt in Jaspers' Thought" (Miron, 2007)

The article examines the conception of guilt in Jaspers' essay "The Question of German Guilt" (1946), and anchors it in wide philosophical themes of his existentialist thought: selfhood, "historicity", and "boundary situations". This article is unique compared with the others in the broad relation existing between the central concept it discusses, guilt, and the nature of the desire for metaphysics as elucidated above. In other words, many of the insights arising in the article regarding guilt are also characteristic of the desire for metaphysics. For example, the shared anchor in freedom and unconditionality as a condition for their appropriate understanding; their clarification is not conducted from a situation of calm and tranquility, but from a sense of necessity, urgency, a personal involvement, and a desire for exhaustion and holism; they are based upon a serious self-search, but the purposes of the search are not exhausted in the realm of the individual but relate to the wider sense of human existence in the world; the lack of acceptance of the existing reality in which the person lives, the desire to escape the concrete level, and the aim to form a relation with a more worthy reality based on higher values. The described relation between the experience of guilt and the desire for metaphysics may serve as inspiration for the examination of other general human experiences (such as dealing with death and loss, religions experiences, and so on) and this desire.

"The Guilt Which We Are: An Ontological Approach to Karl Jaspers' Idea of Guilt" (Miron, 2011)

The article deals with the crystallization of an ontological perception of human experience while relying on Jaspers' perception of guilt, even though he rejected the idea of ontology due to the restriction it imposes on existentialist existence. Like the other article in this collection discussing guilt (Miron, 2007), this article too assumes the holistic nature of Jaspers' perception of guilt that allows us to crystallize from it a broader understanding of human experience. According to the ontological approach developed in the article, just like the desire for metaphysics, so too is guilt not connected to a particular action or behavior, or to abstaining from them, but denotes a mode of facing transcendence that will never achieve complete epistemic transparency.

Afterword

Those who love Jaspers' philosophy share the pain of missed opportunity because his work has largely remained on the margins of philosophical discourse and has not achieved the place it deserves within the history of modern philosophy. There are several reasons for this. First, the prohibition the Nazi regime imposed upon the publication of his writings in 1938 and his dismissal from his teaching position at Heidelberg University due to his criticism of the totalitarian regime, and his loyalty to his Jewish wife, Gertrud Mayer. Precisely in the nineteen thirties and early nineteen forties, when Jaspers' work reached its peak maturity, his path to contemporary philosophical discourse was largely blocked even before his thought had received any real opportunity to face criticism and judgment.

To this we can add the great dominance achieved by Martin Heidegger with the publication of his work *Sein und Zeit* in 1927, five years before the publication of Jaspers' trilogy *Philosophy* in 1932, which made it difficult for Jaspers and other contemporary philosophers to gain their own position and status. This is particularly regarding the monumental oeuvre of Edmund Husserl, Heidegger's teacher, which was pushed aside from the focus of philosophical discourse while Heidegger's work obtained status and importance that was already difficult to dispute at the time, let alone today. Even Heidegger's public support of Nazism did not detract from the status of his philosophical work.

Along with the historical-biographical explanation, the marginal status of Jaspers' philosophy can also be attributed to the style of his writing and the premises on which his thought was founded. Jaspers deliberately avoided coining discrete philosophical concepts, and in practice allowed his ideas and concepts to draw their meaning from the general context in which they appeared. This approach, which led to his being called the "floating philosopher",[18] directly contributed to the unsystematic nature of his thought and made it difficult to understand his already complex ideas, which often impressed his readers as being inaccessible to rational analysis.[19] In this respect, Jaspers' philosophy can be argued to impose upon its readers a task at which he was not successful himself: exposing its basic structures and forming the fundamental concepts in which it is anchored. Thus Jaspers significantly missed one of the central challenges facing him as a philosopher, to present thought patterns of effective tools to help deal with philosophical problems also beyond the boundaries of his own thought.[20]

Despite all this, I hope that the monograph already published and this collection of articles will contribute to the awakening interest in Karl Jaspers' philosophy. I would like the articles included in this collection to be read in a similar way to that in which Jaspers himself wished his book *Philosophy* to be read:[21]

> The meaning of philosophizing is a single thought, ineffable as such: the *consciousness of being* [*Seinsbewusstsein*]. In this work it ought to be approachable from every chapter; each should be the *whole in detail*, though leaving dark what will first illuminate itself through the rest (Ph1, ix).

---

[18] Fritz Heinemann, *Jenseits des Existentialismus*. Stuttgart: W. Kohlhammer, 1957, 65.

[19] See for instance: Von Rinteln, 204; Charles F. Wallraff, *Karl Jaspers: An Introduction to His Philosophy*. Princeton: Princeton University Press, 1970; Heinemann, 1957, 65, 71; Hans Mader, "Das Seindenken bei Karl Jaspers," *Wissenschaft und Weltbild*, 10, (1957), 50–58, 58.

[20] See: Kurt Hoffman, "The Basic Concept of Jaspers' Philosophy." In *The Philosophy of Karl Jaspers*. Paul Arthur Schilpp (ed.). New York: Tudor, 1957, 95–113, 95 ff. Regarding the uniqueness and importance of his philosophical vocabulary, see the discussion in a different context in my article, Ronny Miron, "The Vocabulary of Reality", *Phainomena*, (forthcoming 2014).

[21] A similar principle guided Jaspers when he studied the history of philosophy. See for instance, Jaspers, *Nietzsche, Einführung in das Verständnis seines Philosophierens*. Berlin: Walter De Gruyter, 1950, 9; *Die grossen Philosophen* (1–3). Munich: Piper, 1957, 7-14.

The Covenant between Philosophy and Revelation: David Hartman's Thought in the View of Karl Jaspers' Philosophy

In memory of Moti Etun

In his response to the review of Yeshayahu Leibowitz, one of his most important and stimulating interlocutors, of one of his books, David Hartman described three basic models of referring to Judaism, including the model at the foundation of his approach.[1] This model differs from the two other models, and is founded upon a different religious worldview, but it was formed through dialogue with them. Hartman did not face as an outside observer the two other models, which are, as will transpire, anchored in his interpretation of two fundamental perceptions of deity whose presence he identified in the Bible, Talmud, and in medieval and modern Jewish philosophy. His attempt to understand the different religiosity constituted from them, to sketch the relations between them, and to indicate the implications of their permanent presence in Jewish writing, enabled him to understand also the tension accompanying the existence of the contemporary believer. However, while dealing with these two models stimulated his spiritual world, Hartman's thought was based on different principles. His statement that "These models [constitute] analytical thinking tools rather than labels that should be attached to various periods in our nation's history", allows us to refer to the three models as starting points for his perception of Judaism as a "covenant", which reached its fullest development in his book *A Living Covenant*.[2] The argument at the center of the discussion in this article is that *Hartman's perception of deity in Judaism is motivated primarily by considerations relating to the character of the believer and his attitude to the finite reality*. Hartman's

---

[1] David Hartman, *Joy and Responsibility: Israel, Modernity and the Renewal of Judaism*, Jerusalem, 1978 [hereafter: Hartman 1978]. Leibowitz's review first appeared in *Petachim*, Nisan 5739 (1979), 82-88. Hartman's review also appeared in *Petachim*, Elul 5739 (1979), 78-83. These two articles were republished in: Avi Sagi (ed.), *Yeshayahu Leibowitz, His World and Thought*, Jerusalem, 1995, 47-60 [Hebrew]. The citations of Leibowitz and Hartman are taken from this book [hereafter: Hartman in Sagi].

[2] David Hartman, *A Living Covenant: The Innovative Spirit in Traditional Judaism*, New York 1987 [hereafter: Hartman 1985], 39-40.

statement that "We live in a generation that unfortunately is ruled by the thinking of religious existentialism" reflected his understanding that this trend cannot serve as an inspiration in a religious discourse anchored in commitment to the *halakhah*.[3] However, I believe that existentialist thought, which will be represented in this article by the philosophy of Karl Jaspers, may help expose and elucidate central philosophical aspects arising from the characters of the believer, deity, and reality characteristic of Hartman's thought.

Two Perceptions of Deity: Ontological and Universal

In his aforementioned article, Hartman described two models of perceptions of Judaism: The *first model*, which he described as "self-sufficient", represents a perception of Judaism as a self-standing whole, with the "justification for its thought categories" being internal, and thus they cannot be comprehensible for those who have not been educated accordingly. It appears that the image of deity arising from this model and directed in its actions to a specific audience of believers, matches in its central aspect the one arising from Hartman's interpretation of the biblical story of the exodus from Egypt, which reveals additional features. The deity that declared "I am the Lord thy God, which have brought thee out of the land of Egypt" appears to the enslaved Israelites, who are later freed thanks to his intervention, as an entity whose presence is what creates the reality in which they live. The emphasis given in this approach to the total presence of the deity in reality, serves as a basis for his definition of this model as founded on *an ontological perception of deity*.[4]

The mark of this deity in reality is expressed in various forms: it can save, as described in the story of the liberation Israelites from slavery in Egypt; it can reveal itself through signs and miracles, as happened throughout the years of wandering in the desert; it can sentence annihilation, as on the generation of the flood, the generation of secession, or the people of Sodom and Gomorrah. However, all these forms reflect the same "behavior" pattern of God: a unilateral decision regarding whomever "He finds fit…", for reasons of His own. The Bible refers to punishment expected as a result of "an action that is bad in God's eyes" and "gives commandments embodying moral principles and seeming as aimed at people's best interest".[5] However, the appearances of the unreasonable ratio between the human action and God's response, does not enable the believer to know what he should expect and indicate "a [different] notion of divinity". Hartman uses powerful descriptions to demonstrate the terrifying presence of this deity, called here ontological: "…borders on the demonic… strikes people down, sometimes individually and sometimes on a massive scale, for reasons that seem to be quite trivial, for what may be at most innocent mistakes"; "a destructive force bursting into people's lives".[6] And also:

---

[3] David Hartman, *Maimonides: Halakhah and Philosophy*, Tel Aviv 1976, 9 [Hebrew] [hereafter: Hartman 1976].
[4] Hartman states that this is a general characterization of deity in the Bible. See Hartman 1978, 2.
[5] See, for instance, his treatment of the difference between the reward of the commandments in the Bible and in the Talmud, ibid., 3-4.
[6] Hartman 1985, 44-45.

> ... people who dare to have dealings with God should realize that they are entering a minefield where at any moment they may be blown up...
>
> ... *in God we encounter a furious irrational Force* Whose unpredictability makes it impossible for us to relay on His commitments to us, Whose impatience constantly threatens us with destruction for unwittingly infringing our commitments to Him. Better not to have any mutual commitments, we may feel, than to have commitments that prove ineffective in our greatest moments of need, but threaten us in our slightest moments of misjudgment.[7]

The powerful immanence of God in the world—both as redeemer and rescuer from troubles and as the destroyer of the foundations of human being—is thus revealed as creating factuality from which there is no escape. This quality does not enable the characterization of the ontological deity from the human viewpoint as an absolute transcendence. But if we assume that rationality constitutes one of the essential tools humans have for dealing with reality, then the fact that the believer in the image of the ontological deity has no tools to actually predict its actions, to understand them properly, or even to participate in the decision about their dimensions, makes it in many senses transcendent for him. Assuming the existence of the "self-sufficient" model in the background of the ontological perception of deity thus receives its full meaning: the characterization "self-sufficient" refers not only to the believer but also to God himself, whose image is located above and beyond human horizons. God in the ontological perception, whose entity is embodied in his ability to create facts that form a complete reality, does not require human beings in order to become God, and the existence of such a need could be considered as a disadvantage for him. The believer's status in this approach is marginal, at least in terms of his ability to influence God's hidden plan regarding reality, to the extent that such a plan exists. The focus of a believer's experience of an unclear and chaotic reality is the extensive and profound dependency upon a God he does not understand and does not experience as a person but mainly as a transcendent entity intruding into the world.

The *second model* Hartman presented in his reply to Leibowitz contains an image of God that contrasts in some of its essential aspects to the "self-sufficient" model, and to the character of ontological deity. This model is primarily characterized by the fact that "the legitimate criteria for Jewish self-understanding are only those categories of thought and principles of action that are comprehensible to a universal audience, comprising believers and non-believers, Jews and non-Jews. The universality becomes the final criterion, according to which Judaism must be justified and explained... as serving a universal purpose and as serving a universal audience".[8] The addressing of a non-specific audience typical of this model is also expressed in Hartman's interpretation of the creation

---

[7] Ibid., 45-46. My emphasis.
[8] Hartman in Sagi, 54. The interpretation of the creation story is anchored in the well-known distinction of Joseph Soloveitchik—who was undoubtedly an inspiration for Hartman—between the two descriptions of creation in Genesis. See Rabbi Joseph Dov Halevy Soloveitchik, *Man of Faith*, Jerusalem 1981, 13ff. [Hebrew].

story in Genesis, which he says presents an image of God that "has no private identity, He is a universal God, of the cosmos".[9] Against the background of the *Midrash* noting that the description of creation does not contain any normative dimension, Hartman adds that in the context of creation everything that exists is perceived as an equal creation before God.[10] In this spirit, he states elsewhere that "The account of creation in Genesis admittedly does not involve a covenant with any human being or with any particular historical people".[11] The absence of theogony, which Hartman mentions in his analysis of the meanings of creation, also transpires as playing an important role in emphasizing the dimension of universality in the image of the deity in creation. It appears that precisely the avoidance of clear determinations on issues that have separated different religions throughout history—such as the mode of God's formation, his ability and willingness to intervene in history, and his choice of a particular nation—enable this deity to serve as an object of identification for various nations.[12]

People's ability to talk about the character of God, while discovering what Husserl would have termed "restraint" (*epoché*) regarding his personality traits as crystallized throughout the particular history of their nation constitutes a basis for understanding the image of God in the creation as founded upon a universal perception of deity. To paraphrase Wittgenstein's famous term, we could say that the conversation about deity in this context expresses people's ability to "play" the same game in different languages, meaning to discuss together each about the image of God he imagines in his mind.[13] As with the qualities of the ontological deity, in this context too Hartman notes that the description of creation assumes divine freedom.[14] In his opinion, the image of God arising from this description "involves an irreducible separation between the world and God".[15] However, this basic similarity cannot blur the deep differences between the ontological perception of deity and the universal one: the *first difference* relates to the implications divine freedom, which characterizes both these perceptions, has for human life. While in the ontological perception of deity the freedom may serve as an explanation for God's arbitrariness and unpredictability, in the second model divine freedom is expressed in God's willingness to limit himself and to respect

---

[9] Hartman's interview with Jonathan Ben Dov, entitled "The God of the Communities of Israel", in: Yizhar Hess and Elazar Storm (eds.), *Questions about God: Dialogues*, Or Yehuda 1998, 19ff. [Hebrew] (hereafter: Hartman, "The God of the Communities of Israel").

[10] Hartman calls these relations in the creation an "ontological relationship", but I do not use this term when clarifying the second model, since the meaning he gives it as expressing a continuing relationship does not match the usual philosophical meaning of the term "ontology", and even Hartman himself does not regularly use this term in his clarification of this model. See David Hartman, *A Heart of Many Rooms: Celebrating the Voices within Judaism*, Woodstock 1999, 156-157 (hereafter: Hartman 1999).

[11] Hartman 1985, 22.

[12] On this point, compare also ibid., 133.

[13] On Wittgenstein's concept of "word play", see Ludwig Wittgenstein, *Philosophical Investigations*, trans. G.E.M. Anscombe, Oxford 1958, 18.

[14] Hartman 1985, 22.

[15] Ibid., 259.

finitude "so as to permit human development within the context of freedom".[16] In other words, since the "otherness from God is pronounced good, then our finitude has intrinsic dignity and significance".[17]

The *second difference* deals with the deity's attitude to the world in the two approaches: while the ontological perception stresses God's inclination to intervene in the finite reality, thus disturbing its natural balances, in the universal perception God's image is presented as capable of allowing finitude to sustain itself through its internal power play. Hartman clarifies in this context that the principle of God's self-limitation as a creator is not an expression of ontological mysticism such as the Lurianic theory of *tzimtzum* (contraction), but it enables human independence.[18] To be precise, the presence of God in this perception, compared with the ontological perception, is not necessarily lessened, since his definition as the creator does not prevent in principle the possibility that after creating the world he continued to be present within it. But in the universal divinity characterized by self-restraint a more complex image of the deity is portrayed, revealed only to those who seek it within finitude, while for others finitude is perceived as perfection and totality beyond which there is nothing. In other words: the entity of the ontological deity exhausts it for people who cannot ignore its presence in the world, while the universal deity does not threaten the presence of entities other than it or demand from them recognition of its superiority, but recognizes their existence and accepts them. Paradoxically, perhaps precisely the mystery surrounding the unpredictable behavior patterns of the ontological deity and the human inability to engage with it using the tools of consciousness can serve as a basis for the development of a pantheistic approach. While such an approach blurs the transcendental aspects of God, in contrast to the ontological viewpoint regarding divinity it may help mediate between the believer and God, and perhaps even contribute to establishing his connection with the reality in which he lives and acts. This background sharpens the understanding that the concealed and respecting presence of the deity in the universal perception does not necessarily damage the transcendent nature of the deity and perhaps even contributes to some extent to removing the possibility that the finite reality will be perceived as identical to the deity itself.

In fact, the two differences that distinguish the universal perception of deity from the ontological one stem from the basic understanding of the deity as an amorphous and unqualified figure. The creation story in Genesis focuses on describing what the creator God does rather than on who he is "in himself", and in this respect the absence of God's persona characterizes the universal perception no less than the ontological one. In other words, the clearer and more distinct the qualities of God, the more limited the space he leaves to human beings in which they can express themselves, while a flexible deity figure, or at least one with less defined boundaries, enables people to display a greater variety of modes of

---

[16] Ibid., 24. The descriptions of creation contain, in his opinion, the basis whose full realization is achieved only in the perception of covenant based on the revelation, to be discussed below. He stresses that his understanding of creation is "retroactive" and "The divine self-limitation that allows for human freedom and dignity is a covenantal category, not a cosmic category, even though it first appears in the creation story", ibid., 266.
[17] Ibid., 259.
[18] Ibid., 24.

reference towards it. This understanding of the deity, arising from the description of the creation in Genesis, is somewhat reminiscent of the figure of Demiurgos described in Plato's dialogue *Timaeus*, who from his goodness created the world and then enabled material reality to exist. The subordination of the Platonic deity to the Ideas does not accord with the divine freedom assumed in the creation story. However, in this context it is important that the rationality of the world of Ideas is translated into the world of phenomena and enables the believer to deal with reality and the world using the tools of consciousness. The world of phenomena clarifies a central facet of the universal perception of the deity. The rational facet of reality accompanying the universal perception of the deity, thanks to which God as the creator and the world as a framework in which people live their lives become accessible to the believer, may thus explain Hartman's argument that "Eschatological redemption, then, is not implicit in the notion of creation". This deity "does not aim to redeem the creature from creaturely finitude, nor does it point to an existence not shot through by the problematic of human freedom and temporality".[19] In his opinion, the creation story described in Genesis should be seen as "teaching us to accept our finitude".[20] These features, and the similarity to the Platonic image of divinity, enable the person a not insignificant degree of orientation in the reality in which he exists, lay the foundations essential for the development of various forms of communication with God, and enable its opening to a varied and wide community of believers.

Furthermore, an additional observation of these differences reveals a third difference relating to the question of the philosophical freedom enabled from these two perceptions. This freedom will transpire later as essential for the constituting of Hartman's own perception of Judaism: the ontological deity that sometimes displays irrational and unbalanced behavior to people and reality does not enable the space—in terms of intellectual and mental room for action—that constitutes a precondition for the development of a philosophical personality by the believers. Even if a believer exists who places this figure of the deity as the object of his philosophical investigation, he will have to be gifted with Sisyphean qualities: any mental construction of his will be valid until the attack of rage or mercy of the unrestrained deity to which his philosophizing is directed. The clear contrast between this deity and that of the universal perception, based on rationality and respect for human freedom and finite reality, does not allow us to ignore the potential for constituting a philosophical personality among people referring to it. This sharpens the distinction in the pluralistic depth embodied in the image of the deity arising from the creation story that is the complete opposite of the closedness and fanaticism characteristic of the deity who freed the Israelites from Egypt.

Two Types of Believers: Prophet and Sage

The study of Hartman's interpretation of the two perceptions of deity, the ontological and the universal, enables us to indicate two types of believer that complement them. Hartman describes the believer in the first model as not

---

[19] Ibid., 261.
[20] Ibid., 302.

"feeling the need to interpret faith and the act of Judaism in ways that would make Judaism understood to people outside its special religious framework"[21], may match the image of the believer accompanying the ontological perception of deity. Such a believer cannot, and perhaps needs not, understand the ontological deity. He must subordinate himself to it and fill the practical obligations required of him, whose existence is not dependent upon understanding them. Obedience, submission, and acceptance are the qualities that enable the believer to cope with the figure of the ontological deity. We can imagine Noah, who possessed these qualities, when he was "informed" of God's destructive plan. Hartman marks the difference between the stance of Abraham and that of Noah. The former "walks *before* God" and enters a moral struggle with him, even demanding him to give signs in his promises "whereby I shall know that I shall inherit it". The latter "walked *with* God" willing, without question or condition, to obey any commandment placed upon him.[22] Noah can serve as a model for the ultimate character of the believer who can cope with the ontological deity, but it appears that in light of the terrifying character of this deity, the deity demands even from other characters in different contexts in the Bible who showed clearly different qualities behavior similar to Noah's. Hartman remarks upon this when referring to Abraham's behavior during the *Akedah*,[23] but from God's answer to Moses, "I am that I am", or as the *midrash* describes it bluntly, "Be silent, for such is My decree",[24] it transpires that even when a person dates to demand from God some level of dialogue or sharing, he is pushed back to his finitude while the image of the deity remains unclear to him. To paraphrase the well-known *midrash*, the believer arising from this model can be compared to being pushed the corner where Noah settles and from which he "sees his handiwork drowning in the sea"—meaning his moral world, his freedom, and in particular his urge to grant meaning to the character of the deity that controls his world have their power and vitality diminished—and all that is demanded of him as at least to be silent and certainly not to sing his praises.

However, Noah's submissive nature embodies only one facet of the character of the believer arising from the ontological perception of divinity. Another character portraying the rule of this deity over human reality is the character of the prophet, whose essence is in his authority to testify to the deity's ability to be present in human consciousness and in his role in reporting God's plans regarding the reality itself. In this context, the prophet's multi-dimensional dependence on the God revealed to him is significant. First, his very selection as a prophet is one-sided, and as shown by the midrashic literature regarding the character of Moses according to the words of the book of Jonah, prophecy can be enforced on the person destined to it, who cannot escape it. Second, he is required to transmit the prophecy as it was given to him, without interpretation. He is merely a vessel lacking any influence on the contents poured into him, and he cannot predict the occurrence of the prophecy or promise the acceptance of its messages. It appears that the passivity and submissiveness required of the prophet make him, like

---

[21] Hartman in Sagi, 54.
[22] Ibid., 44.
[23] Ibid., 43-44.
[24] See citation from *Menahot* 29b, ibid., 46.

Noah, an ideal character of a believer who can accept the burden of the ontological deity.

Nevertheless, and despite the deep damage to human freedom, constituting an inevitable outcome of the unrestrained rule of the ontological deity, it seems that from the believer's viewpoint faith in this deity has clear advantages: it does not rely on human freedom that can be negligent in its functioning.[25] The believer can rely on the promises accompanying it to realize in practice the principle of providence according to rewards and punishments and eventually also redemption—a redemption primarily from the arbitrariness and maliciousness filling existence in this world.[26] In essence the theocentric dimension characterizing the ontological perception of deity shows that not only does it subordinate people to the deity without granting them the tools to understand it and does not present such understanding as valuable knowledge, but finitude itself is also subject to the arbitrariness typical of this deity. In any case, when it acts in the person's favor, the ontological deity can create for him a new reality that not only redeems him from the harm of finitude, but also from his own selfhood.

The character of the believer arising from the universal perception of divinity transpires as contrasting with the character of the believer described above in some important aspects. The description of the "universal Jews" in the second model as "stressing the moral importance of ritual and thus indicating the universal importance of unique Jewish rituals and actions"[27] can be reconciled with the description of man in the creation story as created "in God's image". Hartman's argument that "One may understand the concept *tzelem elohim* (image of God) as indicating the similarity between human beings and God with respect to freedom and spontaneity",[28] enables to some extent to include the deity itself within the universal community to which human beings belong. The statement, "This appreciation of creation is antipathetic to the mystic longing to get beyond finitude. It holds that our consciousness of our finitude is not an estrangement from our true being",[29] emphasizes the degree of respect the universal deity possesses toward the finitude of human beings and of reality. The capability in principle of those who were created "in God's image" to understand the universal divinity in creation thus establishes the recognition that "Finite human beings who accept their creatureliness know that they remain separate from their Creator".[30] In contrast to the incessant attempts of the believer in the ontological deity to escape finitude, the believer in the universal perception of divinity is aware of the fact of his being a finite creature, and accepts it. His mature personality allows him to deal better with immanent reality, which in itself is not flawless. But the advantages of the self-awareness of the believer in the universal deity are not limited to this. Along with his recognition of what exists beyond the boundaries of his comprehension, he becomes aware of what the tools of his consciousness, which are also part of his finite reality, enable him: to understand

---

[25] Ibid., 264.
[26] Ibid., 227 ff.; 300 ff.
[27] Hartman in Sagi, 54.
[28] Hartman 1985, 23
[29] Ibid., 259.
[30] Ibid., 259.

himself, his surroundings, and with clear limitations even the deity itself. The respect this believer holds toward finitude and the abilities of his consciousness enable him to turn them into a lever for self-understanding and for creation with an aim to exhaust what they contain as much as possible. In contrast, the believer in the ontological deity, who does not perceive finitude as stable or as valuable, cannot see it as enabling self-realization and self-fulfillment. Therefore, this believer strives to overcome the limitations finitude imposes upon him and hopes to find himself in a completely different being. As a result, not only does he not achieve an understanding of the deity itself, but even aspects that can be known in principle remain vague to him.

The deep connection between the believer in the universal perception of Judaism and the finite reality enable certain aspects of the character of Abraham as representing the typical qualities of this believer. In analyzing Abraham's behavior when he discovered the plan to destroy Sodom, Hartman stresses his conscience and "challenges God by appealing to universal moral principles".[31] From the *Midrash* describing Abraham's hospitality, Hartman learns about "the essential connection between covenantal consciousness and involvement with and responsibility for others. One may not commune with God of the covenant if one is not responsive to the social, economic, and political needs of human beings".[32] These qualities of Abraham's, emphasized in the *Midrashim* Hartman chose to use to establish his position, make him into an example and role model for all people. This interpretation of Abraham's character enabled Hartman to see finitude itself as having weight in creating a wide basis for a more encompassing collectivity of believers that is not dependent on a shared historical experience of a particular revelation. Accordingly, Hartman concludes from the fact that according to the *halakhah* "Abraham's covenant signifies rejection of the idea that covenantal faith commitments are defined by racial and biological conditions" that "In singling out Abraham, God made covenantal religion accessible to all. Abraham is the father of any person who seeks to emulate his way of life and to practice its values, norms, and beliefs".[33] The rainbow that signified the covenant with Noah, the believer typical of the ontological deity perception, is indeed also directed at a universal audience. But the significance of the sign he was given is not so far-reaching, since the rainbow does not determine the reality in which people live, and at most it can be seen as a decoration for life, which we might not notice while involved with everyday concerns. In contrast, what Hartman termed the "universal implications" of the covenant with Abraham[34] have greater weight, and therefore we can argue that the character of Abraham is more suited to the universal perception of deity.

It is completely clear that a perception seeing finitude as its home and considering consciousness, also finite, as one of people's most valuable assets, would crown the sage as the most suitable to deal with the character of a deity that does not guarantee him any redemption from the finitude it respects. The

---

[31] Ibid., 31.

[32] Ibid., 31. While these words are written from the viewpoint of the covenant, the character of Abraham—in other respects connected to the universal perception of deity—clarifies an element that is important also in the universal perception of deity.

[33] Ibid., 31-32.

[34] Ibid., 31.

prophet turns to an exclusive and closed human being that perceives the world's reality in a unique way. By the very role granted him, the prophet embodies the rareness of God's presence, not apparent in everyday reality, but only to the select few, or in dramatic events involving the breach of natural laws. The sage, meaning the person who can identify the possibilities in reality and indicate the ways of exhausting them, sees the fact of his finitude as given. Therefore, he can in principle share his perception of reality with everyone similar to him, meaning with all human beings as such. Since the sage can speak a language understood by a wider collective, each understanding of his about the nature of reality and about the connection between the deity and reality can grant him wider influence in the hearts of more people. So it transpires that while the prophet presents the promise of the realization of another reality that remains far from the grey routine from which his audience cannot escape, the understanding and comprehension of the sage make him an active partner in the creation of a new reality. Precisely because this reality is not separate from the one people inhabit in any case, it enables the believers to exhaust what it contains, and perhaps without the sage's understanding many of its layers would remain as unknown possibilities, which were therefore unrealized.

In many respects, the two perceptions of deity and the types of believers they represent reflect, as presented in Hartman's interpretation of the story of exodus and the story of creation, the dialectic typical of modern Jewish thought.[35] From its inception, in the writings of Spinoza and Mendelsohn, this thought has presented various attempts to examine the unique contents of historical Judaism in light of the universal understanding of people and society in the modern era.[36] However, the connection pertaining, in my opinion, between Hartman's ideas and existentialist philosophy, which will be represented in this paper by Karl Jasper's philosophy, can illuminate the relevance of Hartman's thought to the wider philosophical discourse, which also appears to address philosophical questions similar to those arising from Hartman's interpretation of two of the facets of divinity in the Bible. I would like to clarify that I am not arguing for a direct influence of Jaspers' philosophy on Hartman's thought, and to the best of my knowledge there is no real evidence for this in Hartman's books. Instead of

---

[35] The relation between particularism and universalism has been extensively discussed in the latest studies dedicated to Hartman's thought. See Moshe Holinger, "David Hartman's Covenant Theology: A Model for a Synthesis between Halakhic Judaism and Liberal Democracy in Modern Orthodoxy", in Avi Sagi and Zvi Zohar (eds.), *Renewing Jewish Commitment: The Work and Thought of David Hartman*, Tel Aviv 2001, 131-133 [Hebrew] [hereafter: *Renewing Jewish Commitment*].

[36] The distinction between particularity and universality has appeared in various ways and for various purposes in modern Jewish thought. Thus, for instance, Spinoza distinguished between theology and reason in order to argue against the relevance of historical Judaism in an era of rationalism. See Benedict de Spinoza, *Tractatus Theologico-Politicus*, trans. R.H.M. Elwes, London: Routledge, 1895, chap. XV, 190-199. See also Lewis Feuer Samuel, *Spinoza and the Rise of Liberalism*, Boston 1987. For Mendelsohn this distinction was a means of establishing its legitimacy in an era of the modern centralist state. See Moses Mendelsohn, *Jerusalem and Other Jewish Writings*, trans. Alfred Jospe. New York: Schocken, c. 1969, 32 ff., 61-72. On the relation between particularity and universalism in the thought of German Jews, see in particular George Mosse, *German Jews beyond Judaism*, Bloomington 1985.

arguing for an influence, I propose using the term "hidden dialogue", indicating a certain equivalence of the ideas of the two thinkers, constituted by their very attempt to deal with the possibility of reconstituting a metaphysics in a reality that often played down its importance to the life of free people.[37] I believe that Hartman's focus on establishing his modern views regarding Judaism using Talmudic language left him insufficient room for a systematic clarification of the nature of the philosophical moves at the basis of his arguments. The more structured conceptual system in Jaspers' thought, which is anchored in the tradition of continental philosophy, may therefore help to reveal the philosophical depth that in Hartman's perceptions often exists only implicitly. In this way, Jaspers' philosophy, whose relevant aspects will be presented below, could serve as a tool for a deeper understanding of the unexhausted philosophical possibilities hidden in Hartman's Jewish philosophy.

Karl Jaspers set out in his thought a philosophical path in which the striving for the elucidation of selfhood gradually develops into the constituting of a relation to transcendence.[38] Jaspers defined three languages of metaphysical objectivity, which from the perspective of his entire oeuvre may be seen as reflecting three stages in its development.[39] The first language represents Existenz's unmediated experience of the presence of transcendence as a metaphysical Being existing beyond immanent reality.[40] This experience,

---

[37] Dov Schwartz, who studied the influence of existentialist thought, particularly that of Heidegger and of Paul Tillich, on Hartman's work, defined Hartman's relationship to existentialist philosophy as "a hidden interlocutor, always present". See his article "On Finitude and its Existentialist Origins in Hartman's Thought", *Renewing Jewish Commitment*, 493.

[38] Jaspers and Heidegger are considered the founders of the German stream of existentialist philosophy, but there are many differences between them. There is extensive literature dealing with these differences, but for research that could be relevant, in the broadest sense, to this context, see Alan M. Olson (ed.), *Heidegger & Jaspers*, Philadelphia 1994; Franz Josef Brecht, *Heidegger und Jaspers: Die beiden Grundformen der Existenzphilosophie*, Wuppertal 1948.

[39] For my full interpretation of these three languages, see Miron, Monograph, 2012, 247-261. Samay presents a different interpretation of these three languages. See Sebastian Samay, *Reason Revisited: The Philosophy of Karl Jaspers*, Dublin 1971, 179f.

[40] Karl Jaspers, *Philosophie*, 3, Heidelberg 1994 [1932], 129. The citations taken from the trilogy *Philosophie* will be referenced as follows: Jaspers, Ph1; Jaspers, Ph2; Jaspers, Ph3. The term "Existenz" has many interpretations in the tradition of continental philosophy, but in this article it means: the selfhood of a person that has undergone philosophical elucidation. The concept of transcendence in Jaspers' philosophy has also been given many interpretations. Some have understood it as an expression of the action of transcending by consciousness (*Transendieren*) (e.g., Jeanne Hersch, Hans Kunz), while others as referring to a Being whose reality exceeds the boundaries of immanence (e.g., Hommel and von Rinteln). For purposes of the discussion here, we will adopt the second interpretation. For further discussion, see Miron, Monograph 2012, 8-13, 363-365. See Jeanne Hersch, "Existenz in der empirischen Wirklichkeit", in Jeanne Hersch, Jan Milic Lochman and Reiner Wiehl (eds.), *Karl Jaspers—Philosoph, Arzt, politischer Denker*, München and Zürich, 1986, 50; Hans Kunz, "Critique of Jaspers' Concept of Transcendence" in P.A. Schilpp (ed.), *The Philosophy of Karl Jaspers*, New York 1957, 504f. [Schilpp]; Claus Uwe Hommel, *Chiffer und Dogma: von Velhältnis der Philosophie*

answering one of Existenz's fundamental needs, serves for those who undergo it as real evidence of the existence of an extra-immanent Being.[41] However, Jaspers stressed that the "metaphysical experience [in the first language] lacks any possibility of proof [*Nachprüfbarkeit*] that could have made it into something valid for everyone".[42] The criticism of the closedness and lack of communication typical of metaphysical consciousness that formed during the first period constitute a basis for the establishment of the second language, concentrating on the person's efforts to objectivize his personal experiences that embody an element of reference to transcendence.[43] The main importance of objectivity in this context stems from it helping make transcendence accessible for the world of images and thoughts of those who had not experienced the metaphysical experiences, and also enables communication between people with different metaphysical experiences. The transition from the perception of selfhood as closed within its own boundaries to the development of an ability to communicate that could make the individual's personal experiences into a source of meaning also for those who had not experienced them reflects to a large extent the process of the development of Jaspers' thought. This philosophy, which in its first stages assumed that a complete explication of selfhood necessitated its isolation from the contexts in which it was given, could not permit the entry of the objective viewpoint, and in fact of any other viewpoint into the arena of philosophizing. However, as Jaspers' philosophy developed and accumulated insights into Existenz, difficulties arose from the solipsistic perception of selfhood that had characterized his early thought.

The crisis Jaspers' thought encountered opened new horizons for it, undermining the solipsistic image characteristic of his early perception of selfhood, and in its place he developed a complex perception of Existenz, dealing with the real world reality. At this point he viewed positively the possibility that an objective viewpoint could contribute to self-understanding.[44] The establishment of the understanding that self-realization happens in the world and not in apparent isolation from it eventually led to the conclusion that the framework of the elucidation of selfhood itself would be incomplete unless it included the possibility to communicate with others. As he put it: "placing itself absolutely on itself alone... becomes despair for it".[45] The perception of Existenz as a worldly being, and in particular the appearance of the idea of communication in Jaspers' thought, embodied the maturation of his perception of selfhood.[46] Against this background, the understanding crystallized that the closedness from

---

zur Religion bei Karl Jaspers, Zürich, 1968, 97f.; Fritz-Joachim von Rinteln, *Beyond Existentialism*, London 1961, 207f.

[41] Jaspers, Ph3, 4.
[42] Ibid., 129.
[43] Ibid., 131-132.
[44] These philosophical moves, which have extensive implications for Jaspers' thought as a whole, are mostly concentrated in the first volume of the trilogy *Philosophie*, entitled *Philosophical World Orientation* (Ph1).
[45] Jaspers, Ph3, 4.
[46] On the relation of Existenz to the world, see Ph1, 1-23; Miron, Monograph 2012, 65-80.

others and the world alienates Existenz from itself and detracts from the possibility that its metaphysical experiences would serve its self-realization.[47]

From the perspective of Jaspers' entire oeuvre, it transpires that the concept of communication along with other ideas moderated the drive to achieve a complete and pure elucidation of selfhood, and contributed to the crystallization of a new philosophical inclination directed at obtaining an explication of the world, of Being, and of transcendence.[48] With the concept "Foundering" (*Scheitern*), expressing the peak of this inclination, Jaspers gave sharp expression to his criticism of his earlier perceptions by binding together two philosophical insights that only at this stage transpired as complementing each other. First and foremost this original philosophical concept reflected the recognition that Existenz is not "a being closed within itself", and therefore its elucidation cannot achieve completion. At the same time, awareness formed that "where I myself really exist, I do not exist just as me myself", and as a result Being and transcendence, rather than Existenz, became the foci of the philosophical discussion.[49] This change did not lead Jaspers to detachment from the philosophical insights achieved in the elucidation of selfhood, which remained in the background, but it did open new metaphysical horizons for his thought. The constructive dimension in the concept of Foundering, thanks to which the criticism of the early perception of selfhood did not conclude the philosophical effort to elucidate Existenz, was expressed in the integration of central aspects of the first two languages, into the third language. On the one hand, this language was described as the result of "self-sinking for purposes of contact with transcendence",[50] meaning that like the first language it was also founded on a personal experience in which the introspective element is central. On the other hand, unlike the closedness typical of the first language, in the third language Existenz recognizes the speculative nature of its metaphysical experiences. Its definition as "mediator" (*mitteilbare*), which indicates that the third language is open in principle to communication, also sets the boundary between it and the first language and reveals the element common to it and the second language. The perception of immanence as a cipher (*chiffre*) of transcendence, formulated in the third language, grants new meaning to the main characteristics of the two other languages, which also apply to it: as in the first language, the marks of selfhood's

---

[47] An early version of the idea of communication appeared in the article "Loneliness", which Jaspers wrote in 1915-1916, but which was published only after his death, by his student Jeanne Hersch. See Karl Jaspers, "Einsamkeit", in *Revue International de Philosophie*, Bd. 37, 1983, 390-409. For a presentation of the principles of the perception of communication, see Jaspers, Ph2, 50-117; Miron, Monograph 2012, 109-125. For further discussion, see Fritz Kaufmann, "Karl Jaspers and a Philosophy of Communication", in Schilpp, 210-295; Jürgen Schultheiss, *Philosophieren Kommunikation: Versuch zu Karl Jaspers' Apologie des Kritischen Philosophieren*, Meisenheim, 1981, 97f.; Franz Yosef Fuchs, *Seinverhältniss, K. Jaspers' Existenzphilosophie: Existenz und Kommunkation*, Frankfurt, 1984; Donatella Di Cesare, *Die Sprache in Der Philosophie von Karl Jaspers*, Tübingen, 1996, 11-23.

[48] This development is discussed in the context of the "transition mechanisms", dealing with three ideas: communication, historicity (*Geschichtilschkeit*), and boundary situations. See Miron, Monograph 2012, 103-168.

[49] Jaspers, Ph3, 220.

[50] Ibid., 135.

search for the meaning of its existence are apparent in the third language too, but the individualistic character of this search does not contradict the effort to communicate. In the third language, the cipher language (*Chiffreschrift*), transcendence is no longer perceived only as an expression of existential relations or as a reflection of Existenz about itself and about reality.[51] In fact, Existenz understands itself as directed at the Being existing beyond the familiar boundaries of immanence and of human existence as such, though it knows that only through the symbolic function of language can this experience be accessible to it. As Jaspers put it: "the symbol does not merely clarify, it makes real (*wirklich*) what otherwise would be as nothing".[52]

The character of the selfhood that seeks meaning and significance for its existence, as arises from the general description of the development of Jaspers' philosophy, will transpire below as contributing to the discussion of Hartman's thought. I wish to argue, based on the fundamental similarity between the two first languages described by Jaspers and certain aspects of Hartman's two perceptions of deity, that important sides of the character of the believer in Hartman's discussion can be revealed, but that he did not note all of its qualities himself. The lack of communication in the ontological perception, the awareness of the uniqueness of the metaphysical experience, and the image of "self-sufficient" are largely shared by the character of Existenz arising from Jaspers' first language and the believer in the ontological perception. The absence of a real connection to finitude and the lack of interpersonal communication, which make the continued existence of the solipsistic perception of self typical of Jaspers' early thought difficult, may also explain the problematic existing in the background of the ontological perception of deity arising from Hartman's writings. The believer in the ontological deity, who lives with the expectation of redemption from his finite being and who cannot share his personal experiences with people not included in the closed collective within which he lives, portrays a perception of exclusive and undeveloping faith. The simplistic understanding he has regarding providence leads him to an egoism that does not enable him to see the connection between his personal redemption and the redemption of all. While the ontological deity is presented as capable of sustaining itself without the connection of the believers to it, the believer huddling in its shadow does not develop an independent personality and cannot fulfill himself while he is guided by the perception of reality derived from it. The person's ability to share his beliefs with others is not interpreted in this context as an abstract need of religious faith in terms of the Being itself, but as an essential existential need without which the believer would not only find it difficult to continue holding his beliefs, but also maintaining his self-identity.

In addition to the contribution of Jaspers' philosophy to the clarification of the problematic entailed implicitly in the ontological perception of deity, its relevance can also be found in a more comprehensive clarification of the universal perception of deity. Existenz's ability in the second language to objectivize its experiences expresses the degree of communication and its connection to finitude—an ability so lacking in the character of selfhood reflected

---

[51] Ibid., 135-136.
[52] Karl Jaspers, *Von Der Wahrheit*, München, [1947] 1991, 1032 (hereafter: Jaspers, *Truth*).

in the first language—may clarify important aspects of the universal perception presented by Hartman.[53] Like the Existenz characterizing the second language, the personality of the believer in this approach does not suffer from an illusionary perception of reality that a modern person could not usually accept—whether or not he is a believer.[54] The relation to finitude shared by Existenz and the character of the believer reflected in the universal approach greatly contributes to the connection of these characters with their selfhood. We can also argue, in my opinion, that the "image of God" in the person included in the reality God created in the creation grants him better tools to deal with the complexity afforded by the scientific technological reality to a person committed to a religious worldview.

However, although the universal perception of deity and the second language presented by Jaspers may answer problems arising in the ontological perception and in the first language, it is entirely clear that this does not satisfy the metaphysical yearning at the basis of these two thinkers' philosophies. The unparalleled power of the metaphysical experience and the consciousness of the uniqueness accompanying both the character of the believer in the ontological perception and of the Existenz in the first language are greatly eroded in Hartman's universal perception of deity and in Jaspers' second language. Jaspers' third language, like Hartman's perception of the covenant, aims, as will transpire, to fill the lack in the first two types, thus demonstrating the methodological role they played for each of them.

The Perception of Judaism as a Covenant

The perception of the covenant based on the "synthesis" model appearing in Hartman's reply to Leibowitz, and Jaspers' third language, reflect the fact that both the alternatives presented above did not answer the philosophical needs of these two thinkers.[55] The theocentric perception of deity gave rise to a selfhood characterized by an illusionary view of immanent reality, dependence, and eventually alienation from itself. The universal perception of deity gave people the space required for developing a more mature personality, self-conscious, and capable of maintaining communication relations with its surroundings. However, the disadvantage of this perception stemmed from its not preserving the unparalleled power of the metaphysical experience of the individual personality that experiences it. Jaspers' tendency to express in the third language both the

---

[53] To remove doubt, I wish to clarify that one should not conclude from this that it is the crystallization of the metaphysical experiences in objective patterns that helps a person engage with the world, but rather that the very existence of such an ability may help with this engagement.

[54] I am using the term "illusionary" here in the sense it was given in Goldman's philosophical article, "On Non-Illusionary Faith". See Eliezer Goldman, *Researches and Studies: Jewish Philosophy Past and Present*, Jerusalem 1997, 361-371 [Hebrew]. The non-illusionary dimension in Hartman's thought has received an extensive interpretation in Gili Zivan, "Non-Illusionary Religion—Between Modernism and Post-Modernism: A Study in David Hartman's Thought", in *Renewing Jewish Commitment*, 209-269.

[55] Hartman's perception of covenant receives extensive discussion in *Renewing Jewish Commitment*, see, for instance, David Zohar, "The Covenant in the Thought of Hirschensohn and David Hartman", *Renewing Jewish Commitment*, 170 and n. 3 there.

general and communicative element and the personal and experiential dimension also characterized the "synthesis" model presented in Hartman's reply to Leibowitz, and can be seen as a starting point for his perception of covenant. He says that this model "[indeed] recognizes Judaism's special patterns of thought and action and does not wish to present Judaism as merely an enlightened moral culture, [but] it still believes that Judaism is not a unique species of its own but it participates in the framework of universal wisdom and human psychology". These two facets introduce into the synthesis model "a dynamic tension between the experience of the intimate relation to God through Sinai and the *halakhah*, and the recognition that the *halakhah* should serve the purpose of realizing the basis element of 'God's image' in human beings"—a tension that serves a central role in Hartman's own perception of covenant.[56]

In a way, we can see Jaspers' concept of the cipher (*Chiffre*) and Harman's perception of the Sinai covenant as frameworks containing the human aspect and the diving aspect, which in the first stage were located in different contexts: for Jaspers in the first two languages and for Hartman in the stories of exodus and creation. Jaspers' statement that Existenz "verifies its possibilities when it recognizes itself as based on transcendence" reflects the view that seeks to bridge between the human and the divine without denying the sovereignty of each of them.[57] A similar attempt also arises from Hartman's interpretation of the Sinai covenant in which, he says, "joined the categorical authority of revelation to human moral freedom and responsibility".[58] Thus, unlike the covenant of Egypt and the creation stories, which in Hartman's interpretation present different forms of separation of the human from the divine, the Sinai covenant is presented as a more successful model of a covenant between the divine and the human. As he puts it:

> My reason for preferring the Sinai model is that I do not wish to divide my world into two separate realms, one of which is characterized by autonomous action based upon human understanding of the divine norm and the other by anticipation of and dependence upon divine interventions. I prefer to see God's will for Jewish history, just like God's will for Jewish communal life, as channeled exclusively through the efforts of the Jewish community to achieve the aims of the Torah given at Sinai.[59]

As will transpire later, in addition to the significant similarity between the ideas of these two thinkers, who were active in a different cultural context and in relation to different and even rival historical religions, they also use philosophical strategies that are similar in terms of their basic principle. Three of the central strategies are demonstrated below: the "Foundering", the choice of finitude, and the viewing of interpretation as the basis of the affinity to God.

---

[56] Hartman in Sagi, 54.
[57] Jaspers, Ph3, 4.
[58] Hartman 1985, 39.
[59] Ibid., 231-232.

The "Foundering"

The analysis Hartman proposed to some of the most central biblical stories stressed the uprising of human beings in light of God's demands. It is precisely the ontological deity, which imposed its terror on people and used strong pressure on them, which is unable to restrain the human rebellion against divine authority. Thus, for instance, Hartman explains that "The presentation of the story of the golden calf right after the moment of election may be understood as a reminder that the covenantal community is always liable to fail in its task".[60] Similarly, Hartman states that the beginning of Genesis indicates that "God cannot create a world as he wishes… [and] everything God wants cannot be realized",[61] and he likewise sees the story of the Garden of Eden as an expression of human corruption and failure.[62] His interpretation of these two biblical stories shows that it is impossible to separate the failure of the perception of deity from the failure of the believer to uphold his faith in it. The sin of Adam and Eve expresses uprising against the ontological deity that unilaterally determined the rules of behavior in reality.[63] The rejection of the tranquil reality by Adam and Eve symbolizes the failure of the ontological deity to win the hearts of the believers. This sharpens the understanding that the failure is not only a reaction to realizing the ontological deity's ability for destruction, it also can occur also when the deity is apparently beneficial to human beings and showering them with good things. In this spirit, Hartman interpreted ""The presentation of the story of the golden calf right after the moment of election may be understood as a reminder that the covenantal community is always liable to fail in its task", and saw the "The biblical description of Israel in the desert is a reminder not only of how vulnerable human beings are to idolatry, but also of how willing they are to succumb to the attractions of slavery".[64]

The philosophical concept of Foundering in Jaspers—through which the instability of the solipsistic selfhood and its difficulty in sustaining its evident certainty in the existence of the transcendent Being—can, in my opinion, illuminate the nature of the failure stressed in the interpretation Hartman offered to these stories. The collapse of the solipsistic conception of selfhood, which in Jaspers' philosophy transpired as a condition for constituting a real relation to transcendence, can in this context explain the instability of the two forms of connection between God and his believers in the Garden of Eden and in Egypt. This collapse enables us to argue that the clash between two types of egoistic closedness, that of the deity and that of the human being, prevented the very possibility of constituting a covenant between them. In fact, the meaning of the philosophical concept of Foundering, which in Jaspers reflected an experience of selfhood, is expanded in Hartman's thought and transpires as relevant also for the understanding of the character of the deity. In other words, the closedness, the

---

[60] Ibid., 261.

[61] Hartman, "God of the Communities of Israel", 15.

[62] Hartman 1985, 26.

[63] Clearly this interpretation of Hartman's reveals the "ontological face" of the creator God who shapes reality in the Garden of Eden, but this should not be seen as a contradiction of the nature of the universal divinity of creation.

[64] Ibid., 261-262.

solipsism, and the egoism characterize the ontological deity no less than they characterize its believers. Hartman's interpretation of the sin of the golden calf and the story of Adam and Eve in the garden of Eden demonstrates not only the failure of the ontological perception of deity in determining the boundaries of the reality human beings would inhabit, but also the believer's inability to adhere to such a deity. In this respect, God's failure to win the hearts of Adam and Eve and the rebellious behavior of the Israelites in the sin of the golden calf represent two sides of the same coin: they express the long-term instability of the ontological perception of deity.

The philosophical term "Foundering", found to be relevant for the elucidation of Hartman's thought in this context, is not synonymous with 'failure'. While the latter usually indicates the missing of certain possibilities, Foundering as a philosophical concept is revealed in Jaspers' thought as the origin of a positive consciousness enabling achievement of a new understanding.[65] The sharp awareness of the boundaries of his perception of selfhood, on which the concept of Foundering rests, served Jaspers as a foundation for constituting a more mature metaphysical consciousness that helped him overcome the solipsism that ensnared his early thought. Similarly, in Hartman's thought, "God's repeated confrontation with human corruption", reflecting the failure of his relations with his believers, is presented as a starting point for the search for "new ways of relating to human beings in history"[66] against the background of the failure of exile and the consciousness of organic existence typical of the Bible.[67] The lesson arising from Hartman's interpretation of these two stories thus becomes a constituting element of the perception of covenant expressing a way of relating preferable to that arising from the ontological and universal perceptions of deity. On the one hand, the deity is required to restrict its freedom in order to allow human beings to express their selfhood. On the other hand, human beings are also required to limit their freedom in order to constitute a conscious situation that would enable them to face the deity. In this context, one can see certain facets of the character of Abraham as reflecting the image of the ideal believer in the perception of the believer formed in Hartman's thought. Hartman learned from the *Midrash* about Abraham:[68]

> Abraham represents the shift from God the solitary Creator of Nature to God the self-limiting covenantal Lord of History. Abraham is not simply an instrument of the omnipotent Master of Nature; he stands over and against God as an other; his importance as a historical figure is marked by divine self-limitation, that is, by God's becoming the 'God of the earth' only through the efforts of Abraham. [...] whereas Noah was

---

[65] For more on the concept of Foundering in Jaspers, see Miron, Monograph 2012; and also Johannes Thyssen, "The Concept of 'Foundering' in Jaspers' Philosophy", in: Schilpp, 297-335.
[66] Hartman 1985, 26.
[67] Hartman 1978, 2.
[68] Midrash Sifre, Genesis 24:2, cited in Hartman 1985, 29.

incidental to his covenant with God, Abraham was a full-fledged partner".[69]

These words help establish the argument that the covenant model involves elements of the two languages Jaspers described. Like the selfhood accompanying the first language, in this context Abraham's character is characterized by an aspiration to leave its personal mark on reality and not to be controlled by forces with which it cannot communicate. They also reflect the effort, central to Jaspers' second language, to normalize the metaphysical experience in the finite reality and make it into an integral part of it. It is clear that defining Abraham's God as "the God of History" indicates a certain proximity between Hartman's perception of the covenant and the universal perception of deity. This perception, which was based on respect toward finitude, indirectly enables history meaning a worldview in which reality is perceived as managed in accordance with the rules of nature and human initiatives.[70]

However, while the covenant with Abraham has universal implications, his relations with God are based on commitment to certain values and in the end have a particular character. Much as universalistic perceptions can serve as a solid basis for the pluralism Hartman considered a religious value, he clarifies that a Jew committed to the biblical tradition cannot be committed to "the element of being" as in the deistic approach, which did not recognize the authority of revelation or its value in shaping the believer's consciousness of reality, but rather he is committed to the God involved in history rather than in nature.[71] In this respect we can state that making history—a more limited realm than nature, whose phenomena are phrased in more general terms—into the arena where the covenant between human beings and God is realized indicates a process of individuation that both the deity and the believer undergo in the perception of the covenant. On the one hand, the God of Abraham is not presented as realizing his power in the entire universe like the God of creation. The dialogue with him focuses on his plans aimed at the particular human collective destined to develop from Abraham's seed. On the other hand, Abraham himself appears as a real character with a name, certain life conditions (married to Sarah, living in a certain place, etc.). The implications of this process, apparent in God's dialogue with Abraham, for the character of the communication between the deity and the believer are clear: the deity must assume the possible occurrence of the believers' sin and rebellion, while the believer himself must accept the possibility that

---

[69] Ibid., 29, my emphasis.

[70] For more on the meaning of human autonomy in Hartman's thought, see Moshe Halinger, "Halakhah and Human Autonomy", in: Avi Sagi, Dudi Schwartz, and Yedidia Z. Stern (eds.), *Judaism: A Dialogue Between Cultures*, Jerusalem 1990, 336-345. See also D. Singer, "The New Orthodox Theology", *Modern Judaism*, 9, 1989, 38-48.

[71] Hartman 1999, 154-155. On the pluralistic element in Hartman's thought, see David Dishon, "Pluralism between Religions: David Hartman on Jewish-Christian Dialogue", in *Renewing Jewish Commitment*, 107-120; Ronen Lubitz, "The Theological Structure for the Constituting of Tolerance and Pluralism in David Hartman's Perception of Judaism", ibid., 227-309; Einat Ramon, "Secular Judaism and Secular Jews in David Hartman's Religious Thought", ibid., 425-443. For comparison with the structure for religious pluralism in Jaspers' philosophy, see John F. Kane, *Pluralism and Truth in Religion*, Michigan, 1981.

natural hazards and in general the arbitrariness and chance involved in reality, might not pass him by thanks to his faith in God. This is the depth of religious faith anchoring the believer and his God in history, and this is also its inevitable cost.

The process of individuation can explain Hartman's argument that sin denotes the start of the process that leads to divine revelation and election. According to him, the egalitarian and non-discriminatory approach of the God of creation toward reality, which later encountered human rebellion, "frustrate God", who succeeded in creating the whole world with his speech but not to make Adam accept the goodness in the Garden of Eden. In his opinion, the "solution" to God's frustration arises only later in Genesis, when God appears as seeking to create a community that will preserve the primal relations of the Being not through the consciousness of creation but through choice and commitment.[72] This means that the admission that human beings have their own particular identity from which the possibility inevitably arises that they might not choose God was a decisive stage in God's "understanding" that the pattern of his connection with the believer must express his personal relation toward his believers. Therefore, Hartman states that the revelation to a particular nation or a particular person was essential for the biblical deity of history.[73] The election and the revelation aimed at a certain group of people, itself composed of individuals with independent personalities, do not express only the understanding that the covenantal relations must be grounded on recognition of the partner's particularity, but also the admission of the possibility that people could feel separate from and even alien to God and reject the relationship he offers them. Hartman goes far in his efforts to establish the particular dimension in the covenantal relationship, and argues that even "God of the earth" himself becomes a God "only through the efforts" of human beings.[74] Against this background, we can argue that the deity's particularity not only constitutes an essential requirement for the very establishment of the relations with his believers, it was also essential for the very determining of God's status as such. In this spirit, Hartman sought to demonstrate the centrality of the particular dimension in the relationship between the believer and his God through the institution of marriage. He argues that when there is love mature between the couple, "They learn [...] that love cannot compensate for human weaknesses and failures... A mature relationship is based on respect for human frailty and weakness... They appreciate the problematic of human finitude and the fact that separateness is a permanent feature of any love relationship".[75] Much as marriage still usually constitutes a universal model for a relationship between adult people, it is never structured according to a defined pattern and always has a particular form of realization. Just as in mature love there is no expectation that the very existence of the relationship will lead to a complete change in the personality of the partners, so in Hartman's perception of the covenant the believer has no expectation of redemption that will change the world

---

[72] Hartman, 1999, 157-158.
[73] Ibid., 155.
[74] Hartman, 1985, 29.
[75] Ibid., 273.

order, and in parallel the deity does not expect his believers to be perfect and answer his demands at any time.[76]

However, after Hartman established the essentiality of the particular dimension in the covenantal relations between God and his believers, an additional trend can be observed in his words that qualified the particularity through anchoring it within the framework of general principles. Thus, for instance, Hartman states that the "concrete sign [of Abraham's covenant]—circumcision—signified to later generations that commitment to particular norms and values must define a person's identity".[77] Elsewhere, he describes the *mitzvoth* (commandments) as providing the structure for regular relations to the deity. He argues that the interpretation of the Sinai revelation in terms of the revelation of God's laws to the community necessarily restricts the spontaneity of the revelation[78] that expresses the personal dimension in the relationship between the deity and the believers and anchors it within a more general context. The marriage example that served to demonstrate the personal and particular in the covenantal relationship is harnessed in this context to stress their general dimension. At this point, the maturity and the secret of the stability of the marriage covenant is presented as stemming from the absence of a conditioning factor in the relationship between the parties. Just as "Mature lovers no longer fear they will be condemned or rejected because of failures or mistakes", so the covenant whose institutions the Sages worked to establish grants the "feeling that the relationship is too firm to admit the possibility of its termination. The covenant is certain". "Specific actions may be judged"—an agreed process that defines the relations between two independent parties—"but not the vitality and significance of the relationship itself".[79] In other words, like a marriage, the stability of the mature relationship of a person with the deity is also based on the fact that each of the parties in it remains within the boundaries of his being—the person does not escape his finitude and the transcendent deity does not delve into finite reality and manage it instead of human beings. Precisely within this framework, preserving the *general principle* that people and the deity remain what they are, can a system be enabled in which each particular personality can find the form of relationship that suits him or her. The unconditionedness demonstrated through the marriage relationship sharpens at this point the understanding that the particularity in the covenantal relations is itself contained within the boundaries of a general framework whose parties are not motivated by the desire to breach it.

The understanding that sees the *mitzvoth* and the general norms, in which the covenantal relations are anchored, as means that qualify the particularity of these relations, did not in Hartman's thought reach the point of removing this element of his thought or making it into a marginal facet. The anchoring of the covenant in finitude, which I will discuss later, guarantees that the revelation itself will always appear to human beings in an incomplete and fragmentary form, and thus every human situation in the present will always require a renewed interpretation of the contents of revelation. On the other hand, even the interpreter himself does

---

[76] On the element of mutuality in revelation faith, see also Hartman 1999, 155.
[77] Hartman, 1985, 32.
[78] Hartman, 1999, 158-159.
[79] Hartman, 1985, 274.

not create an independent and original creation, but always starts from an existing datum.[80] Like Jaspers' concept "situation Being" (*Seinsituation*), in which the necessity of world reality is intertwined with the freedom entailed in its possibilities, so too the particular character of finitude granted by the believer's experiences has a background and depth exceeding the boundaries of the existence and consciousness of the individual interpreter.[81] Therefore, the meaning granted to texts and *mitzvoth* is not perceived as *derived* from them, but as something the person creates from data that are themselves open to a variety of interpretations. In addition, the constraints the interpreter encounters may prevent him from presenting his interpretation as a universal understanding of the revelation.[82] In this respect, precisely the individual's effort to understand the contents of the revelation—mainly expressing the attempt to establish his faith not only on a religious experience but on a meeting with a text that requires him to employ intellectual skills that are not subject to this experience and that also serve him for other purposes—can help release him from the presumption to make general and universal claims about the revelation.

Against this background, Hartman is revealed as seeking to have things both ways: he uses *particularity* as a means to preserve the person's relation to his selfhood and to the concrete finitude typical of his situation, and also to protect the interpretation from the interpreter's tendency to present it as absolute and universal. In parallel, the *element of generality*, typical of the covenantal relations anchored in the legality of the *mitzvoth*, serves as a means of making religious consciousness and the interpretation that constitutes it communicative and into a foundation for constructing a pluralistic and tolerant community. Clarifying the complex relationship between the particular element in Hartman's perception of covenant and its general element, which restrict and balance each other, enable us to argue that his perception of covenant does not simply constitute a "synthesis" composed of aspects taken from both of the other perceptions of deity Hartman discusses in his interpretation. The analysis I have presented above shows that the isolated selfhood and the transcendent God in the ontological perception, and the universalistic viewpoint on which his interpretation of the God of creation is based, were unable to join together in Hartman's approach until they had undergone a profound transformation that restricted the dimensions of each component in the perceptions and omitted the original implications attributed to them. In other words, the selfhood appearing in the model Hartman termed "synthesis" is not characterized by a tendency to accept the ontological deity or

---

[80] First and foremost this statement is founded on the fact that the person interprets not only within a given cultural context but also within an existing interpretative tradition. Hartman expands this statement to the question of God's existence. See Hartman, "The God of the Communities of Israel", 13 ff.

[81] The concept "situation Being" in Jaspers' philosophy plays a decisive role in rescuing his perception of selfhood from its early solipsistic image and in its perception as a worldly being. See Ph1, 1-4. However, it should be noted that the element of possibility embodied in this concept is not exhausted by the interpretation possibilities of finitude but relates first and foremost to the ontological multifaceted nature of immanence. An early version of this term appears in his book: Karl Jaspers, *Die Geistige Situation der Zeit*, Berlin-Leipzig 1931, 23f.

[82] Hartman 1999, 159-160.

the solipsistic personality demonstrated in the description of Jaspers' first language, which matches it. On the other hand, the presence of the transcendent deity is not similar to the ontological deity or to the universal deity that is related to the second language in Jaspers' approach, but its special connection to the specific collective destined to arise from Abraham's seed is stressed. The particularity of the covenant, enabled through the effort taken by both parties to restrict themselves, transpires as contributing to both of them. The ontological deity that restrains its own impetus for immanence thus achieves a more stable and profound connection from the believers. Thanks to this, the believer who becomes capable as an individual of transcending closed forms of thinking creates a connection with the reality in which he lives and achieves a more mature self-understanding. In parallel, the universal image of the deity in the creation does not remain distanced from finite reality and no longer displays an impersonal relation to human beings, and the rational element it contains becomes an essential tool in the formation of communicative relations between it and human beings.

However, while the covenant made at Sinai serves as an ideational framework in which the fundamental principles that constitute Hartman's perception of faith and deity are crystallized, it transpires that it is not a substitute for the two first positions presented above. Moreover, it seems that Hartman's commitment to the Jewish tradition as a whole and as historical continuity spurred him to fix the weight of the two forms of connection between God and the believers in the creation and in Egypt within his perception of covenant, anchored in elements related to the revelation at Sinai. He argues that "the biblical story in Genesis serves as a framework for the covenant at Sinai by suggesting that the realization of God's design for history, as opposed to His design for nature, involves human beings". [83] Regarding the role of the relationship between God and his believers in Egypt in his perception of covenant, Hartman states:

> While the Exodus story is never negated or denied, it is now retained as a memory, like the memory of our early relational intimacy with our parents, which is fondly retained in later years as we build our life around mature friendships and voluntary commitments. Just as the memory of childhood dependence is imprinted in one's mature consciousness, so too can the Exodus from Egypt remain as a permanent memory".[84]

In addition to the exodus from Egypt existing in the collective memory on which religious consciousness is based, Hartman believes that God's relationship with his believers in Egypt contains several essential insights that complement his perception of covenant. It shows that the covenant of Sinai can be fully realized only when social and political conditions enable human beings freedom and self-respect; it "prevents the misunderstanding of the *mitzvah* as an inward spiritual category, unrelated to social and political conditions", and finally, "the Exodus

---

[83] Hartman, 1985, 25.
[84] Ibid., 270-271.

counteracts the temptation of escaping into otherworldliness because it anchors the covenant in history and in the social and political life of the community".[85] The framework originating in the character of the deity in creation, and the memory and acceptance granted by the exodus story to the perception of the covenant based on Sinai demonstrate once again the relevance of the philosophical concept of Foundering in elucidating Hartman's approach. As we have seen, the criticism expressed in Jaspers' concept of Foundering regarding his early solipsistic perception of selfhood did not deny the importance of Existenz in constituting the later and more mature metaphysical approach, and it was even based on parts of it. Similarly, Hartman's concept of covenant, with all its criticism of the characters of the deity and the believer arising from the stories of exodus and creation, did not negate the value of the forms of connection they express, and even indicated their contribution to the religious communication it supported. It appears that thanks to the continuity to which Hartman's viewpoint regarding Judaism is committed, it saw itself as free to appropriate certain aspects of the various appearances of the Jewish tradition and to turn them into part of his independent perception, using them to grant Judaism a new face.

The Choice of Finitude

The ontological deity and the universal deity and the characters of believers that accompanied them in Hartman's interpretation portrayed different forms of contempt for finitude. More precisely, they expressed an unwillingness to accept the gap between the deity and the human being. The ontological approach stresses God's intervention in the processes of natural reality, and similarly, the believer expecting miracles and signs hoped to escape from finitude. The emphasis on the deity's accessibility in the universal approach expressed the striving to overcome the gap between the divine and the human. A similar principle exists in the first two languages in Jaspers' thought: Existenz's unmediated experience of the presence of the deity in the first language, and the translation of transcendence into objective language in the second language, also largely negate the gap between the divine and the human. In contrast with these two approaches, in Hartman's perception of covenant "our finitude is appreciated for its own intrinsic value",[86] and thus it denies any basis for the assimilation of the everyday human existence into the divine Being, or turning it into its follower. Indeed, like the events accompanying the story of the exodus from Egypt, the Sinai revelation too is presented in the Bible as a miraculous occurrence, but the *mitzvoth* given at this event, which largely defined the essence of the covenant between God and his people, determined in Hartman's opinion "limitations upon the subsequent occurrence of miracles in history". Instead of "spontaneous divine miracles in history... an immanent communal framework that enables an orderly development of history based on the human freedom to act" is adopted.[87] Hartman presents the central motive behind his perception of covenant in the following passage:

---

[85] Ibid., 271.
[86] Ibid., 259.
[87] Ibid., 235-236.

> It is the development of this metaphysical picture of reality that allows *us* to value the covenant even without the certainty of eschatological redemption... Acknowledging the dignity of finitude, one learns to accept death as a permanent feature of the human condition. This appreciation of creation is antipathetic to the mystic longing to get beyond finitude. It holds that our consciousness of finitude is *not an estrangement from our true being* and that we do not need to anchor our existence in the eternal before we can discover *authenticity, legitimacy, or "redeemedness"*... the immortality of the soul or the physical resurrection of the dead... are therefore not essential for us to stand as dignified finite creatures *before our Creator. Finite human* beings who accept their creatureliness know that they remain separate from their Creator.[88]

Hartman concluded from the fact that the covenant took place in the desert, where, as the biblical stories showed, the disadvantages and weaknesses of human beings were revealed, that the covenant is not "made with intellectual or spiritual geniuses or with persons of exceedingly great moral capacity, but with persons who are prepared to ignore God's scheme for history when their fundamental biological needs are not satisfied".[89] Against this background it transpires that the choice of finitude reflects first and foremost the requirement that the filling of human needs, existential and emotional, will serve as a basis and condition for the constitution of the covenant, rather than serving as a reward for it.[90] Hartman's proposal to separate human beings' basic needs from the real content of the faith does not reflect the believer being above these needs, but wishes to negate the worldview perceiving faith as a means for their fulfillment. Thus, only when the basic conditions stemming from human beings' finitude are met can they turn to constituting the faith, which in itself reflects the no less human need to transcend their finitude, and to "anchor their existence in an eternal Being". In this context, Hartman mentions the fact that "faith in the certainty of God's acting in history irrespective of human initiative and action is thus found in both the prophetic and rabbinic tradition". However, he writes: "I have chosen to take up a different strand of the Judaic tradition and to construct a covenantal anthropology in which the essential role of human freedom and responsibility in the realization of the covenantal vision of Judaism is never suspended or neutralized", thus indicating the conscious nature of his choice of finitude as the key element in religious faith.[91]

---

[88] Ibid., 259, my emphases.

[89] Ibid., 262.

[90] On this point, Hartman's position is very similar to that of Leibowitz, whose main points are in the article "Practical Mitzvoth". See Yeshayahu Leibowitz, *Judaism, the Jewish Nation, and the State of Israel*, Jerusalem and Tel Aviv 1979, 13-36 [Hebrew] (hereafter: Leibowitz 1979). For further reading regarding Leibowitz's approach to the *Mitzvoth* see: "The possibility of religious subjectivity - its defense and critique", in Anne Koch (ed.)., *Watchtower Religionswissenschaft. Standortbestimmungen im wissenschaftlichen Feld*, diagonal-Verlag, Marburg, 2007, 95-118.

[91] Hartman, 1985, 264-265. Hartman's choice well reflects the shift characterizing modern Jewish philosophy from dealing with the entity of the deity to clarifying the character of

Hartman's discussion of the arguments for choosing finitude as the anchor of the covenantal relations and the implications of this choice clearly indicate his awareness of the problematic arising from the two other perceptions of deity. Against the background of our discussion of Jaspers' philosophy, this discussion is interpreted as the philosophical consciousness of Foundering accompanying this choice. But beyond this, Hartman's words lack a real explication regarding the nature of finitude itself, which he sought to support as an essential part of faith. Nor does Hartman provide an answer to the question why a person should see religion and general and Judaism in particular as a framework within which his self-realization and self-fulfillment can be enabled. In this context, the characterization of the covenant "in terms of a complete interaction between God and man in which humanity is not denied"[92] is important, since it makes the person's existential journey to himself relevant for clarifying Hartman's ideas. It is precisely Jaspers' thought—demonstrating a process of development from recognizing finitude as a medium in which a person can realize himself to seeing finitude itself as anchored in a transcendent Being—that can help clarify philosophical processes that remained implicit in Hartman's thought. This means that the transition from dealing with selfhood to elucidate transcendent reflected in Jaspers' philosophy could fill with contents the vacuum Hartman's thought left between the finitude in which the person conducts his life and the deity as a transcendent Being in relation to which religious faith is constituted. At this point, it is relevant that the choice of finitude typical of Jaspers' thought results from the collapse of the solipsistic perception of selfhood. Existenz's acquaintance with finitude as the Being that surrounds it not only revealed to it possibilities that were hidden from it while it was entirely devoted to clarifying its selfhood, but also led to the exposure of the metaphysical depth in which immanence itself is anchored. In fact, only immanence that is not merely immanent, meaning immanence that is perceived as containing metaphysical depth, can serve as a framework for the self-realization of the Existenz that does not wish to be trapped in the boundaries of its selfhood. In other words, metaphysics appears from Jaspers' words as an element of openness, space, and depth. This is how it can serve as a substrate to connect between a more mature selfhood and immanence that has wide and distant horizons, to which Hartman's thought was also directed.

This insight is the basis, in my opinion, of Jaspers' definition of immanence as a cipher of transcendence. On the first level, this statement means that immanence is not self-standing but is connected with a certain relation to a wider Being,[93] and so it is clear that the boundaries of selfhood's realization in

---

the believer within the boundaries of finitude. A clear example of this shift is the thought of Franz Rosenzweig, seeking to see death as the appropriate starting point of philosophy. See in particular Franz Rosenzweig, *Star of Redemption*, University of Notre Dame Press, 1985. However, the thought of A. J. Heschel, M. J. Berdyczewski, H.N. Bialik and others also demonstrates this trend. For the cultural and historical background for this, see for example Eliezer Schweid, *Rethinking*, Jerusalem 1991, 283-305 [Hebrew]. For more on Hartman's interpretation of Heschel's thought, see Hartman 1999, 169-180.

[92] Hartman in Sagi, 55.

[93] Jaspers developed this fundamental idea within his idea of the encompassing (*Umgreifende*), at the center of his great book *On Truth*. See in particular Jaspers, *Von der Wahrheit*, Piper: München, (1947) 1991, 47-222 (hereafter: *Truth*).

immanence are not finite, just as immanence itself does not embody the boundaries of Being. But with a deeper observation, the meaning of the definition of immanence as a cipher of transcendence is that transcendence or the deity itself has an immanent dimension. Therefore, immanence itself should be seen as embodying forces that are not exhausted within it as an existential reality in which people live as finite beings. The concept "immanent transcendence" (*immanente Transzendenz*) reflected this profound vision that enfolds a dual commitment: both to immanence as a finite reality that has its own existence and that constitutes a framework in which human beings live, and to the self-realization of human beings, which transpired as unobtainable in isolation and detachment from immanence, which in itself is not exhausted in its being a finite entity.[94] Jaspers' thought paves the philosophical way from the person's egoistic and closed selfhood to the personality striving to constitute a relation with the transcendent entity through two complementary processes. These are the formation of recognition of finitude as a medium for self-realization and as anchored in the metaphysical depth existing beyond it, and in parallel the maturation of the selfhood portrayed, among other things, in the formation of the person's awareness of his need for transcendence as a source of meaning and significance in existence. This also clarified both the person's turning to elucidate finitude, and finitude itself becoming a source and support in the process of constituting the consciousness of standing in the face of the deity.

It appears that elucidating the nature of the relation to transcendence in Jaspers' thought, in a process that neither serves as an answer to a person's egoistic needsnor involves breaching the boundary separating people as finite creatures from transcendence as an infinite being can illuminate important aspects in the character of faith at the basis of Hartman's perception of covenant. This faith constitutes an expression of a more mature and conscious humanity that has a wide influence on the entirety of human existence. The covenant that "reaffirms the dignity conferred upon human existence by creation",[95] does not free the person from his obligations in this world and does not enable him to establish his existence outside the boundaries of some regularity, and in particular not outside the rules of nature.[96] However, it seems that the qualities a person acquires in the process of crystallizing faith, which in fact is not separate from the very recognition of the reality in which he lives, can help him face the demands of existence. In his polemic with Leibowitz, who saw Judaism, or more precisely the Jewish *halakhah*, as "creating a sector of things and actions in life that have a meaning of sanctity" along with the secularity that is essentially in contradiction to the demands of religion,[97] Hartman presented his position more sharply when he argued:

---

[94] On the concept of "immanent transcendence", see Jaspers, Ph1, 35 ff.

[95] Hartman, 1985, 261.

[96] Unlike the "relative boundaries" that constitute a constant challenge for human wisdom. In this context, see Jaspers' distinction between the "relative boundaries" (*Jeweilige Grenzen*) and the "boundaries in principle" (*Grenzen Prinzipielle*), in Jaspers, Ph1, 45. On this point, Jaspers continues Kant's distinction between two concepts of boundaries: the barrier (*Schranke*) and the boundary (*Grenz*). See Immanuel Kant, *Prologomena to any Future Metaphysics,* trans. and ed. Gary Hatfield, Cambridge 1997, 111-112.

[97] Leibowitz, 1979, 31.

> Since *I argue that the entire personality participates in the worship of God*, and not only the human will, I attempt to phrase the human feature revealed in the *halakhah*... My argument is that if the person does not develop *certain attitudes to life*, he will lack the conditions to live as a man of faith in accordance with the *halakhah*. For this reason I make the effort to phrase *the human characteristics of faith*. Whoever believes in God as the creator must recognize his limitations as a human being; he must treat life as a gift, recognize the "other" beyond himself... in other words, *faith in creation not only entails a cognitive commitment to the doctrine regarding the origin of existence, it also involves the approach according to which you organize your relation to yourself, to your surroundings, and to your world in general*.[98]

Affirming the finitude and the powers of the complete personality, which were the central pillar of the philosophical relation to transcendence in Jaspers' thought, are revealed in these words as suiting the perception of faith presented in Hartman's thought. It, too, is not only a religious faith but portrays a way of facing existence, or what Jaspers called, following the German tradition, a "worldview" (*Weltanschauung*).[99]

Interpretation as the Basis of the Relation to the Deity

Hartman's choice of finitude as the space of existence and self-realization of the person and as the medium in which religious consciousness is constituted, as described above, extricated the believer from the constant expectation of divine revelation. Faith founded upon the choice of finitude does not guarantee the person an escape from the difficulties of existence or from the arbitrariness and disappointment that await him. Precisely the separation between the divinity and the world, or the loosening of the connection between the fact of God's existence and his tangible embodiment in natural reality, is what allows people to identify the dynamic of reality and to find their way within it. However, the choice of finitude not only did not silence the person's metaphysical urge to transcend his selfhood and natural reality, it even exposed the person to the existence of a hidden metaphysical layer in reality. This enabled him to notice the transcendent dimension accompanying his experiences in the world. Thus, Hartman's dual commitment to finitude and to the experiential and creative dimension of religious faith enables his perception to be viewed as denying both the pantheistic approach focused on immanence alone, which leads to the trapping of the deity itself within the boundaries of finitude, and also the ascetic position that abandons the world as a reality that has its own value due to its being a finite reality.

However, granting respect to the independent dynamic of the immanent reality that was dependent on the restriction of the deity no longer enabled direct revelation or even its expectation to be seen as a source for the constituting of faith. The concealment of the divinity within immanence made the gap between

---

[98] Hartman in Sagi, 57, my emphases.

[99] For the definition of the worldview in Jaspers and in his contemporary Max Scheler, see: Karl Jaspers, *Psychologie der Weltanschauungen*, Heidelberg, 1985 [1919], 1f. (hereafter: *Psychology*); Max Scheler, *Philosophische Weltanschauung*, Bern, 1954, 5-15.

the divine and the human into part of the factuality of immanence itself, invited the believer to decipher the mode of the deity's presence in reality, and thus opened a way for an equivocal understanding of the deity itself. On the one hand, the choice of finitude as the place and context where faith develops, and as portraying the necessity with which it must contend, directed the person to the Being existing beyond the boundaries of his selfhood, thus also avoiding the identification of faith with the person's selfhood. On the other hand, the necessarily individual viewpoint of each person experiencing differently the presence of God in the world preserved the dimension of human freedom and ruled out the possibility of pouring faith into defined patterns as expressed in Jaspers' second language. Such patterns are also expressed implicitly in the tendency to anchor divinity into universal thought patterns that would preserve the connection to the universal character of the deity of creation. These two elements related to the "situation Being" characterizing Judaism following the destruction of the second temple joined together in the model of the covenant for which the rabbinical culture that developed in the Talmud served as a paradigm for Hartman.

Hartman saw the rabbinical culture that developed in the Talmud as a post-prophetic culture that created a new medium enabling a different type of faith than that enabled by the universal and ontological perceptions of deity. While in the Bible God is identified with his immediate presence in nature as expressed in his ability to intervene in the rules of nature, in the Talmud God is present in the medium of writing, and thus becomes a text. In other words, God turns from a being interpreted through itself into a Being that can be interpreted by human beings. The wisdom of the sages is not represented by Hartman just as the only source and support remaining in the era after revelation, but it is also perceived by him as a no less reliable substitute for it. As he puts it: "Human beings can, through their own reasoning, *compensate for the absence of God's active involvement* in revealing the Torah".[100] The reliability of the text in delivering God's presence, and thus replacing revelation, is also demonstrated in Hartman's argument that the Torah, no less than nature, contains "multiple layers of meaning and complexity... [and] delivers the power and abundance of the higher reality"[101]. In this respect, there is no place for an understanding that sees the removal of prophecy from Israel and the destruction of the temple as a source or reason for the inevitable shallowness of faith and the weakness of the religious consciousness that is apparently forced to rely on the limited abilities of human beings. The rabbinical culture that makes the text into God's word in a way that the two cannot be separated sees, according to Hartman, the Torah itself as a sort of "incarnation of God's will and love".[102] In other words, the sages in their wisdom participate in the process of replacing the immediate presence of God with the written word, which according to the principle of "Torah from heaven" is perceived as God's word, since "the word... contains God's living reality".[103] Hartman argues that the interpretation of the students of the Torah not only mediates between them and God's word, but by studying faith itself becomes

---

[100] Hartman, 1985, 34, my emphasis.
[101] Hartman, 1999, 9.
[102] Ibid., 7.
[103] Ibid., 8.

dependent on the written medium that receives a life of its own to the extent that the person imagines himself speaking directly with God and "experiencing the existential immediacy of being in God's presence".[104] Eventually, not only do the study and interpretation of the Torah replace divine revelation in reality through prophets and miracles, Hartman states that in fact "Revelation finds its continuation in the rabbinic application of human wisdom".[105]

However, the embodiment of the deity in the medium of test is not a technical means enabling the believers to experience God's presence, since this medium itself constitutes part of the message the deity has to its believers. In this context, Hartman attributes importance to the fact that in contrast to the Bible, the Talmud is full of disagreements and different opinions, and even the speakers themselves do not present their positions as the only truth. In his opinion, the uniqueness of the Talmudic heritage stems from it not understanding revelation as "pure and simple" but as equivocal, rough, and complicated. Much as the image of revelation can raise difficulties for religious faith that is sometimes considered as requiring and dependent upon absolute certainty, in Hartman's opinion it teaches the person to contain vagueness and multiple meanings, and by this shows him that religious fervor and internal persuasion do not have to rest on absolute certainty.[106] In addition, the influence of the medium of test on the nature of religious truth also shapes the divine authority of revelation. Hartman argues that the Talmud and *Midrash* release God's "speech" from the verbal cables that characterized it during revelation. While it is "based on divine revelation", following the development of the oral tradition the Torah itself is inseparable from the wealth of the Talmudic interpretation, and as a result the believers become participants in the development of the revelation itself.[107] Hartman's words show that in addition to the legitimacy given to "the Jewish community... to decide for itself how it should understand the commandments that it had received from Him in the Torah"[108] expressing the faith of God himself in the power of human wisdom to reveal the truth of revelation, it also denies the very divine authority as subject to its mediation by human beings.

Turning to the Talmud rather than the Bible[109] shows that wisdom, no less than the mental maturity of the personality capable of overcoming the need for immediate understanding, is what creates the difference between the viewing of the world as a finite reality exhausted in the tools of empirical consciousness and its understanding as containing transcendent meanings.[110] It seems that while revelation prevents the person from connecting to finite reality by disputing its regularity and order and threatens the human being's ability to influence it, the interpretation developed against the background of the absence of revelation is

---

[104] Ibid., 8.
[105] Hartman, 1985, 7, my emphasis. On the perception of the *halakhah* as a human creation, see Avi Sagi, "Rabbi Soloveitchik and Prof. Leibowitz as Theoreticians of the *halakhah*", *Daat* 29 (1982), 131-148 [Hebrew].
[106] Hartman, 1999, 20-22.
[107] Hartman, 1985, 36-37.
[108] Ibid., 229.
[109] Ibid., 6.
[110] Jaspers too indicated the essential link between a person's ability to decode the ciphers of transcendence and the state of Existenz. See *On Truth*, 1037, 1041.

decisively influenced by the character of the finite reality in which the interpreter lives. Hartman notes in this context a historical fact that the boundaries of the interpretative freedom in the tradition "are simply what the community is in fact prepared to accept as Torah".[111] He also states that understanding God's laws must reflect at least to some extent the individual's understanding of reality and moral approach.[112]

The centrality of interpretation in constituting the faith and crystallizing the religious personality also reflects another facet of the role of finitude in Hartman's perception of covenant. Immanence as an existential reality, which participates in the shaping of Hartman's perception of faith and divinity, is thus joined by another dimension related to the human consciousness founded upon the texts of the tradition that are not themselves separable from the reflection accompanying the routine of existence. The two facets of immanence, as existence and as consciousness, do not leave any doubt regarding the centrality of finitude in Hartman's perception of Judaism. The statement regarding the relevance of the third language described by Jaspers, centered on the concept of the cipher, to the understanding of Hartman's thought, now receives its full meaning in this context. Just as through the concept of cipher Jaspers' metaphysical approach was anchored in immanence as a real reality,[113] so too did Hartman's perception of faith, constituting part of the person's relation to himself and his surroundings,[114] not enable it to be detached from existence in the world. Viewing immanence as a cipher of transcendence constitutes an interpretation and expresses the role of human consciousness in exposing the hidden metaphysical presence embodied in immanence.[115] So too does the Talmudic interpretation and the Jewish creation that developed later reveal the divine presence hidden in the text of the Torah. Hartman gave direct expression to his perception of religiosity as a reflection of the relationship that mediates between God and man through the various facets of finitude in the following passage:

> Real understanding of God requires that He exist in a community, and be sanctified and profaned within it… what can we do, God needs the community… He is dependent, therefore he is excited and angry when the community behaves criminally. This is what the prophets decried. The cry of the prophets is the cry of God, Who is dependent on the community's way of life. If there is no justice within society and you torment orphans and widows, God is profaned. He is dependent upon you! This is the God of Judaism… *perfection is in dependence, being dependent is the framework of perfection. God's perfection is not in*

---

[111] Hartman, 1985, 8.

[112] Hartman, 1999, 20. Hartman expresses this opinion in: Hartman, "The God of the Communities of Israel", 17. He also applies this approach in his interpretation of Maimonides' Letter of Apostasy, which expresses, in his opinion, "a position opposing purely formal legalism, and focusing on the total personality of the follower of God's path". See David Hartman, *Leadership in Times of Trouble: On Maimonides' Letters*, Tel Aviv, 1989, 57 [Hebrew].

[113] Jaspers, Ph3, 140.

[114] Hartman in Sagi, 57.

[115] Jaspers, Ph3, 170.

> *living alone, but in living in a relation, together. Perfection of relation and not perfection of "I am self-sufficient".*[116]

The theology of relation that Hartman sketches in his thought is thus based primarily upon mutual relations in which each party recognizes the essentiality of the relations themselves in order to maintain its self-identity. Just as God is dependent upon the existence of a community of believers who treat him as such, so for the individual the relation to God serves as a framework for realizing the possibilities entailed in his own humanity.[117] Just as the person cannot shape his relation to God only in accordance with his wishes and emotions, but must ask himself "what God wants from him", so too God understands that he cannot create the world as he wishes, but must take into consideration the character of the believer intended to live in this world.[118]

Hartman's thought, presenting interpretation as mediating between man and God and as a reliable substitute for revelation, inevitably raises the question: does his interpretation, presenting the Talmudic creation as participation in revelation and its continuation, not lead to cancelling the gap between the deity and the human being, and thus to the loosening of the connection between the believer and the finitude in which he exists? I do not believe it does. Hartman argues explicitly that the criticism expressed in the existence of different alternative understandings of the text in tradition grants a feeling of distance from the past, and this includes distance from the revelation.[119] Unlike the positivistic viewpoint often typical of traditional interpretations of the biblical stories that see them as an ontological description,[120] the symbolic critical view that Hartman adopted consciously,[121] could not deny the limitations of representation of consciousness regarding the Being of God. Hartman's words, "The modern-day recognition of the human sources that influence religious outlooks", testify to his awareness of the gap between God and man that remained despite the interpretative efforts. Due to this awareness, he says, the interpreter avoids "giving the convictions of faith an absolute epistemological status".[122] The comparison between Hartman's thought and that of Jaspers shows that not only is the effort to preserve the transcendent dimension in the perception of faith common to both these thinkers, the implications of this effort on the character of the believer arising from their thought are remarkably similar. Just as the hidden presence of God in the post-revelation era is perceived by Hartman as projecting onto the believer and as a result he becomes capable of postponing his drive for an immediate and unmediated experience of God's presence,[123] so too for Jaspers the ability of Existenz to decode the cipher of transcendence is dependent upon postponing its drive for immediacy, or as Heidegger called it, "the eagerness for the new"

---

[116] Hartman, "The God of the Communities of Israel", 22, my emphasis.
[117] On the element of mutuality, see Hartman, 1985, 133-134.
[118] Ibid., and also Hartman, "The God of the Communities of Israel", 15.
[119] Compare Hartman, 1999, 3.
[120] On this issue, compare ibid., 20.
[121] Compare Hartman, 1978, 4.
[122] Hartman, 1985, 257. See also Hartman's identification with the words of William James cited on p. 258.
[123] Hartman, 1978, 3.

(*Neugierigkeit*).[124] At the same time, the experience of transcendence was nourished by the ability to experience wonder and fascination with immanent reality.[125] So it appears that not only does experience in the interpretative position not cancel the gap between God and human beings, dealing with it in this way establishes its presence in consciousness and even deepens it. Thus, in shaping the way human beings face their deity it naturally contributes to preserving the gap between the human and the divine as a permanent factor in the relationship between people and God. In this respect we could argue that to the extent that interpretation succeeds in building a bridge between the believer in the present and the revelation that is no longer, it reminds him of the inescapable fact that human beings and the deity are and will continue to be on opposite sides of this bridge.[126]

The Foundering, the choice of finitude, and the place of interpretation in constituting the relation to God constitute central pillars in Karl Jaspers' metaphysics and transpired as establishing elements of Hartman's perception of covenant. These elements demonstrate the determined philosophical effort of both these thinkers to constitute a spiritual world in which accepting the existence of a metaphysical Being does not involve alienation to the modern ethos, in which the human being is positioned as a personality striving to understand itself through independence and responsibility.[127] The vision of religious pluralism arising from the thought of Hartman and Jaspers required them to consciously distance themselves from religious worldviews that perceived revelation as a factual event that occurred at a particular point in time, a perception that has separated religions throughout history, and in the modern era has encouraged the closedness and degeneration of religious consciousness.[128] Instead of focusing on the "revelation itself", Hartman and Jaspers sought to conduct a constant dialogue with *the revelation faith as a phenomenon*, which in their opinion reflects one of the important channels through which people have sought to grant meaning to the reality in which they live, and through this to clarify their own selfhood to themselves. Unlike the revelation that demands unreserved submission and acceptance of the practical demands accompanying it, the revelation faith, which in fact does not distinguish between the faith and its contents, or as Jaspers put it, "the subject and the object of faith are one",[129] can enable modern people who are not willing to accept a religious way of life to identify with it or at least to show respect and appreciation toward it. In addition, the revelation faith can serve as a fruitful source for the development of philosophical creations based on the

---

[124] Jaspers, Ph3, 153. On the term "eagerness for the new", see Martin Heidegger, *Sein und Zeit*, Tübingen, 1993 [1927], 143f., 182f.

[125] Jaspers, *Truth*, 1048, 1031.

[126] Awareness of the necessarily particular nature of interpretation constitutes a central element in the pluralistic vision regarding the possibilities of present-day Jewish identity, which appears as a theme throughout all his books. See in particular David Hartman, *Conflicting Visions: Spiritual Possibilities of Modern Israel*, New York, 1990, 225-270.

[127] In this context, see Sagi's definition of Hartman as an "*a priori* modernist", Avi Sagi, "David Hartman: Modernistic Jewish Philosophy—Introductory Chapters", *Renewing Jewish Commitment*, 445-491.

[128] This is the central purpose of Jaspers' last great book: Karl Jaspers, *Der Philosophische Glaube angesicht der Offenbarung*, München, 1962.

[129] Ibid., 49.

interpretation of the sources of religious tradition, which would indicate new possibilities for self-fulfillment, thus answering the human need to transcend the boundaries of existence—a need that has been marginalized in modern being.

However, from the renewed pairing of philosophy and revelation in the thought of Hartman and Jaspers we should not conclude that these two are based on one common source or that they portray one truth in different ways. Hartman's deep modern consciousness barred the entry of harmonistic or mystical elements that guarantee people release from everyday reality and its ills. The modern consciousness based on a break or even alienation between a person and himself, his world, and God, is reflected in the thought of Hartman and Jaspers in the undecided tension between striving to defend the status of the religious experience and of philosophical intuition as explicitly particular elements typical of the believer's character. At the same time, they try not to damage the possibility that this tension could contribute to the constituting of a language that would connect different people seeking for meaning and significance in their world. Apart from this tension ensuring the preservation of the philosophical praxis as a permanent component in the consciousness of these thinkers, awareness of it served for them as a living testament that the argument for the absolute validity of a particular religious worldview has not basis. In this spirit, Hartman sought to establish the understanding in principle that one cannot derive from people's unconditioned attitude to the constituting assets and events of their culture any unequivocal understanding. Therefore, the believer is entitled, or perhaps even required, to find his way through the blending of personal responsibility and philosophical freedom towards the truth of revelation.

From Psychiatry to Philosophy: The Concept of Self in Karl Jaspers

In memory of Moti Etun

"The practice of the physician is concrete philosophy".[1] This statement by Karl Jaspers at the opening of the Centenary Conference of the German Association for Natural Science and Medicine, held in Wiesbaden in 1958, many years after he had left his practice and research in the field of psychiatry, indicates a connection between his practice as a psychiatrist and his philosophical conceptions. The fact that Jaspers started his academic career as a researcher of mental diseases and an active psychiatrist, and even afterwards as a philosopher continued to deal with the issues that had interested him as a scientist, will serve as a basis for the discussion of the connection between his early ideas about mental patients and the perception of Existenz that he developed in his philosophical writings. The article's central argument is that Jaspers' perception of the field of psychopathology and of mental illnesses as a particular expression of the individual's world, as it appeared in his early writings (1910-1913a), served as a foundation for the perception of subjectivity in his book *Psychology of Worldviews* (1919). This perception was developed and expanded in his philosophy of Existenz, as presented in his philosophical writings (1931-1947). This interpretation of Jaspers' work differs from the approach usually reflected in the research literature, which focuses on his philosophical writings and does not generally attribute any real importance to his early writings for understanding his philosophy.

The following discussion is anchored in a developmental methodology that aims to reveal the main milestones in the formation of Jaspers' perception of selfhood. This method is appropriate for illuminating the issue of the individual's subjective being in Jaspers' thought, since this interested him continuously over many years. Various concepts—such as "mental", "self", "subjectivity", and "Existenz"—which denoted subjectivity in Jaspers' writings, expressed different stages in his search for a viewpoint that would illuminate this being in its particular fullness. As will transpire, the turnover of concepts reflects the

---

[1] Cited by Schipperges 1986, 88.

profound changes that occurred in Jaspers' perception of selfhood and in his philosophy in general, as well as his basic view of a person as a being yearning for better and wider self-understanding. However, just as only as a philosopher could Jaspers comprehend the connection between medical practice and philosophy, so also in the discussion below, the relevance of his early thought to his perception of self transpires only through the explicit discussion of it in his later philosophical writings.[2] The hermeneutical circularity arising from the interpretation presented to Jaspers'' thought below is an inseparable part of the phenomenological viewpoint in which it is anchored. Indeed, the very nature of the circularity requires the issue to be viewed as one whole, and thus the discussed issue is clarified only after the presentation of its stages of development within Jaspers' thought is completed. In other words, the interpretation presented below will reveal both the development of the issue of selfhood in Jaspers' thought and the research method through which the understanding of the issue itself was achieved.[3]

Mental Illness as an Expression of the Individual's World

Jaspers' attempt to form a viewpoint that would enable access to the individual's subjective being is apparent already in his basic distinction between the psychopathologist and the psychiatrist, with which he opened his first book, *General Psychopathology* (1913).[4] Jaspers described the psychopathologist as someone who "wants only to identify and recognize, characterize and analyze not the individual person, but the general", and to anchor him in the conceptual framework of the science of psychopathology. In contrast, the psychiatrist, who experiences practical work with mental patients, aims his gaze at "the person with his singularity and his completeness". In other words, the psychiatrist aims to form an understanding regarding the entirety of the patient's personality and world, and only according to them does he examine the relevance of the scientific definitions to his concrete needs and situation (Psychopathology1, 1). The definition of the psychiatrist's art as an "expertise" (*Kennerschaft*) does not contradict the perception of his field as a "science" (*Wissenschaft*) (ibid., 2), but adds to it a personal and unique facet that is not expressed in the structured approach of psychopathology.[5] It appears that precisely the personal approach

---

[2] An immanent elucidation of Jaspers' text often and inevitably tends to use a style that anthropomorphizes the various concepts discussed in it, particularly Existenz. Clearly this style does not change the abstract nature of the concepts.

[3] For more on the issue of circularity, see Golomb 1980.

[4] This approach was already apparent in the articles (1909-1913a) that preceded the appearance of his first book, *General Psychopathology* (1913) (hereafter: Psychopathology1). This book was published in nine editions. The first (1913) is the most limited, and there are very few changes in the second and third editions. The fourth (1942) (hereafter: Psychopathology4), which significantly expanded upon the first, expresses the philosophical substrate that had accumulated in the years prior to its publication. After this edition, five more editions in the same format as the fourth were published. The citations to Jaspers' writings refer to abbreviations of the titles, as listed at the end of this article.

[5] Jaspers described psychiatric practice using the term *Beruf* (profession, calling). This concept originates in the writings of Max Weber, whose influence upon him Jaspers often admitted. In his Protestant perception of ethics, Weber granted this term a religious

displayed by the psychiatrist toward his patients and his personal experience that exposes him to the varied appearances of mental illnesses in different people may fill with understanding the gap between the conceptual framework of the science of psychopathology and the real reality, which is more complex and richer.

Against this background, he also defined the difference between the boundaries within which the psychopathologist operates and those that exist for the psychiatrist. The former is subject to "limits" (*Beschränkungen*), meaning barriers originating in the system of rules and concepts of the science of psychiatry. The latter is presented as encountering the fundamental "bounds" (*Grenze*) stemming from the fact that the person as an individual cannot be exhausted through concepts that are subject to knowledge and reflection (ibid., 1-2).[6] Unlike the concepts of science that are subject to change and development, the boundary the psychiatrist faces is finite in essence and cannot be removed or overcome. Jaspers attributed the reason for this to what he called the person's quality of "singularity" (*Einselnheit*). This quality, which in his early writings expressed the inseparable cohesion between the person's physical and mental powers, requires, in his opinion, granting importance to the unique character of the mental patient within the general understanding of his illness.[7]

Furthermore, this viewpoint, which placed the mental patient's subjectivity at the focus of psychiatry's interest, is essential not only for a better understanding of his condition but also for the perception of the psychiatrist himself (ibid., 2). This shows the influence of Dilthey's basic perception that sought to connect the "direct experience" (*Erleben*), the "understanding" (*Vestehen*), and the ways it is expressed (*Ausdruck*). Dilthey stated that any experience belongs in advance in a concrete context, since only there can it be understood and can it become possible at all. He presented the understanding of the experience, the subject striving to achieve this understanding, and the thing or object to which his consciousness is directed as belonging to the same context. In any case, the understanding aimed at objects is simultaneously the subject's self-understanding.[8] In the spirit of these words, we can note that unlike the approach at the basis of the science of psychopathology during his period, Jaspers sought to loosen the sharp distinction between the experiencing subject, in this case the psychiatrist, and the object on which the experience is focused, the mental patient seeking treatment. Jaspers

---

meaning and linked it to the perception of science in modern German culture. See Weber 1958, 79-92; Weber 1919, 524-555.

[6] Jaspers' use of the concept of "boundary" to demonstrate the particular nature a mental illness make take on for people who experience it is largely equivalent to Kant's distinction between limits (*Schranke*) and bounds (*Grenze*) . Later in his philosophical writings, Jaspers made this distinction into one of the central parameters in the philosophizing method that led him to its peak crystallization in the concept of "boundary situations". In this context, see Jaspers' basic distinction between 'relative bounds' (*jeweilige Grenzen*) and 'principle bounds' (*prinzipielle Grenzen*) (1932a, 45). On Kant's influence on Jaspers' psychiatric method, see Walker 1993a, 1993b, 1994, 1995a. For further discussion, see also Golomb 1981.

[7] For more on the mental patient's quality of singularity, see Jaspers, Psychopathology1, 408.

[8] Dilthey discusses this issue in what was called the "methods polemic", dealing with the differences between the methodologies of the humanities and that of the natural sciences. See Dilthey 1927, 79-88; 315 ff.; Schnädelbach 1984, 54 ff.

strove to reveal the context the two shared and to establish a treatment approach that would be anchored in a wide understanding of this context.[9]

Against this background, we can also understand Jaspers' attempt to connect the psychiatrist's very choice of the occupation of psychiatry with his personal character traits and perhaps also with his typical nature, as we can see from his argument that "in the absence of the ability and desire to observe the mental and imagine it before our eyes in its fullness, one cannot engage in psychopathology" (ibid., 12). It transpires that the psychiatrist's personality has importance not only in the attitude he displays to his patients, but also for his understanding of the mental illness itself. Therefore, the psychiatrist, according to this approach, must harness to his professional work not only the scientific socialization he has absorbed during his years of training, but also the entirety of his personality and his world. Thus, understanding mental illnesses and determining ways of treating them cannot rely only upon objective criteria derived from the conceptual system of the science of psychopathology; they must also be based on a system of subjective considerations originating in the interaction that is formed between two human beings in a concrete situation. Focusing the attention on the subjective being of the two people located on either side of the therapeutic situation—patient and therapist—actually makes the pathological aspect in the meeting between them secondary. Just as the mental patient does not cease to be a human being when he experiences a mental illness, so too does the psychiatrist not remove other sides of his personality just because he has studied medicine. As Jaspers put it:

> We want to feel what actually happens *in the human soul*, to grasp the thing and think about it. In psychopathology the general drive for reality means the drive to the real mental life, which we want later to know in contexts that can only *partially* be distinguished sensorily like the objects of science (ibid., 12).[10]

Jaspers' description of what he called "the mental in its real reality" (ibid.) using general expressions such as "reality", "the person", "mental life", compared with "the patient" or "the mental illness", demonstrate his viewpoint that granted priority to the mental patient's humanity in relation to the clarification of the reasons and conditions that cause the mental illness, on which the science of psychopathology focuses. Jaspers' need to translate the drive to observe the human soul to the psychopathological viewpoint—as if this were not the explicit subject of the discussion—accords with his far-reaching statement that the starting point of psychopathology exists factually in the realm of normality (ibid., 3).[11] The basic understanding on which the science of psychology relies, whereby

---

[9] On Jaspers' role in this polemic, see Walker 1995b.

[10] All the emphases in citations from Jaspers' writings are my own. I have omitted Jaspers' own emphases because of their relative frequency.

[11] The contribution of the phenonemonolgical approach to blurring the traditional distinction between "normal" and "abnormal" was the basis for Jaspers' positive attitude towards it. Jaspers and the psychiatrist Binswanger are considered in the mental health research literature as key figures who introduced phenomenological thinking into the field of psychopathology. On this issue, see Jaspers' programmatical article on phenomenology

there are individual differences between people, makes it essential for psychopathology no less than physiology. The fact that in certain cases psychology cannot serve the psychiatrist in his work with mental patients should encourage psychopathology to create its own psychology (ibid., 4) that would complement what is lacking in the psychology aimed at understanding people defined as normal.[12]

Jaspers believed that the decision regarding the normality or pathology that one should attribute to a particular mental phenomenon will in any case remain an inaccurate estimate. If based only on the physical aspects, it would prevent a uniform understanding of the individual personality and thus would harm the correct perception of the patient's condition (ibid., 3). In his words, psychopathology can do justice to its task as a scientific discipline "only if its starting point is in the boundary-less search, in the infinite variance of reality, in the wealth of subjective approaches and objective facts, in the multiplicity of methods and the uniqueness of each of them" (Psychopathology4, 460).[13] Precisely this wider viewpoint could enable Jaspers to achieve the goal he had set himself, as a person and not only as a psychiatrist: to establish contact with the infinite being of a person who had a mental illness (Psychopathology1, 2).

It appears that the viewpoint that placed the patient's subjective selfhood at the focus of psychiatric practice helped Jaspers form his approach in principle whereby the understanding of the phenomenon of mental pathology should be based only on analysis of its physiological aspects but also on reference to the mental patient's subjective personality. Jaspers' attempt to make the particular features of the individual's subjective being into part of the system of considerations in treating mental illness expressed primarily the critical image he formed around the positivistic scientific method focused on the physiological and general aspects of the illness and adopting an impersonal attitude toward the patient.[14] But in his writings from this period, Jaspers was unable to develop the appropriate tools to characterize subjectivity as a particular being. Hence

---

(Causality). On Binswanger's attitude to Jaspers, see Binswanger 1913. For further discussion of the history of phenomenology in psychiatry, with an emphasis on the German philosophical discourse that developed around it, see Schneider 1926; Kronfeld 1922; Spiegelberg 1967, xxvii-xlv. See also research dealing with the relations between mental health and the various approaches taken from existentialistic thought: Van Kaam 1961; Sonnemann 1954; Tymieniecka 1962.

[12] On this matter, Jaspers indicated approaches that could serves as a basis for a psychology book that would complement the psychopathology studies (Psychopathology1, 4, n. 1).

[13] On his retrospective attitude to the mental health profession from a philosophical viewpoint, see also his two essays "The Idea of the Physician" and "Physician and Patient", in Philosophy and the World, 169-207.

[14] The background for this is Jaspers' criticism of the positivistic viewpoint that ruled the science of psychopathology during his period. Jaspers termed this approach "prejudices" of psychiatry, and defined as "mythologies of the brain" the approaches based on the assumption prevalent in those days that saw mental illness as a brain disease (Psychopathology1, 8). In this context, it seems that the criticism was directed mainly at the German psychiatrist Griesinger; see Griesinger 1876.

subjectivity appears from these writings as an enigmatic being inaccessible to the formal tools on which the science of psychopathology relies.[15]

In the end, while dealing with the scientific worldview helped Jaspers clarify his position regarding the appropriate treatment of mental illness and the desirable character of the psychiatrist, it also showed him the way out of psychopathology and science in general. However, the perception of human nature at the basis of these early writings laid the first foundations for the philosophical perception of selfhood that he developed later on. Just as he believed that the science of psychopathology could not grant a complete understanding of mental illness, let alone enable a comprehensive understanding of the person experiencing it, as we will see later, he argued that philosophy, which is also bound by the representation restrictions of consciousness, cannot reveal the person's complete and particular being.

Selfhood in "Worldviews"

After he no longer saw himself as committed to formulate an approach that would provide, among other things, an immediate response to the suffering of ill people, suffering that sometimes also included physical problems, the possibility opened up for Jaspers to place subjectivity at the focus of a discussion dealing with it from a wider perspective. The subjective being to be elucidated in *Psychology of Worldviews* (1919) was no different in essence from the one that interested him in his early days, since within psychiatry too Jaspers considered the particular dimension exceeding the boundaries of pathology. But in *Psychology* subjectivity was placed at the focus of a more systematic and structured discussion dealing with describing and elucidating the experiences that determined, through the choice of the individual subjectivity, its perception of itself, of its "worldview" (*Weltanschauung*).[16] Unlike knowledge (*Wissen*), which is acquired within a professional setting that determines its boundaries and posits "objective" criteria for its testing, the worldview was presented by Jaspers as expressing the entirety of a person's world. It simultaneously portrays the entirety of the person's concrete experiences and his ability to objectivize these experiences in order to achieve a wider understanding of himself in reality (Psychology, 1-2).

In *Psychology*, Jaspers also dealt with worldviews as "multiplicity", meaning a phenomenon that has general characteristics relating to people's very attempt to grant meaning to their existence. In this framework, he referred to the objective dimensions involved in the process of constituting worldviews—a process in which a general human phenomenon was revealed involving people's attempts to objectivize their experiences. Jaspers stated in this context that "the psychology

---

[15] We can notice a certain influence of the enigmatic and covert perception of selfhood appearing in Jung. See Jung 1996.

[16] The concept "worldview" is one of the most central in German culture, and contains wide philosophical and psychological meanings. The tension between "world-knowing" (*Welterkennen*) and "self-knowing" (*Selbsterkennen*) characterizes the various thinkers who addressed the issue of worldviews, including Jaspers. For further discussion, see Heidegger's interpretation of *Psychology* and the interpretations of Dilthey and Max Scheler to the issue of worldviews, which had many connections with Jasper. See Saner 1973, 70-100; Dilthey 1962; Scheler 1954.

of worldviews means less research that is constructed on details but delineating the field we perceive conceptually" (ibid., 6). He also declared that his book does not deal "with the empirical case in itself" (ibid., 13-14), that deals with a certain worldview, but presents a "catalog" (ibid., 18) or "a gallery of worldviews" (ibid., xi). The analysis of the various worldviews presented in the book aims to grant the reader a rational understanding of the phenomenon of worldviews and to "slay a disguised and false form of existence" (ibid., 5) on which particular worldviews may rest. In other words, observing the multiplicity of worldviews helps identify in this phenomenon the basic foundations and thus to grant a sort of external perspective for the examination of individual worldviews.

However, like his early position criticizing systems with pretensions of providing an exhaustive understanding of mental diseases, and which as a result miss the understanding of the patient as an individual person (Psychopathology1, 8), in this context Jaspers was concerned about the possibility of the "catalog" missing the specific truth entailed in the *private* worldview as such (Psychology, 14-15). Jaspers' wish to respond to the infinite and inexhaustible nature of the particular human experience, represented in the worldviews of individuals, was expressed in the argument that although "one should be unceasingly systematic... one should still allow no method to reach control to enable as many systematic thoughts as possible—if possible, all of them—to have influence" (ibid., 19). This statement shows Jaspers' worry that too close acquaintance with a particular system would lead to identification with it and thus block the possibility of understanding individual worldviews that cannot be explained through the system, or would force upon these worldviews a distorting interpretation. This possibility could be relevant precisely for the approach whereby a multiplicity of worldviews represents different modes of expression for one general phenomenon, and thus Jaspers wished to express his reservations about this approach, arguing that "it is futile to talk about the unity [of the worldview phenomenon]. To prove it—is impossible. To disprove it—equally impossible" (ibid., 18). This means that the infinite variance reflected in the ways people experience reality and the ways they perceive themselves does not enable the achievement of an exhaustive and complete understanding of the person as an individual being. It appears that the drive "to feel what actually happens in the human soul" (ibid.,12), the basis of Jaspers' interest in the subjective being of the mental patient, found its continuation in *Psychology*, and to a great extent also a wider arena for its realization, precisely through the observation of the particular dimensions of worldviews. Just as in his discussion of mental illness he focused on the *person* as a real being, in this context too Jaspers was interested more in the *person* who had a worldview rather in the worldviews themselves, as though they were entities with a separate existence from the people who possessed them. As he put it:

> We are not looking for the frequent or the average... We are seeking the specific patterns even if they are completely rare. Our field... [is] what we notice in the historical, internal, living experience and the [experience] present in the particular thing, even if it is unique. (ibid., 14).

These statements pushed into the margins of the discussion the handling of the general and structural aspects typical of worldviews as such, in favor of an observation focusing on the elucidation of the subjective being that constituted the worldview. So it is not surprising that Jaspers chose to establish the understanding of the individual worldview on *instincts* (ibid., 16-17), which portray the observer's personal viewpoint, rather than on the rational perspective that guides the relativistic viewpoint examining worldviews as a general phenomenon. The requirement for openness toward a variety of approaches that examine the particular dimension in individual worldviews is necessitated from the fact that worldviews are not formed in accordance with a fixed and defined pattern. Jaspers' statement that when observing worldviews we must "*move ourselves around the thing*" (ibid., 18) demonstrates the viewing of the individual worldview as an ontological representation of the original and complete being of the person who constituted it by processing his various experiences.[17] Not only did Jaspers not separate between the experiential and subjective experience and the action of its objectivization, neither did he deduce from it epistemological conclusions.[18] For him the objectivization was primarily an ontological representation of the subjectivity in its individual realization. Therefore he could also view the individual worldview a subject constitutes as "*a means of self-consciousness*" (*Selbstbesinnung*) (ibid., xiii) or as a tool providing "clarifications and possibilities that can constitute means for self-reflection" (ibid., 5).

These statements, granting precedence to observing individual worldviews over observing the phenomenon of the multiplicity of worldviews, do not negate the value of the relativistic understanding. This is because the fact that different people form different worldviews can indicate the infinite and open nature of the human experience, which can be represented in different ways, which Jaspers defined as different "positions" (*Stellungen*) of the person in existence (ibid., 18). In this respect, the various worldviews can be seen as different examples of the possibilities of a person's granting expression to his individuality. We discover that observing the worldviews may help understand the individual's particular being, not just because it constitutes a framework within which he expresses his experiences of reality, but also because through the very constituting of a worldview the individual constitutes himself.

Selfhood in the Face of Immanence

The discussion of Jaspers' early writings clearly indicates that his interest in the self being was mainly in revealing its particular and unique dimensions. However, as will transpire, clarifying these dimensions could no longer satisfy Jaspers' interest in the issue of selfhood. In his philosophical writings published after *Psychology* (1919), he expanded significantly the boundaries of the discussion of it and formulated a more complex perception. However, these writings clearly maintained the connection to his earlier perception of selfhood, a connection that

---

[17] On the ontological meaning of psychological terms, see for instance May, 1983.

[18] In the separation between the subjective experience and its objectivization we can find an expression of Kant's influence on Jaspers; see the appendix to *Psychology*: 465-486.

introduces tension into it and explains some of the difficulties Jaspers had to deal with.

Against this background, we can define the discussion of selfhood in *Psychology* as an intermediate stage: between abandoning his practice and scientific engagement in psychiatry and the start of crystallizing his philosophical thought. On the one hand, in *Psychology* Jaspers liberated himself from the boundaries imposed by the scientific discussion context and placed at the center of his discussion what was previously a deviation from it: the individual's subjective being. In this framework he was able to fill with content the perception of subjectivity, and it did not remain as an intuition referring to an enigmatic and hidden being to which access is essentially limited. On the other hand, Jaspers' attempt in *Psychology* to focus on the particular fullness of this being made it difficult to examine it in relation to other objects of thought, and greatly restricted its predication. Finally, the discussion of selfhood in *Psychology* led to the detaching of selfhood from the world it apparently wished to observe, and revealed the tendency to solipsism that was inherent in its perception. This means that selfhood was perceived as a being constituting itself through reflection about its experiences in reality, but after processing these experiences they are once again assimilated into its consciousness as various reflections derived from its selfhood as one whole. To be precise, the solipsistic tendency apparent in Jaspers' early perception of selfhood did not crystallize into radical solipsism like that of Berkeley or into methodical solipsism like that of Descartes, since Jaspers did not see the contents of consciousness as a single portrayal of reality or as an exclusive source of certainty. In other words, the tendency to solipsism in the perception of selfhood was not based on the metaphysical premises typical of a solipsistic position, but was largely a side-effect of Jaspers' aim to focus on the individual's subjective being, and also of the lack of sufficient tools to express additional dimensions of human existence. This distinction, which moderates to some extent the solipsistic nature of Jaspers' pre-philosophical perception of selfhood, also explains his ability to overcome it, as will transpire from the following discussion of this perception in his philosophical writings.

In *Philosophical World Orientation* (Ph1), the first volume of the trilogy *Philosophy* (1932), Jaspers wished to deal with the possibilities of philosophically elucidating selfhood in relation to reality in the world (*Welt*) and "formal knowledge" (*Bewusstsein überhaupt*). It seems that his early understanding of philosophy, as dealing with questions related to the reality of the world and the nature of knowledge, turned them into main axes around which the philosophical discussion of the individual's subjective being was crystallized. Jaspers' aim, having previously been known as a psychiatrist or psychologist, to enter the mainstream of philosophy, was apparent also in moving to new terminology. The concepts of "mental", "selfhood", and "subjectivity" typical of his earlier writings were replaced at this stage by the philosophical term "Existenz", which occupied a central position in his writings. These changes reflected both his search for a new point of view through which it would be possible to form a philosophical perception of selfhood, and also Jaspers' self-criticism of his early perception of subjectivity.[19]

The new viewpoint regarding selfhood was anchored in the understanding that a person "fundamentally does not exist in any form of existence that becomes conscious [of itself]" (Ph1, 12), meaning that the basis of a person's being is not embodied in his self-consciousness, and thus this cannot serve as a basis for the elucidation of selfhood. This new understanding served as a basis for examining the individual's subjective being in light of two factors external to it: the external reality of the world and the objective viewpoint of knowledge. The entry of the concepts "world" and "knowledge" into the philosophical discussion of selfhood challenged the solipsistic tendency typical of Jaspers' early perception. Beyond the implications of these concepts for the entirety of his thought, which will not be discussed here, they served as a basis for developing the philosophy of Existenz, in which selfhood was considered as a *worldly being*. There is no doubt that in this context new aspects of the individual's subjective being were revealed, which enabled its more complex understanding. However, as will transpire below, even at this advanced stage in the development of Jaspers' perception of selfhood, its early solipsistic substrate was apparent within it. This argument will be demonstrated through an examination of Jaspers' discussion of "world" and "knowledge".

Existenz and the World

Jaspers anchored the existence of Existenz in the world in what he called the "situation being" (*Situationsein*).[20] This term denotes both the human freedom to experience and act in the world and also the restrictions that limit it and demand that it adapt itself to a reality external to it (ibid., 1). The term "situation being" actually defines the two points of contact Existenz has with the world: freedom and necessity. In other words, within the discussion in *Philosophical World Orientation*, Jaspers did not address the wider philosophical meanings of the concept of world, but limited his discussion to what he perceived as the framework of Existenz's experience of the reality surrounding it. Moreover, Jaspers did not attempt to elucidate concrete situations, but discussed the elucidation of the fundamental phenomenon of a person's being in these situations.[21] The choice of a limited framework of discussion enfolded Jaspers' argument in principle that Existenz does not experience the world as a whole but only certain sides or parts of it.

---

[19] Looking back, Jaspers called *Psychology of Worldviews* "a hasty book of my youth"; see Report, 392 ff.

[20] For an early version of the idea of "situation", see Spritual Situation, 23 ff. The meaning of the term "situation" is expanded within the discussion of the "boundary situations" (*Grenzsituationen*), see Ph2, 201 ff.; 1919, 229 ff. On the formation of selfhood in boundary situations, see Salamun 1985, 64-72.

[21] The only context where Jaspers tried to elucidate specific situations is in his discussion of "boundary situations" (Ph2, 201-245). However, precisely these situations are an exception that does not indicate the rule, since they mainly point to what is beyond people's routine existence, while the "situation being" embodies the context in which people's experience of existence occurs.

Against the background of the perception of subjectivity that preceded the constituting of the "being of Existenz" in Jaspers' writings we can state that this philosophical move, which limited "world" to the boundaries of "situation being", enabled a gradual transition from the perception of selfhood, ruled almost absolutely by particular parameters, to a perception anchoring selfhood in an external world reality. In this respect, the concept of "situation being" can be seen as the start of an important development in Jaspers' thought, which began to overcome the solipsistic tendency typical of his early perception of selfhood. But it appears that the very constituting of a wider viewpoint regarding selfhood, which in this context was termed "Existenz", opened to Jaspers' philosophy wider horizons whose significance exceeded the boundaries of the discussion of the individual's subjective being. In Jaspers' words:

> *The situation has become a starting point and a target*, since it alone is real and present. However, it itself becomes meaningful for me only through thinking about the objective world reality [*Weltdasein*]. I must think again about this reality as self-standing. I cannot perceive my situation without progressing to the world thought [*Weltdenken*], nor can I perceive the world without always returning to my situation, only in which does confirmation of the reality of what was placed in thought occur... This movement is not absolute, [since] there remains *a connection within the restrictions of existence*. (ibid., 69).

The concrete reality surrounding the person, i.e., the "situation", is determined at this stage as a starting point for the explication of the individual's subjective being, but this explication is also simultaneously directed at explicating this being itself. Moreover, expanding Jaspers' viewpoint beyond the direct discussion of selfhood cannot be exhausted in the discussion of "situation being" that surrounds it. Existenz's consciousness that its experience of the world is limited to particular situations does not silence its drive to understand the world as a reality independent of the consciousness referring to it.[22] Accordingly, the philosophical explication of selfhood cannot be exhausted in examining the relation of Existenz to the "situation being", meaning to the close reality in which its various experiences occur. This explication is required to form a more general understanding of the "objective world reality" or of the "world thought", a thought that is not derived from Existenz's direct experience in the concrete reality that surrounds it.

Jaspers expressed the requirement that the explication of selfhood would deal simultaneously with elucidating the "situation being" in stating that a person "must think about the two meanings of 'world': 'as a whole of the other that can be investigated as one thing and that has general validity' and as 'not-I' [*Nichtich*] encompassing the self-being [*Ichsein*]" (ibid., 63). The first meaning of

---

[22] This interpretation differs from the position common in the research literature, which generally did not view the discussion in *Philosophical World Orientation* as an expression of Jaspers' attempt to elucidate the immanent being. Also, immanence is not usually perceived as a significant part of the perception of Existenz, and sometimes it is not perceived as an important factor in Jaspers' perception of being. See Räber 1955, 30 ff.; Olson 1979, 10 ff.; Schneiders 1965, 167.

the world necessitates its examination objectively and independently of the person, while its second meaning is derived from the relation between it and the self-referring to it. In this respect, we can distinguish two levels of otherness in the concept of "world": one is closer to the person and maintains a relation toward him, although this is defined as its negation and contrast; the other embodies a deeper otherness, which no longer expresses the relationship between it and the person.

The duality of the two concepts of world, indicating the expansion of the boundaries of Existenz's consciousness, cracks the early solipsistic understanding of selfhood. Unlike the latter, Existenz is now presented as a being that can observe the existence of a reality external to it. However, this change does not detach Existenz from its basic and deepest relation to the reality closest to itself, and the movement between thinking about the "situation" and that directed at the "objective world reality" does not distance it from itself. In other words: the "connection in the restriction of existence", as Jaspers put it, is preserved. The split between the two concepts of world also emphasizes this relation, since it makes apparent Jaspers' difficulty in assimilating into the concept of selfhood the recognition of the independent existence of another being. From this point of view, the two meanings granted to the concept of "world" demonstrate the dependence of the perception of world on the attitude of Existenz toward it: as an otherness that it faces as a separate object, or as its negation. In this respect, the recognition of the world's external reality was unable to blunt the solipsistic tendency entirely, since it left the reality of the world and that of Existenz as intertwined.

Existence and Knowledge

Jaspers' attempt to expand the boundaries of the discussion of selfhood and its perception is expressed in the discussion of the question whether formal knowledge could help explicate Existenz. In fact, the question under discussion in this context was whether in addition to the subjective and particular sides, Existenz had sides that were accessible to the objective viewpoint of consciousness. Jaspers answered this question in the negative, but as will transpire below, dealing with it enabled him to clarify the particular aspects of Existenz. In this context, his argument in principle was that since Existenz is not an object but "a being that refers to its possibility, it *no longer* exists as such for knowledge as such" (ibid., 14).[23] In other words, the perception of Existenz does not rely only on clarifying the possibilities that it has already realized in practice, but also those it has yet to realize, but which it perceives as belonging to it. However, the potential dimension in the being of Existenz is not accessible to formal knowledge that directs its ability to organize and generalize toward defined objects in the world (ibid., 10). Jaspers argues that Existenz constitutes

---

[23] Some Jaspers scholars argue that there is a significant influence and similarity between Kierkegaard's perception of Existenz and that of Jaspers regarding the restriction of formal knowledge in relation to Existenz (see Young-Breuhl 1981, 5-9; Heinemann 1954, 61-83; Olson 1979, 45 ff.). Against the background of the connection between Kierkegaard's concept of self and his criticism of Hegel's perception of subject, it is worth also examining the relationship between Jaspers and Hegel on this issue; see Sagi 2000, 7-16.

for knowledge a "boundary" that it cannot cross, since instead of the objects it is used to see, when examining Existenz it encounters only vacuum (*Leere*) (ibid., 11-12). Formal knowledge as a whole cannot reveal its objective and general aspects, if it even has such aspects. Knowledge's inability to express the particular being of Existenz does not stem from Existenz itself being outside the boundary of immanence, but from the basic limitations of knowledge that do not enable it to express Existenz's unique form of experience as a world being in immanent reality.[24]

The rigidity Jaspers attributed to formal knowledge, as a framework referring only to objects, did not enable him to grant it a positive role in explicating Existenz. But in this his perception of selfhood did not regress to its earlier stages of development, where it was perceived as a completely particular being. The discussion of formal knowledge in this context shows that it can contribute to the elucidation of Existenz through elimination. This means that from the fact that formal knowledge cannot testify to Existenz, we can draw positive conclusions regarding the character of this being. This interpretation of the role of the discussion about formal knowledge in the explication of Existenz is anchored in Jaspers' basic distinction between two concepts: "ability to be known" (*Erkenntbarkeit*), portraying the status of objects in the world, and "ability to be elucidated" (*Erhellbarkeit*), characterizing Existenz (ibid., 17-18).[25] In fact, there are two basic functions of knowledge: as knowing it is characterized by activity, control, and the ability to plan, and as elucidation it mainly constitutes a mental stance characterized by its ability to allow the thing to become clarified through itself.[26] The very limitation formal knowledge shows regarding Existenz—a limitation that stems from the basic fact that Existenz cannot become "knowable [*erkennbar*] as a world-being [*Weltsein*]" (ibid., 17)—testifies to this being's uniqueness in comparison with the other things that exist in the world, and at the same time to its special status in the process of philosophizing. Existenz is not only different from other things in the world, which are accessible to formal knowledge, but from a philosophical point of view it is prior to them and is not subject to formal knowledge's restrictions of representation (ibid., 14). This statement does not make the discussion of knowledge within the context of explicating Existenz worthless, since even the act of knowing embodies a mode of standing in existence that Existenz experiences. In this respect, Existenz is not constituted only through the unique stance it displays towards existence, meaning: its perception as an arena in which it can find options for self-

---

[24] The gap between the being of Existenz and what objective consciousness can testify to is expressed in various interpretations given to Jaspers' perception of Existenz, in which it was understood as a relativistic, irrational (Bollnow 1939, 136-139, 157; Bollnow 1960 [1942], 11 ff.; Lenz 1951, 32 ff.), idealistic (Gabriel 1951, 20; Stegmüller 1960, 233 ff.), and opposed to any scientific knowledge (Kempski 1964, 235 ff.).

[25] For more on this issue, see Miron 2004c.

[26] The use here of the verb "elucidate" (*erhellen*) rather than "explain" (*erklären/erhläutern*) or "illuminate" (*erleuchten*) also demonstrates the particular stance of consciousness facing Existenz compared to its stance facing objects. In German, this stance was defined as "*hell werden lassen*". On this issue, see Marcel Gabriel's remark that the use of the verb *erhellen* is uncommon in philosophical language; Gabriel 1932/1933, 160.

realization. The uniqueness of Existenz is revealed, by elimination, also through the mode of existence in which its uniqueness as an individual being cannot be expressed, meaning formal knowledge.

The discussion of knowledge reveals the complexity of Jaspers' perception of Existenz, which feeds simultaneously from both the early perception of selfhood, emphasizing the particular dimensions of the individual's being, and from the perception of being (*Sein*) that started to form in his writings at this stage. His negative attitude to the possible contribution of knowledge to the philosophical understanding of selfhood constitutes a continuation of his early criticism of the positivistic position, which saw what was reflected in knowledge as the be-all and end-all. This criticism is implied in Jaspers' argument that since knowledge is not the only means through which a person's experience in the world can be examined, it should not be used as the primary means of evaluating the philosophical arguments about Existenz. However, we can see the very dealing with the viewpoint of knowledge as a new beginning that heralded Jaspers' philosophical reservations about the idealistic and mystical worldviews in the realm of philosophy. These reservations would accompany his later philosophical writings and especially influence his perception of being, characterized by a positive attitude to the objective viewpoint of knowledge.[27] In this respect, although objective knowledge *cannot* serve as a sole or main means of evaluating Existenz, it *is not* entirely removed from its explication.

But although Jaspers recognized the relevance of the discussion of "world" and "knowledge" to the constituting of the philosophical conception of selfhood, and assimilated these concepts into his philosophy of Existenz, it appears that he did not cease dealing with the tension they created with his early perception of selfhood. One of the clearest expressions of this is in the following worlds from *Elucidation of Existenz* (Ph2):

> *What satisfies me in world-knowing is ambiguous*: either the world is desired as my realized existence-desire [*Daseinlust*]... indeed it is inevitable for me to desire the world since I exist in it; but as an absolute drive this desire will become destructive for me; *against* [this desire] *I hear the demand* [*Anspruch*] *from my possible Existenz*: to detach myself from the world I am in danger of sinking into... as such the world is not known but has already lost itself in existence [*Bestand*]. (Ph2, 3).

In these words, Jaspers revealed the two motives that Existenz might have in knowing the world reality external to it: it can wish to know it because it can find its existence in it. In this respect, knowing the world has a positive motive, and can be seen as part of Existenz's self-knowledge, or as complementing this knowledge. Existenz's attempt to know the world can also be motivated by a negative motive. Here Existenz's main motivation is to identify the differences between it and the reality surrounding it in order to establish a self-consciousness of a being that is separate and distinct from the world. These motives lead to two alternatives that Existenz faces. The first, appearing implicitly, directs Existenz to

---

[27] This approach enabled Jaspers to grant a central role to knowledge in the perception of the "encompassing" (*das Umgreifende*); see Truth, 225-449.

see itself as part of the world and to act within it from this knowledge. This alternative is derived from the fundamental perception of Existence as a worldly being. The second, more explicit, faces Existenz with the radical option of detaching itself from the world, and should be understood against the background of its uniqueness as revealed through the discussion of formal knowledge.[28] These alternatives portray the two balance points that were subject to constant mutual temptation in the philosophical explication of selfhood at this stage: on the one hand, Jaspers continued to perceive Existenz as a unique and particular being, similar to the early perception of subjectivity. On the other hand, in his philosophical writings the perception of selfhood was granted the additional understanding that it is a world being, and therefore its self-consciousness must include reference to the reality external to it, a reality whose objective aspects are accessible to formal consciousness.

It appears that the drive for detachment from the world that is raised at this stage of the discussion primarily reflected Jaspers' difficulty in giving up his earlier perceptions, and shows that the discussion of the world and formal knowledge was mainly functional: the discussion of the world helped understand Existenz as a worldly being, and the discussion of formal knowledge clarified its perception as a unique being in relation to all the other objects in the world.[29] This interpretation receives support from the fact that after revealing the abyss between the perception of Existenz and the independent generality typical of the world perceived through consciousness, Jaspers stated that "possible Existenz distinguishes itself from the world in order to really enter it *later*" (ibid., 4). This means that the perception of Existenz as a world being does not contradict its perception as a unique being, but coexists with it. So it is not surprising that when he sought to examine the possibility of returning Existenz to the world Jaspers presented a positive reference to the possible contribution of objectivity and generality in explicating Existenz. He argued that since the thought that elucidates Existenz is aimed in advance at concrete situations, it requires objective thought that would examine the possibilities existing in the world that Existenz faces. However, we must be precise here: Jaspers did not argue that realizing a certain possibility in existence is directly derived from logical or objective understanding of the world reality. Existenz becomes acquainted with the possibilities entailed in the world through objective knowledge, but it is the only one that determines their meanings for it. As he put it:

> If I want to know what I am then I present myself my objective existence, the thought patterns I experience, as a scheme of my being. I perceive myself within it, but *I experience that I am not completely identical to it*: what thus becomes an object does not reach compete

---

[28] The discussion of the possibility of detaching Existenz from the world consistently left its mark upon the interpretations of Jaspers' perception of Existenz, which tended to present it as extreme subjectivism. See for example Bollnow 1960 (1942), 11-26; Lenz 1951, 14, 32; Kempski 1964, 235-250; Müller-Schwefe 1961, 39 ff.; Reis 1950; Hersch 1965, 120 ff.; Imle 1926, 503; Imle 1937, 186 ff.

[29] Like the interpretations that emphasized the limitations of the discussion of the concept of world in Ph1, the limited discussion of formal knowledge in this context also received different interpretations. See Samay 1971, 146; Olson 1979, 20; Young-Breuhl 1981, 2.

identity with me myself, since in my expansion I must lose myself in these scheme. (ibid., 32).

The dialectic discussion of the relations between Existenz and the world finds in these words one of its most formulated phrasings in Jaspers' writings. Existenz sees the reality external to it, or in his words "objective existence", as part of itself. In other words, the process of constituting its self-consciousness does not occur in a vacuum, but in reference to the external reality forced upon Existenz, in light of the necessity dimension that constitutes an inseparable part of situation being. However, Existenz does not identify itself with this reality, since there is no identity between the access ways of clarifying this reality, meaning between the objective viewpoint of knowledge and the explication of Existenz. The perception of Existenz as a world being now receives its precise meaning: Existenz exists in the world and is constituted through conscious connections directed at itself and at this world. However, the element of freedom—the other facet of the situation being—enables Existenz to exceed the necessity entailed in the situations to which it finds itself subject. Thus, the same necessity or objectivity in which its perception as a world being is anchored can be pushed aside in favor of a speculative possibility that does not yet exist in practice in reality, but which Existenz strives to realize in its existence. The potential embodied in the existential choice to transcend situations thus prevents the identity between Existenz and the situations in which it exists. So we can describe the existential existence as a conscious movement between the reality that exists in practice and a possible reality, or as a movement between two languages—the particular existential language with which it refers to itself, and the objective thinking language with which it refers to the reality external to it.[30] This movement is presented by Jaspers as a process spread over an entire lifetime, which a person experiences as long as he attempts to live as an Existenz:

> The separation is always performed anew. For existence as such, the empirical forces constitute an only condition [while] the existential [forces] reach consciousness and reality only through pushing and penetrating: the process of separation, which in an eye blink is fully clear, will never reach its entire completion. (ibid., 21).

This *in and out dynamic*, typical of the relation of Existenz to the world, or what Jaspers termed "penetrating" and "pushing", demonstrates the struggle for supremacy and perhaps even exclusivity that arises in his discussion between the two representations of Existenz. However, no less than this, this dynamic expresses the establishment of the philosophical insight whereby Existenz *is anchored in the same world to which objective knowledge refers*, and hence the relevance of objective knowledge to a more complete understanding of Existenz as a world being. It seems that although the discussion of the concepts of knowledge and world in the elucidation of Existenz disputed the early perception of selfhood that tended toward solipsism, the functional nature of the discussion

---

[30] On the perception of existential freedom in Jaspers, see Ph2, 175 ff., and also Tennen 1977, 47-47.

of these terms affirmed this perception, or at least the difficulty in letting it go. In any case, even if the separation from the early perception of selfhood was not completed, the tendency to solipsism that characterized it remained as a naïve or unconscious position in Jaspers' thought.

The "Foundering" of Selfhood and the Transition to the Discussion of Being and Transcendence

The philosophical explication of selfhood revealed, as we have seen, a connection between the perception of Existenz and the early perception of subjectivity, but also the attempts to overcome it due to the solipsistic dimensions that accompanied it. The process of distancing from the solipsistic thinking pattern had two main implications: *in terms of the content* it was expressed in the perception of Existenz not relying only on clarifying its patterns of reference to itself, but being presented as having a relation to an external reality. *In structural terms*, the discussion did not revolve around selfhood as an only object, and in fact a new axis of philosophizing started to emerge in Jaspers' thought, directed at explicating the concepts of being and transcendence. This structural aspect also had an influence on the contents, since at this stage Existenz was no longer perceived as a decisive factor that determined the framework of discussion of additional subjects or the meaning granted to them. These changes greatly expanded the perception of selfhood in Jaspers' thought, and allowed him to discuss several important philosophical issues, such as communication, historicity (*Geschichtlichkeit*), boundary situations, and "foundering". The complete explication of these issues exceeds the boundaries of the discussion in this article.[31] Despite this, we can clearly state that their discussion revealed additional facets of the being of Existenz and contributed to forming a more complex perception of selfhood than the one characterizing Jaspers' early thought. Moreover, these issues helped in the transition from philosophizing focused on clarifying selfhood to one aimed at elucidating being and transcendence.[32] In the following passage, appearing in the discussion of communication, Jaspers listed—consciously or unconsciously—the reasons for the change that occurred in his perception of selfhood, and in fact in his philosophy as a whole:

> Against the tendency for self-sufficiency, against satisfaction with the knowledge of consciousness in general, against the individual's self-desire, against the drive for self-closure in a life closed in upon itself, against the erring in the existing tradition as a routine way of life, philosophizing wishes to illuminate the freedom that catches the being in

---

[31] These issues are extensively discussed in my monograph on Jaspers, see Miron, Monograph 2012, 109-140; 171-184.

[32] It should be noted that a certain basis for Jaspers' discussion of communication and boundary situations appears already in his early writings (prior to *Philosophy*, 1932), but these ideas only reach real crystallization in *Elucidation of Existence*. See, for example, Jaspers' early discussion of boundary situations in *Psychology* (229-280). Jaspers' idea of communication also appears in his article "Loneliness", written by Jaspers in 1915-1916, and first published (edited by his student Hans Saner) in 1983.

its origin through communication, before the always threatening solipsism or the universalism of existence. (Ph1, 61).

Communication, as a possibility Existenz can realize, is located between two poles that accompanied the maturation of Jaspers' perception of selfhood: solipsism that threatens the isolation of selfhood and its detachment from the world, and universalism that threatens to erode its particular element. In other words, communication is anchored on the one hand in the understanding that "I cannot become myself without entering into communication" (ibid.), because "what is really from itself still does not exist from itself alone" (ibid., 50). In this respect, communication fills with contents the perception of Existenz as a worldly being. On the other hand, this understanding did not completely remove the image of Existenz as a being isolated from its surroundings. Evidence for this is contained in the definition of communication as "an internal struggle for the possibility to stand by myself... [and] to be capable of living as an interpretation of myself [*selbst unantastbar*]" (ibid., 56). In this respect, we can state that Jaspers' desire to grant philosophical representation to selfhood as an independent and self-sufficient being continued to motivate his thought even when he already recognized that this perception damages the possibility of obtaining a more complete understanding of self-being.[33]

Jaspers' statement, "you and I, who are separate in existence, are one in transcendence" (ibid., 71), enables a more accurate understanding of the meaning he granted to the idea of communication in his philosophy of Existenz. This statement means that in existence (*Dasein*), that is in the arena of meeting of two Existenzes, they remain separate. In contrast, the relation these two Existenzes form toward transcendence, portraying an entity or dimension beyond both existence and the Existenzes, loosens or perhaps even eliminates the differences between them.[34] In this respect, we can say that the two Existenzes are "one thing in transcendence". It appears that communication represents a speculative possibility and not necessarily an order Existenz is required to realize in order to obtain more complete self-understanding. The main importance of communication in Jaspers' philosophy of Existenz is that it constitutes an important intermediary stage aimed at leading Existenz to form a relation toward another being, whose otherness is even deeper than that of the other Existenz. This being is transcendence. It is no wonder that in the discussion of communication no expression was granted to the character of the other toward which the communicatory relation is constituted. This context discussed only the conditions that formed it on Existenz's part and presented the changes that the very possibility of communication creates in the way in which Existenz perceives itself. As Jaspers put it:

---

[33] The research literature has deal extensively with the perception of communication in Jaspers' philosophical writings and in his later writings published after World War II. In this context, see Arendt 1958; Kaufmann 1957; Schneiders 1965, 150 ff.; Jean Marie 1989, 49 ff.; Fuchs 1974.

[34] There is a controversy regarding the meaning of the concept of transcendence in Jaspers' thought. For our discussion of the perception of selfhood, the immanent interpretations of this concept are particularly important. See for example Hersch 1978, 36-37; Hersch 1986, 50 ff.; Kunz 1957, 504-513.

> Making itself stand absolutely upon itself alone is for Existenz the truth of its independence on the reality of time, but this [truth] becomes despair for it. Existenz itself is conscious that as something completely self-standing it must sink into vacuum. To the extent that it is appropriate for it to form actually from itself, *it transpires to it that what fills it comes toward it*. It is no longer it itself if it happens that it remains outside; *it stands for itself, as though it were given to itself. It affirms its possibility only if it knows itself as based on transcendence*. (Ph3, 4).

In these words, Jaspers noted the roots of the crisis experienced by the perception of Existenz, but also indicated the general direction in which its solution would be found. This means: the perception of selfhood as a being independent of what exists outside it—a perception typical of Jaspers' early thought—transpires as pointless and thus it "becomes despair for Existenz". But if Existenz recognizes that it is based on what exists beyond it, meaning on transcendence, it will achieve a more complete and true self-consciousness and thus be able to realize itself. The basic understanding on which the idea of communication is based, whereby Existenz cannot be satisfied only with itself (Ph2, 59), is rephrased at this stage and presented by Jaspers in *Metaphysics* (Ph3) as experiencing "insufficiency in any being that is not transcendence" (ibid., 3).[35] These changes make the explication of transcendence into an inseparable part of Jaspers' perception of selfhood, which included a discussion of the meaning transcendence has for Existenz's perception of self even before it presented an elucidation of the concept of transcendence itself.

The primary concept Existenz has regarding transcendence is of the contrast between them. It perceives transcendence as a being in which "there is no freedom and there is no lack of freedom" (ibid., 5). This means that on the one hand, the being of transcendence does not rely on the very possibility that Existenz would form a conscious relation toward it, but it exists in itself, independently, meaning not only for Existenz. On the other hand, Existenz's viewpoint is the one at the basis of the definition of transcendence through the term "freedom"—a term serving first and foremost to characterize Existenz. This definition enfolds the two facets of the existential consciousness that are revealed in light of its becoming acquainted with the being of transcendence. On the positive side, Existenz recognizes itself as being formed outside itself (*von Ausserichsein*) by transcendence (ibid., 47).[36] But on the negative side, this

---

[35] Another interpretation of Existenz's sense of insufficiency appears in Hans Kurz (1957), who attributed it to knowledge of its mortality, thus leaving Jaspers' framework of philosophizing within the boundaries of immanence.

[36] This understanding would serve later in Jaspers' discussion to extricate the relations between Existenz and transcendence from the level of contrast, and it would help form a positive and more direct relation towards it. In Kantian terms, this understanding can be seen as a basis for the "unthinkable" not becoming for Existenz a "boundary" (*Grenze*), where consciousness ceases to be capable of containing everything it encounters, but only a "limit" (*Schranke*), from which progress toward constituting direct knowledge of transcendence is not necessarily prevented. Thus the upheaval Existenz experienced following its becoming aware of the existence of transcendence can represent the contrast between transcendence and Existenz and simultaneously serve as a "starting point" (Ph3,

definition indicates that the self-consciousness of Existenz is still not capable of allowing itself to achieve a direct characterization of transcendence (ibid., 67). Still, the entry of transcendence into the discussion of selfhood made Existenz no longer be perceived by Jaspers as "bothered" by itself, but as having a mature self-consciousness that enabled it to turn away from itself and constitute a relation toward a being existing beyond it.[37] The changes in Jaspers' perception of self reach their peak crystallization with the formation of the philosophical concept of "foundering", presented as follows:

> Foundering [*Scheitern*] is the absolute [*Letzte*]: so proves the proximity of the cruel reality of world orientation… Knowledge sees itself placed on the antonymous boundaries in which the possibility of thinking without contradiction is lost; *beyond knowledge and outside it floats as a thing that embraces any truth that it not rational*. It founders [in terms of] world orientation of the world as existence, because it cannot be understood outside itself and within itself; this is because it does not become a being closed within itself and beyond which can be seen, however the process of consciousness cannot realize itself as a complete thing. It founders in explicating Existenz, in Existenz's self-observation; *where I myself really exist, I do not exist only as myself*. (ibid., 220).[38]

While the term "failure" indicates that certain possibilities have been missed, the philosophical concept of "foundering" denotes not only a change in the existential consciousness but also a more radical turning point in Jaspers' philosophy.[39] In its most direct meaning, this concept denotes the philosophical ability to face the final boundary of the explication of Existenz and the world. In other words, philosophizing encounters at this stage the necessity for antonyms that by their very definition as such cannot be solved within its boundaries. Thus it cannot create a whole perception of Existenz or of the world, but only face the irrational and all-embracing truth that does not contribute to the direct understanding of these objects. The very possibility of continuing the philosophizing depends at this stage on the ability to contain contradictions in thought. If we can define the stages of the development of Jaspers' perception of selfhood as also based on the previous failures, these were local, relative, and each time an exit from them was

---

48) and "origin" (ibid., 47) for the constituting of transcendence later as a uniform being that would embody identity between possibility and its real reality (ibid., 51).

[37] In this context, it is worth comparing Jaspers' words with Heidegger's discussion in his later writings. See especially Heidegger 1959; Heidegger 1954 ; Heidegger 1993. There has been extensive research comparing Jaspers' thought with that of Heidegger. In this context, see Wisser 1995, 51-221; Löwenstein 1988; Wisser 1988, 341-361; Brecht 1948.

[38] Jaspers addresses the criticism of *World Orientation* and *Elucidation of Existenz*—the two frameworks of philosophizing in the first two volumes of the trilogy *Philosophy* (1932)—in other contexts. Compare, for instance, Ph1, 58 ff., and Ph2, 4 ff.

[39] For additional interpretations of Jaspers' concept of 'foundering', see Miron 2012, 171-184; Salamun 1985, 64 ff., 146 ff.; Thyssen 1957; Rintelen 1961, 197 ff.; Pfeifer 1952, 41 ff.

found within the boundaries of the elucidation of selfhood.[40] In contrast, there can be no escape route from the philosophical consciousness of foundering, and thus it necessitates the constituting of a new framework of philosophizing—a framework that would suit the new self-perception of Existenz, but primarily enable a direct elucidation of the two concepts of being and transcendence.

The accumulation of changes in the perception of existential consciousness made the awareness of the enforcing, isolating, and restrictive character of individuality (Truth, 221) a primary datum from which Jaspers turned to explicate the concepts of being and transcendence. The perception of Existenz as a being that perceives itself in light of transcendence created an irreversible change in Jaspers' perception of selfhood. Now a new starting point was established for the elucidation of selfhood, whereby "Existenz exists only from a relation to transcendence, or else it does not [exist]" (Ph3, 6). However, the fact that the disputing of solipsism has already occurred within the philosophizing framework aimed at selfhood was greatly important not only for a more complete understanding of Existenz, but also for the discussion of being and transcendence. Precisely because the disputing of solipsism did not lead to the complete removal of Existenz from the philosophizing framework, but only to it being pushed aside from the center, is what enabled Jaspers to continue revealing additional facts of the self-being and also to largely maintain continuity with his earlier philosophical insights.

Understanding Existenz as aimed at transcendence not only posited a new focus in Jaspers' thought, it also retroactively projected on the earlier insights regarding the nature of existential self-understanding. Now Jaspers was able to state that "the means of searching for being from possible Existenz are ways to transcendence, and their explication is philosophical metaphysics" (ibid., 3). During the elucidation of being and transcendence important aspects were also added regarding Existenz, but these were indirect and no longer stood in the focus of Jaspers' discussion. The process of revealing the metaphysical anchor on which the perception of selfhood relies, leading to the understanding of the philosophy of Existenz itself as metaphysics (Ph1, 27), was not only enabled thanks to the maturation of the existential self-consciousness, but also portrayed its very maturation. In the end, the diversion of the emphasis in Jaspers' thought from selfhood to being and transcendence reflected the transition between two different modes of existential existence: from "existing as Existenz" to "existing as Existenz in face of transcendence".

Conclusion

The perception of selfhood as an internal reality hidden within the depths of the mental patient's soul underwent deep changes throughout Jaspers' writings, which extricated it from the closedness typical of it in his early thought and gradually expanded its circle of reference. At the peak of the philosophical journey aimed at elucidating selfhood, the understanding formed in Jaspers'

---

[40] This tendency was particularly prominent in the discussion of the encompassing in *Psychology* (51-216), where Jaspers found new types of worldviews that answered problems characterizing the preceding types.

thinking that the real origin of existential self-consciousness was actually revealed through the formation of a philosophical connection to transcendence. This laid new foundations for an additional elucidation of selfhood from a more accurate starting point. In other words, revealing transcendence as the real datum of the philosophical explication did not denote the locking of the philosophization axis aimed at elucidating selfhood, but rather enabled the more accurate establishment of its starting point. In this respect, the most important philosophical achievement of the explication of selfhood in Jaspers' writings is discovering the correct datum from which the elucidation should begin. Just as in the philosophical perception of selfhood Jaspers did not distance himself from his early intuitions as a scientist, so later on his path to explicating being and transcendence was not accompanied by alienation from the basic insights he had formed during the elucidation of selfhood. In fact, not only in the perception of selfhood but in Jaspers' entire oeuvre the simultaneous presence of tendencies of continuity alongside tendencies of change and development is apparent.

The article opened with a discussion of Jaspers' early writings and gradually moved to his later writings. But the display of the discussion in genealogical form does not exhaust the thought process in which the critical understanding of the perception of selfhood in Jaspers thought was crystallized. This is because only after studying his philosophical writings was it possible to note the relevance of the perception of psychiatry in his early days to the perception of selfhood developed in his philosophical writings. Only then was it possible to indicate the traces his early perceptions left in his philosophy of Existenz. Following the changes and developments in the viewpoints regarding selfhood revealed not only Jaspers' ability to realize philosophically his early intuitions as a scientist, when as he put it, he was possessed by "a desire to observe the mental in its fullness" (Psychopathology1, 2); it also revealed the completeness of the world from which he created—first as a psychiatrist and later as a philosopher.

References

Jaspers' writings and their abbreviations

1909-1913a. "Heimweh und Verbrechen" (Dissertation), *Archiv für Kriminal-Anthropologie und Kriminalistik* (1909) 35 (Doctoral Dissertation); "Ein Beitrag zur Frage: 'Entwicklund einter Persönlichkeit' oder 'Prozess'?", *Zeitschrift für die gesamte Neurologie und Psychiatrie* (1910) 1:567-637 (Development); "Die Methode der Intelligenzprüfung und der Begriff der Dimenz", *Zeitschrift für die gesamte Neurologie und Psychiatrie* (Referatential) (1910) 1:402-452 (Method); "Zur Analyse der Trugwahrnehmun (Leibhaftigkeit und Realitätsurteil), *Zeitschrift für die gesamte Neurologie und Psychiatrie* (1911) 6:460-535 (Trauma Analysis); "Kausale und 'verständliche' Zusammenhange", *Zeitschrift für die gesamte Neurologie und Psychiatrie* (1913a) 14:158-263 (Causality).

1913. *Allgemeine Psychopathologie: Ein Leitfade für Studierende, Ärzte und Psychologen*, 1st ed., Berlin (Psychopathology1).

1919. *Psychologie der Weltanschauungen*. Heidelberg, 1985 (Psychology.

1931. *Die geistige Situation der Zeit.* 1st ed., Berlin and Leipzig (Spiritual Situation).
1932. *Philosophie.* 3 vols. Heidelberg, 1994. Vol. 1: 1932a. *Philosophische Weltorientirung* (Ph1). Vol. 2. 1932b. *Existenzerhellung* (Ph2). Vol. 3: 1932c. *Metaphysik* (Ph3).
1935. *Vernuft und Existenz.* München, 1987 (Wisdom and Existenz).
1937. *Existenzphilosophie.* Frankfurt a.M. 3rd ed. Berlin, 1964 (Philosophy of Existenz).
1942. *Allgemeine Psychopathologie.* 4th ed. Berlin and Heidelberg. 8th ed., 1965 (Psychopathology4).
1947. *Von der Wahrheit.* München, 1991 (Truth).
1950. *Nietzsche: Einführung in das Verständnis seines Philosophierens.* Berlin (Nietzsche).
1958a. *Philosophie und Welt: Reden und Aufsätze.* München (Philosophy and the World).
1958b. *Rechenschaft und Ausblick: Reden und Aufsätze.* Tübingen (Report).
1962. *Der philosophische Glaube angesichts der Offenbarung.* München (Philosophical Faith in the Face of Revelation).
1983. "Einsamkeit", *Revue International de Philosophie* 37: 390-409 (Loneliness).

Other authors

Arendt, Hannah. 1958. "Karl Jaspers", in *Reden zur Verleihung des Friedenspreises des Deutschen Buchhandels*, 27-40, München.
Binswanger, Ludwig. 1913. "Bemerkung zu der Arbeit Jaspers: Kausale un 'verständliche' Zusammenhange zwischen Schicksal und Psychose bei der Dementia praecox (Schizophrenie)", *Internationale Zietschrift für ärzliche Psychoanalyse* (Leipzig) 1:383-390.
Bollnow, Otto Friedrich. 1939. "Existenzerhellung und philosophische Anthropologie", *Bulletin für Deutsche Philosophie* 12/2:133-174.
Bollnow, Otto Friedrich. 1960 (1942). *Existenzphilosophie.* Stuttgart.
Brecht, Franz Josef. 1948. *Heidegger und Jaspers: Die beiden Grundformen der Existenzphilosohie.* Wuppertal.
Dilthey, Wilhelm. 1927. *Der Aufbau der geschichtlichen Welt in den Geisteswissenschaften.* Leipzig.
Dilthey, Wilhelm. 1962. *Weltanschauungslehre: Abhandlung zur Philosophie der Philosophie. In Gesammelte Shcriften.* Vol. 8. Stuttgart and Göttingen.
Ehrlich, Leonard H., and Richard Wisser, eds. 1988. *Karl Jaspers Today: Philosphy at the Threshold of the Future.* Lanham, MD.
Fuchs, Franz Josef. 1984. *Seinverhältnis: Karl Jaspers' Existenzphilosophie Existenz und Kommunikation.* Frankfurt a.M.
Gabriel, Leo. 1951. *Existenzphilosophie von Kierkegaard bis Sartre.* Vienna.
Gabriel, Marcel. 1932/1933. "Grundsituation und Grenzsituationen". In Saner 1973, 155-180.
Golomb, Jacob. 1980. "From Phenomenology to Hermeneutics: On Paul Ricoeur's Hermeneutic Method", *Iyyun* 29: 22-36 [Hebrew].
Golomb, Jacob. 1981. "On the Crisis of Science and Psychology in Husserl's *Crisis*", *Iyyun* 29: 264-279 [Hebrew].

Griesinger, Wilhelm. 1876. *Pathologie und Therapie der psychischen Krankeiten.* 4th ed. Braunschweig.
Heidegger, Martin. 1959. *Gelassenheit.* Tübingen.
Heidegger, Martin. 1954. "Überwindung der Metaphysik', in: Martin Heidegger, *Vorträge und Aufsätze,* Günther Neske Pfullingen, Tübingen, 71-99.
Heidegger, Martin. 1993. "The Question Concerning Technology", in: *Martin Heidegger, Basic Writings,* William Lovitt (trans.) Harper Collins, San Francisco, 307-341.
Heinemann, Fritz. 1954. *Existenzphilosophie—lebendig oder tot?* Stuttgart.
Hersch, Jeanne. 1965. *Die Illusion: der Weg der Philosophie.* Basel.
Hersch, Jeanne. 1978. *Karl Jaspers: eine Einführung in sein Werk.* Basel.
Hersch, Jeanne. 1986. "Existenz in der empirischen Wirklichkeit", In Hersch, Lochman, Wiehl, eds., 47-58.
Hersch, Jeanne, Jan Milic Lochman, and Reiner Wiehl, eds. 1986. *Karl Jaspers: Philosoph, Artzt, politischer Denker.* München and Zürich.
Imle, F. 1936. "Jaspers als Existenzphilosoph", *Philosophisches Jahrbuch der Görresgesellschaft* 49: 487-504.
Imle, F. 1937. "Jaspers als Existenzphilosoph", *Philosophisches Jahrbuch der Görresgesellschaft* 50: 178-193.
Jean Marie, Paul. 1989. "Der Weg des Menschen oder Kommunikation und Liebe bei Jaspers". In *Karl Jaspers: Denken zwischen Wissenschaft, Politik und Philosophie,* ed. Dietrich Harth, 43-64.
Jung, C. G. 1996. *Persönlichkeit und Übertragung.* In *Grundwerke.* Vol. 2. Zürich and Düsseldorf.
Kaufmann, Fritz. 1957. "Karl Jaspers and a Philosophy of Communication". In Schilpp, ed., 211-295.
Kempski, Jürgen von. 1964. "Philosophie als Anruf'. In *Brechungen: Kritische Versuche zur Philosophie der Gegenwart.* Hamburg.
Kronfeld, Arthur. 1922. "Über neuere pathologisch-phänomenologische Arbeiten", *Zentralblatt für die gesamte Neurologie und Psychiatrie* 28: 441-459.
Kunz, Hans. 1957. "Critique of Jaspers' Concept of Transcendence". In Schilpp, ed., 499-522.
Lenz, Joseph. 1951. *Der moderne deutsche und französische Existentialismus.* Trier.
Löwenstein, Julius L. 1988. "Das Bleibende von Jaspers und Heidegger". In Ehrlich and Wisser, eds., 317-340.
May, Rollo. 1983. *The Discovery of Being: Writings in Existential Psychology.* Norton: New York.
Miron, Ronny. 2004. "From Opposition to Reciprocity—Karl Jaspers in Science, Philosophy and What Lies Between Them". *International Philosophical Quarterly* , 44/2, (2004), 147-163 (Miron, 2004c).

Miron, Ronny. 2012. *Karl Jaspers: From Selfhood to Being.* Rodopi: Value Inquiry Series (Miron, Monograph, 2012).

Müller-Schwefe, Hans Rudolf. 1961. *Existenzphilosophie: Das Verständnis von Existenz in Philosophie und christlichem Glauben.* Zürich.

Olson, Alan M. 1979. *Transcendence and Hermeneutic: An Interpretation of the Philosophy of Karl Jaspers*. Boston and London.
Pfeifer, Johannes. 1952. *Existenzphilosophie: Eine Einführung in Heidegger und Jaspers*. Hamburg.
Räber, Thomas. 1955. *Das Dasein in der "Philosophie" von Karl Jaspers: Eine Untersuchung im Hinblick auf die Einheit und Realität der Welt im existentiellen Denken*. Bern.
Reis, Johannes. 1950. "Menschliche Existenz bei Jaspers", *Die Neue Ordnung* 4: 418-426, 527-531.
Ringer, Fritz K. 1969. *The Decline of the German Mandarins: The German Academic Community 1890-1933*. Cambridge, Mass.
Rintelen, Fritz-Joachim von. 1961. *Beyond Existentialism*. Trans. Hilda Graef. London.
Sagi, Avi. 2000 *Kierkegaard: Religion and Existenz: The Voyage of the* Self, Batya Stein (trans.), Rodopi, Amsterdam-Atlanta.
Salamun, Kurt. 1985. *Karl Jaspers*. München.
Samay, Sebastian. 1971. *Philosophische Weltanschauung*. Bern.
Saner, Hans, ed. 1973. *Karl Jaspers in der Diskussion*. München.
Schilpp, Paul Arthur, ed. 1957. *The Philosophy of Karl Jaspers*. Dublin.
Schipperges, Heinrich. 1986. "Medizin als konkrete Philosophie". In Hersch, Lochman, and Wiehl, eds., 88-111.
Schnädelbach, Herbert. 1984. *Philosophy in Germany 1831-1933*. Trans. Eric Matthews. Cambridge and New York.
Schenider, Kurt. 1926. "Die phänomenologische Richtung in den Psychiatrie", *Philosophischer Anzeiger* 4: 382-404.
Scheniders, Werner. 1965. *Karl Jaspers in der Kritik*. Bonn.
Sonnemann, Ulrich. 1954. *Existence and Therapy: An Introduction to Phenomenological Psychology and Existential Analysis*. New York.
Spiegelberg, Herbert. 1967. "The Relevance of Phenomenological Philosophy for Psychology". In E. N. Lee and M. Mandelbaum, eds., *Phenomenology and Existentialism*, 219-241. Baltimore.
Stegmüller, Wolfgang. 1960. *Hauptströmungen der Gegenwartsphilosophie*. Stuttgart.
Tennen, Hanoch. 1977. *The Perception of Existnetial Ethics in the Thought of Karl Jaspers*. Ramat Gan [Hebrew].
Thyssen, Johannes. 1957. "The Concept of 'Foundering' in Jaspers' Philosophy". In Schilpp, ed., 297-335.
Tymieniecka, Anna-Teresa. 1962. *Phenomenology and Science in Contemporary Thought*. New York.
Van Kaam, Adrian L. 1961. "The Impact of Existential Phenomenology on Psychological Literature of Western Europe", *Review of Existential Pscyhology and Psychiatry* 1: 63-92.
Walker, Chris. 1993a. "Karl Jaspers as a Kantian Psychopathologist, I: The Philosophical Origins of the Concept of Form and Content", *History of Psychiatry* 4: 209-238.
Walker, Chris. 1993b. "Karl Jaspers as a Kantian Psychopathologist, II: The Concept of Form and Content in Jaspers' Psychopathology", *History of Psychiatry* 4: 321-348.

Walker, Chris. 1994. "Karl Jaspers as a Kantian Psychopathologist, III: The Concept of Form in Georg Simmel's Social Theory: A Comparison with Jaspers", *History of Psychiatry* 5: 37-70.

Walker, Chris. 1995a. "Karl Jaspers and Edmund Husserl—III: Jaspers as a Kantian Phenomenologist", *Philosophy, Psychiatry and Psychology* 2/1: 65-82.

Walker Chris. 1995b. "Karl Jaspers and Edmund Husserl—IV: Phenomenology as Empathic Understanding", *Philosophy, Psychiatry and Psychology* 2/3: 247-266.

Weber, Max. 1919. "Wissenschaft als Beruf". In *Gesammelte Aufsätze zur Wissenschaftslehre*. Tübingen, 1958.

Weber, Max. 1958. *The Protestant Ethic and the Spirit of Capitalism*. Trans. Talcott Parsons. New York.

Wisser, Richard. 1988. "Aneignung und Unterscheidung: Existenzphilosophie im Kampf um die Existenz der Philosophie". In Ehrlich and Wisser, eds., 341-361.

Wisser, Richard. 1995. *Karl Jaspers: Philosophie in der Bewährung. Vorträge und Aufsätze*. Würzburg.

Young-Bruehl, Elisabeth. 1981. *Freedom and Karl Jaspers' Philosophy*. New Haven.

From Opposition to Reciprocity: Karl Jaspers on Science, Philosophy, and What Lies between Them

Abstract

This article deals with the relationship between philosophy and science in the writings of Karl Jaspers and with its reception in the wider scholarly literature. The problem discussed is how to characterize the relationship that exists between science—defined on pure Kantian grounds as a universally valid knowledge of phenomenal objects—and philosophy—conceived by Jaspers as the transcending mode of thinking of personal Existenz rising towards the totality and unity of Being. Two solutions to that problem arise from Jaspers's writings. The oppositionist view is based in his earlier philosophy of Existenz. It describes the discrepancy between determinateness, bestowed by science to its objects, and freedom of self-determination, which is both a synonym and a condition of possibility for Existenz. The reciprocal view is based in Jaspers's later works, where he focuses on exploration of his concept of Being (*das Umgreifende*). By contrast with most of Jaspers's commentators, the present interpretation is anchored in a developmental and contextual understanding of Jaspers's thought. Showing the transcendental background of this topic, the proposed interpretation allows us to abstain from viewing the two solutions as incoherent or contradictory and instead to see them as constitutive of a single philosophical course.

Foreword

Since the return of the twentieth century, philosophers have dealt with the question of the boundaries between philosophy and other fields of knowledge. This article deals with the relationship between philosophy and science in the philosophical writings of Karl Jaspers and with its reception in the wider scholarly literature. Actually, his discussion of this subject is not based on a conception of science and philosophy as two differentiated disciplines but focuses on the viewpoints that he grasped as typical of them.[1] Consequently, Jaspers's attitude towards science also contains his views regarding objectivity, relativity, method, generality, conscious reason, and even epistemology. On the other hand, philosophy in his thinking also manifests subjectivity and particularity, the absence of method, and openness, as well as the pursuit of unity, perfection, totality, and evident certainty. As will be made clear, the wide range of meanings on which the concepts of "science" and "philosophy" are based in Jaspers's thought also has bearing upon the understanding of his philosophy as a whole. However, the broad understanding of the terms "science" and "philosophy"—on which Jaspers never presented a consistent conception—leads to the great complexity of the issue in his thought. As will be seen, this complexity is well reflected in the reception of the subject in the literature.

Three different scholarly approaches have attempted to resolve what seem to be contradictions in Jaspers's stand on the issue. Most of the scholars who have dealt with the relationship between science and philosophy in Jaspers's thinking have defined it as one of opposition. Sebastian Samay, for instance, contends that philosophy in Jaspers's thought is opposite to science in two basic senses: first, philosophy is not meant to convince others of its rightness, and second, "it does not have a certain object but a comprehensive foundation."'[2] In his view, they first must be presented in their pure form in order to reveal any possible cooperation between the two. This means that, on the one hand, philosophy does not constitute scientific knowledge, but on the other, scientific knowledge does not exhaust the whole truth. In Samay's opinion, Jaspers held that science could be of help to philosophy only if the latter relinquished its scientific pretensions, while philosophy could be of help to science if it abandoned its metaphysical claims.'[3]

Elisabeth Young-Bruehl expresses a similar position on this issue.[4] She contends that, in contrast to scientific thinking, which strives after conceptualization and objectivity, Jaspers presents a type of thought that searches for a basis, an origin from which antinomies develop. In her opinion, this approach is apparent in the concepts by means of which Jaspers sought to clarify

---

[1] Thanks to Prof. Avi Sagi from Bar Ilan University for his critical reading and for his useful notes. This article is based on Jaspers's writings published during the years 1932-1947, including: Jaspers books and their abbreviations: *Die Idee der Universität, Schriften der Universität* (Berlin-Heidelberg: Springer, 1946) (hereafter, IdU); *Nietzsche: Einführung in das Verstandnis seines Philosophierens* (Berlin: Walter de Gruyter & Co., 1950) (hereafter Nietzsche); *Philosophie*, vols. 1-3 (München: Piper, 1994 [1932[): *Philosophische Weltorientierung* [Ph1]; *Existenz Erhellung* [Ph2]; *Metaphysik* [Ph3]; *Philosophie und Welt, Reden und Aufsätze* (München, Piper & Co., 1958) (hereafter, PW); *Psychologie der Weltanschuungen* (München-Zurich: Piper, 1985 [1919])(hereafter, Psychology); *Rechenschaft und Ausblick, Reden und Aufsätze* (München: Piper, 1958) (hereafter, Report); *Vernunft und Existenz, Fünf Vorlesungen* (München: Piper, [1935] 1987) (hereafter, Wisdom and Existenz); *Vernunft und Widervernunft in Unserer Zeit* (München: Piper, 1950) (hereafter, VuW); *Von Der Wahrheit, Philosophische Logik* (München: Piper, [1947] 1991) (hereafter, Truth).
[2] Sebastian Samay, *Reason Revisited: The Philosophy of Karl Jaspers* (Dublin: Gill and Macmillan, 1971), 108-09 (hereafter, Samay).
[3] Samay, 111.
[4] Elisabeth Young-Bruehl, *Freedom and Karl Jaspers's Philosophy*, New Haven and London: Yale Univ. Press, 1981) 7-8 (hereafter, Young-Bruehl).

Existenz (such as freedom, will, and so on) that are not anchored in the dichotomy of subject and object typical of scientific thought.'[5] In a similar vein Hoffman claimed that Jaspers called for the establishment of total and completely separate sciences because he assumed that it was impossible to unite all the different types of consciousness that accompany human existence into a universal science or a single systematic and coherent philosophy.[6]

Another interpretation holds that science and philosophy in Jaspers's thought are anchored in a common foundation and therefore mutually interdependent on each other. Hanoch Tennen, for instance, contends that the methodical awareness of basic assumptions, which leads to the recognition of their limits and relative meanings but also fosters a desire to overcome the restrictions and seek out perfection, is common to both science and philosophy in Jaspers's thought. Besides this common foundation, Tennen also emphasizes the contentions by means of which Jaspers depicted science and philosophy as mutually interdependent on each other. In his opinion, this dependency stems from Jaspers's conception, according to which science needs the ideas that originate in philosophy in order to formulate its own questions, goals, and values. However, science, as a mode of critique, has to serve as a prior assumption for philosophy.[7] Alan Olson presents a similar approach when he concludes that the boundary between science and philosophy in Jaspers's thought is epistemological, i.e., that it reflects an awareness of the different forms of consciousness in human existence.[8] In the same spirit, James Collins defines the difference between

---

[5] Ibid., 21-22. A similar conclusion to Young-Bruehl's regarding the relationship between science and philosophy can be drawn from other interpretations. See: Fritz Heinemann, *Existenz philosophie—lebendig oder tot?* (Stuttgart: Kohlhammer, 1954) 72-74 (hereafter: Heinemann); Fritz-Joachim von Rinteln, *Beyond Existentialism*, trans. H. Graef (London: George Allen & Unwin, 1961) 204f (hereafter: von Rinteln).

[6] Kurt Hoffman, "The Basic Concepts of Jaspers's Philosophy" (hereafter, Hoffman) in *The Philosophy of Karl Jaspers*, ed. P. A. Schilpp (New York: Northwestern Univ. Press, 1957) 95f. Compare also to Charles F. Wallraff, *Karl Jaspers: An Introduction to his Philosophy* (Princeton: Princeton Univ. Press, 1970) 38-65.

[7] Hanoch Tennen, "Jaspers's Philosophie in kritischer Sicht—Das Verhaltnis zwischen Philosophie und Wissenschaft," *Zeitschrift für philosophische Forschung* 28 (1974) 542-44. It appears that behind Tennen's interpretation lies Jaspers's distinction between two concepts of limit: *Prinzipielle Grenzen* and *Jeweilige Grenzen* (Ph1: 45). Jaspers's distinction was parallel to Kant's concepts, which distinguished between *Grenze* and *Scharnke*. See Immanuel Kant, *Prolegomena to Any Future Metaphysics*, ed. Beryl Logan (London and New York: Routledge, 1996) 111. A different formulation of the foundation common to science and philosophy is presented by James Bennet in the framework of what he calls the "inclusive position." See James O. Bennett, "Karl Jaspers and Scientific Philosophy," *Journal of Philosophy*, 31 (1993) 441-42. The understanding that awareness of the limits of science leads to philosophy appeared also in Kurt Rossmann, "Wert und Grenze der Wissenschaft" in *Weiler Horizont, Festschrift für Karl Jaspers, zum 70. Geburtstag*, ed. Klaus Piper (München: Piper, 1953) 144; Dietrich Harth, "Grenzen der Wissenschaft" in *Karl Jaspers, Denken zwischen Wissenschaft, Politik und Philosophie*, ed. Dietrich Harth (Stuttgart: Metzlersche, 1989) 207-26.

[8] Alan M. Olson, *Transcendence and Hermeneutics: An interpretation of the Philosophy of Karl Jaspers* (Boston and London: Martinus Nijhoff, 1979) 13-16.

science and philosophy in Jaspers's thought as "a conflict between siblings involved in a competition to expose the truth."[9]

Besides these two paths of interpretation, an additional approach appears in the literature that deliberately abstains from deciding among the different positions expressed by Jaspers on this issue. Thus, for instance, James Bennet contends that Jaspers's philosophy presents a dualistic position stemming from the simultaneous presence of two dimensions: the personal-existential and the impersonal-scientific.[10] Bennet therefore concludes that there is little room for separating science and philosophy in Jaspers's thought since the subjectivity of *Existenz* requires the objectivity manifested by science, although scientific knowledge itself is grasped as leading to the "non-knowledge" crucial to philosophy.[11]

Indeed, the fact that Jaspers never presented a coherent and consistent conception in his discussion of science and philosophy provides a reasonable textual basis for each of the above interpretations. However, against the background of the obscurity that characterizes Jaspers's own writing on this issue, it is hard to rest content with any one of them, for each of them gives room to just one of the voices that appears in Jaspers's writings and offers no explanation for the presence of other voices. Furthermore, none of them properly addresses the broader context of the discussion, in the framework of which Jaspers expressed his positions on science and philosophy, or the marks they have left on his conceptions of other issues.

In contrast to these approaches, the interpretation of the issue suggested here will attempt to meet the challenge posed by Jaspers himself when faced with a philosophical text that arouses difficulties in understanding: "To experience contradictions in their vitality. Instead of randomly prodding contradictions, we must look for the source of contrariety [*Widersprüchlichkeit*]" (Nietzsche, 17). Accordingly, the following discussion will neither strive to determine the centrality of one of the positions expressed by Jaspers on the subject nor avoid this by seeking the haven of contradiction.

The phenomenological approach on which the discussion is based consists of examining the *viewpoints* in which Jaspers's various references to science and philosophy were anchored in their immanent contexts. As in any phenomenological discussion, it is impossible to illuminate the entirety of the subject at once without spreading it out over several stages. Moreover, the suggested interpretation of this issue also reflects an overall understanding of

---

[9] James Collins, "Jaspers on Science and Philosophy" in Schilpp, 136. Additional interpretations that expand upon the dimension of dependency: J. Rudolf Gerber, "Karl Jaspers and Kantian Reason. " *New Scholasticism*, 43 (1969) 400-23; Joseph W. Koterski, "Jaspers on Freedom and Truth in Science" in *Karl Jaspers Today, Philosophy at the Threshold of the Future*, ed. Leonard H. Ehrlich and Richard Wisser (Washington D.C.: Center for Advanced Research in Phenomenology and University Press of America, 1988) 133-52.

[10] The conception of the polarity between subjectivity and objectivity is widely treated of in Jaspers. See Ph2: 336-49.

[11] Bennet, 446-49. On the standing of the personality in Jaspers's thinking, see Richard Wisser, "Karl
Jaspers: The Person and His Cause, Not the Person or His Cause, " *IPQ* 36 (1996) 413-27.

Jaspers's thinking. Hence my attempt to consolidate a thematic understanding of this issue will seek to accomplish what Jaspers himself failed to do: to formulate an explicit and broad understanding of the issue of the relationship between science and philosophy in his thinking.

Discussion

In understanding Jaspers's conception of science and philosophy, the importance of context lies in the fact that it was not generally discussed in his writings as part of his discussion of Being and *Existenz*, the two principal objects around which his philosophical writings took shape. The idea that science is opposed to philosophy, which will henceforward be termed "the oppositionist position," appears as part of his philosophical explication of selfhood, which he termed *Existenz*. Additionally, we find in Jaspers the view that the relationship between the respective viewpoints of science and philosophy is one of reciprocity, stemming from their common foundation, from the fact that they complement one another. This idea, which will henceforward be termed "the reciprocal position," is more prominent in those contexts where Jaspers discusses "Being." Although Jaspers himself never pointed to any connection between these two positions and the broader contexts of his thinking, such a connection, as will become evident, clearly arises from his conceptions of *Existenz* and Being.

The Typology of the "Oppositionist Position"

The "oppositionist position" appears directly in several contexts wherein Jaspers conducts a typological comparison between "science" and "philosophy." Thus, for instance, he defined modern science as a *methodical consciousness*, the contents of which are *certain* and *universally applicable* [*allgemeingültig*] (IdU 12-13, Report 241) but which are dependent on its basic assumptions and, therefore, cannot claim to possess an absolute truth (Report 249-50, 254). In other words, science presents a generally valid truth that is not yet the entire truth because beyond it lies essential truth that cannot be grasped by science (Truth 256). Under the influence of Max Weber, Jaspers determined that modern science bestows knowledge and a framework for the realization of the powers of human reason, but it cannot provide it with a source for determining values and goals—this is not its purpose at all (Ph1: xxv).[12] In parallel, philosophy was presented as opposite to science in "the lack of the general validity of its persuasions," but at the same time as having the potential to be unconditional and certain for those who see it as an absolute truth (Ph1: 319).[13] For the individual, philosophy may become a faith in which one sees the source of directly experiencing Being in its entirety (Report xxvii, 247).[14] Jaspers contended that philosophy, specifically

---

[12] See also IdU 18. On Weber's conception of science and its influence on Jaspers's own, see Max Weber, "Wissenschaft als Beruf [1919]" in *Gesaminelte Aufsatze zur Wissenschaftlehre* (Tubingen, J. C. B. Mohr, [1922] 1968) 524-55; Heinemann, 61-66; Ernst Moritz, "Max Weber's Influence on Jaspers" in Schilpp, 369-93.

[13] Compare also to IdU 13; Report 254-55.

[14] The conception of philosophy as a faith was further developed in his thinking in *Der Philosophische*

because it is not directed at a defined object or a particular field that can shape experience (Ph1: 318-19) but is presented as a universal viewpoint, may consolidate an approach towards human experience as a whole wherein different aspects of Being express themselves (Reason and Existenz 22).[15] It follows that even if philosophy cannot provide us with knowledge about reality or experience, it does contribute to a broader understanding of human beliefs, aspirations and self-awareness (Ph1: 323-24; Report 255). On the basis of these contentions about the uniqueness of science and philosophy, Jaspers also pointed to certain latent drawbacks, drawbacks that are nothing but the converse of these advantages. Thus science is presented as "incomplete" and particularistic in its cumulative advance, while philosophy is depicted as lacking any real assets or knowledge that might serve as a basis for any kind of ontological understanding (Ph1: 323, 325).

The Context of the "Oppositionist Position"—the Idea of Existenz

The "oppositionist position" is manifested fully in contexts in which Jaspers consolidated his conception of philosophical selfhood as *Existenz*. One of the most prominent characteristics of *Existenz* concerns the discrepancy between the "world" [Welt] and "conscious reason" [*Bewußtsein Überhaupt*]. Whereas Jaspers grasped *Existenz* as being that constitutes itself by means of reflexive action, the concepts of "conscious reason" and the "world" were presented as having objective meaning that extends beyond subjective references directed towards them. Therefore, Jaspers sought to establish his conception of philosophical selfhood on the basis of several dichotomous statements that locate *Existenz* on one side, with the world, conscious reason, generality, and objectivity on the other. Thus, he contends that whereas "the world as known Being [*Gewußtsein*] is generally valid for every man... *Existenz* in and of itself is *not general*"; it cannot be represented as a private case that is obedient to a general rule of law, but is "the individual of a concrete particularity" (Ph2: 4). Since the conception of *Existenz* refers to the actuality of a particular entity that *may* or *may not* be realized in concrete reality, Jaspers frequently uses the expression "possible *Existenz*."[16] However, because conscious reason is grasped by Jaspers as being able to represent only what actually exists [*Dasein*], it cannot provide access to *Existenz* (Ph1: 14).

Glaube (München: Piper, 1948) and in *Der Philosophische Glaube angesichts der Offenbarung* (Munchen: Piper, 1962). On this topic, see also Leonard Ehrlich, *Karl Jaspers: Philosophy as Faith* (Amherst: Univ. of Massachusetts Press, 1975).

[15] See also Reason and Existenz 14. Like Kant, Jaspers refers to a perfection that does not constitute an object, and as such it is opposite to science as a field that deals with the particular (Ph1: 322; Report 253). Kant's influence on Jaspers is a thing of renown, In this context, see Greber, 406f; Erich Grünert, "Der Einfluss Kants auf Karl Jaspers: Zugang zur Transzendenz bei Kant und Karl Jaspers," *Freiburger Zeitschrift für Philosophie und Theologie* 3 (1956) 21-28.

[16] Compare this also to the two concepts of the "world" presented by Jaspers in a different context: the
"world" as otherness that can be investigated and is of general validity, and the "world" as "not-I" (*Nichtich*) (Ph 1: 63).

The above-described awareness of the limitations of formal conscious reason in representing human phenomena is largely a continuation of Jaspers's earlier views. As a young psychiatrist, Jaspers was confronted with the limitations of the science of psychopathology in representing the subjective dimension of mental disease. He later developed this approach in his book *Psychology of World-Views* (1919) by emphasizing the importance of the world-view in revealing the subjective dimension of a normal personality.[17] The principles of his approach are already evident in these earlier writings, which point to the connection between the limitations of science and those of human conscious reason: just as the science of psychopathology cannot provide us with a complete understanding of mental disease, so too any type of thinking that is anchored in objective standards cannot reveal the full and unique Being of man.

These positions are of great importance in understanding the development of Jaspers's conception of selfhood, which lies beyond the scope of this article. For the purpose of this discussion, the important thing is that even though Jaspers grasped *Existenz* as worldly being and assumed that he was committed as a philosopher to discussing concepts of the "world" and modes of objective reason, he still distinguished between the philosophical viewpoint and the objective one. His main contention in this context was that "being able to be grasped by conscious reason" [*Erkenntbarkeit*] is characteristic of objects (Ph1: 17-18) and could be applied to everything outside *Existenz*, or in his terms to the "not-I" [*Nichtich*],[18] whereas what he termed "being able to be clarified" [*Erhellbarkeit*] was more relevant to the philosophical discussion aimed at explicating *Existenz* as particular being (Ph1: 17-18).[19]

I believe that Jaspers's deliberate choice of the term "elucidation" [*Erhellung*]—rather than "explanation" [*Erklären/Erläutern*] or "enlightenment" [*Erleuchtern*], for example—was specifically meant to demonstrate the qualitative stance of philosophy towards the objects of its inquiry, in comparison to the stance of conscious reason towards objects. Whereas the operation of reason expresses one's active regulation, the philosophical viewpoint, which is directed in this context towards *Existenz*, first and foremost reflects a state of

---

[17] See *Allgemeine Psychopathologie: Ein Leitfaden für Studierende, Arzte und Psychologen* (Berlin:
Springer, 1913), 8, 14f: Psychology 10-11, 14-15.
[18] This distinction, between "I" or *Existenz* and what he termed "not-I," as well as between their different approaches, is also of great importance in understanding the ontological conception that underlies Jaspers's conception of selfhood. There are different interpretations regarding this issue. See Olson, 10: Werner Schneiders, *Karl Jaspers in der Kritik* (Bonn: Bouvier, 1965) 167; Thomas Raber, *Das Dasein in der "Philosophie" von Karl Jaspers, Eine Untersuchung im Hinblick auf die Einheit und der Realitat der Welt im Existentiallen Denken* (Bern, Francke, 1955) 33f, 133f.
[19] This contention has been variously interpreted, See Samay, 146-47: Olson, 20; Jürgen von Kempski,
"Philosophie als Anruf" in *Brechungen, Kritische Versuch zur Philosophie der Gegenwart* (Hamburg:
Rowohlt, 1964) 243; Hans-Rudolf Müller-Schwefe, *Existenz philosophie, Das Verständniss von Existenz in Philosophie und christlichem Glauben* (Zurich: Vandenhoeck & Ruprecht, 1961) 39: Johannes Reis, "Menschliche *Existenz* bei Jaspers," *Die Neue Ordnung* 4 (1950) 418-26, 527-31.

mind that is characterized by an ability to allow things to elucidate themselves.[20] Yet from a different viewpoint we could contend almost the exact opposite regarding the activity or passivity attributed to these two positions. Whereas reason requires man to limit his observation in accordance to rationality, Jaspers makes the philosophical viewpoint of "elucidation" much more flexible in order to be able to express the dimension of freedom, which is central to the conception of *Existenz* as being that constitutes itself. From this viewpoint, it is "elucidation" that appears to be an active position, which determines both its objects and the modes of approach to them by itself. In any event, the dichotomy between "conscious reason" and "elucidation," as a philosophical viewpoint directed towards *Existenz*, is maintained.

Having established the gap between *Existenz*, "conscious reason," and the "world," and out of a continuing disposition to defend the centrality of *Existenz* to his discussion, Jaspers attempts to take another step by presenting the advantages of the philosophical viewpoint, which is directed towards the *Existenz*, over the objective viewpoint that deals with the "world." In his own words:

> In philosophizing the I of possible *Existenz* has the decidedly dominant function of which in that circle can be only negatively defined. Possible *Existenz* may perhaps open the positive way that is closed to conscious reason in the world of objects. This kind of philosophizing is as nothing for empirical existence, and a groundless figment of imagination for conscious reason. But for possible Existenz it is the way to itself and to genuine Being. (Ph1: 14-15)

What emerges from this remark is that philosophizing, which is directed towards explicating "*Existenz*," may reveal what "conscious reason" is unable to arrive at because of its bondage to the "being of the object." In other words, what is revealed as "Being-in-itself" to philosophizing, which is directed towards *Existenz*, simply does not exist for conscious reason because of the limitations of representation of the tools at its disposal. The tension between the philosophical viewpoint and the objective one is taken to the extreme of presenting the objective viewpoint of reason as verily undermining the possible actuality of the particular being of "*Existenz*" (Ph2: 5). It appears that Jaspers's commitment to refer to the actual reality revealed by means of conscious reason was at this stage defeated by a contrary inclination, i.e., that which sought to give philosophical expression to the particular being of *Existenz*. The identification of the objective viewpoint with the concept of the "world" led Jaspers to the presentation of *Existenz* as being that desires to separate itself from the world, or, in his words: in "reasoning the world the world is desiderated as a craving of existence": however, "as an absolute urge this desire will become destructive to me; counter to [this desire] I hear the demand out of my possible Existenz: to detach myself from a

---

[20] In German, this position could be defined by the phrase *hell werden lassen*. In this matter, see Gabriel Marcel's remark, according to which the use of this verb is not common in philosophical language, in his article, "Grundsituation und Grenzsituationen [1932/1933]" in *Karl Jaspers in der Diskussion*, ed. Hans Saner (Munchen: Piper & Co. 1973) 160.

world, sinking into which puts me in danger."[21] Objective reason's inability to express the qualitative being of "*Existenz*" and the latter's craving to separate itself from the world do not stem, of course, from a conception of *Existenz* as being that is outside the world, but express conscious reason's inadequacy in helping to perform philosophy's labor of "elucidation." Furthermore, since the determinations of *Existenz* with regard to itself are impossible for conscious reason (Ph2: 12-14), Jaspers concluded that there is no possibility of establishing the Being of *Existenz* on the basis of objective perceptibility.

Unlike conscious reason, which gives man satisfaction stemming from his ability to organize the world, the self consciousness of "*Existenz*" rests only upon insights that it itself arrives at in the course of the reflexive process. Only thus can *Existenz* meet the ultimate demand "to be from the source of my selfhood" (Ph2: 6).[22] From this aspect, "dissatisfaction" can be seen as expressing the stance of philosophizing that is directed towards the clarification of *Existenz* in the face of the tools, upon which, according to Jaspers, science in general relies, namely, the objective viewpoint or conscious reason.[23] The fact that Jaspers did not move back from the conception of *Existenz* as worldly being allows us to assert that Existenz constitutes itself from the space of its existence [*Dasein*], but its self-consciousness takes shape in alienation and disjunction from this world.

---

[21] The philosophical step whereby Jaspers sought ostensibly to "withdraw" *Existenz* from the world is dialectical, since ultimately "possible *Existenz* separates itself from the world in order to truly enter it later." However, in the scholarly literature there is reference mainly to the first part of this maneuver. By extension we may point out prominent examples of an approach, according to which Jaspers's conception of *Existenz* constitutes an irrational position or expresses an idealistic world view: Otto Friedrich Bollnow, "Existenz Erhellung und Philosophische Anthropologie," *Bulletin für Deutsche Philosophie*, 12 (1939) 136-39, 157; F. Imle, "Jaspers als Existenz philosoph," *Philosophisches Jahrbuch der Görresgesellschaft* 4 (1936) 503; Joseph Lenz, *Der moderne deutsche and französische Existentialismus* (Trier: Paulinus-Verlag, 1951), 54; Leo Gabriel, *Existenz philosophie von Kierkegaard bis Sartre* (Wien: Herold, 1951) 221-22; Wolfgang Stegmtiller, *Hauptstromungen der Gegenwartsphilosophie* (Stuttgart: Kroner, 1960) 233f; Marcel Reding, *Die Existenz philosophie, Heidegger, Sartre, Gabriel Marcel und Jaspers in kritischer-systematischer Sicht* (Dusseldorf: Schwann, 1949) 96-109.

[22] Many scholars who have studied Jaspers's thinking view this conception of philosophy as the reason for the lack of influence of his work. See Heinemann, 66; Bennet, 246 n45; Tennen, 560-61; Schneiders, 263-64; Hans Saner, *Karl Jaspers, Werk und Wirkung, zum 80. Geburtstag* (München: Piper, 1963); Charles Wallraff, "Jaspers in English: A Failure in Communication," *Philosophy and Phenomenological Research* 37 (1977) 537-48; A. Lichtigfeld, "Jaspers in English: A Failure not in Communication but rather in Interpretation," *Philosophy and Phenomenological Research* 41 (1980) 222. Jaspers himself referred to his commentators in his essay "Reply to my Critics" in Schilpp, 748-869.

[23] In Jaspers's discussion of the discrepancy between "*Existenz*" and the limits of expression of formal reason, the influence of Kierkegaard's critique of the Hegelian subject is evident. In this matter, see Olson, 45; Young-Bruehl, 5-9; Heinemann, 61-83. On Kierkegaard's conception and its scholarly interpretation, see Søren Kierkegaard, *Concluding Unscientific Postscript*, trans. D. F. Swenson and W. Lowrie (Princeton: Princeton Univ. Press, 1974) 545; Avi Sagi, *Kierkegaard, Religion and Existence: The Voyage of the Self*, trans. B. Stein (Amsterdam-Atlanta: Rodopi, 2000) 12-13.

As a result of this discussion, we can interpret the philosophical move that was focused on the being of *Existenz* and that emphasized the discrepancy between it and the "world" and "conscious reason" as a comprehensive application of the "oppositionist position." The meaning of this position is that there is an opposition between the viewpoint of "philosophy" (or to be more precise the conception of "*Existenz*" with which Jaspers's philosophy dealt) and the objective viewpoint of "conscious reason," which is directed at the world and in which "science" is anchored. In other words, the "oppositionist position" realizes its full philosophical potential in Jaspers's conception of *Existenz*. This enables us to conclude that no less than the "oppositionist position" testifies to the conception of the relationship between "philosophy" and "science" in Jaspers's thinking; it constitutes the existential part of his philosophy.

The Typology of the "Reciprocal Position"

Alongside the "oppositionist position" there appeared in Jaspers's philosophical writings a "reciprocal position." According to this position, there are reciprocal relations between these two viewpoints stemming from a common foundation, the fact that they complement one another. This position sees scientific knowledge as mainly concerned with various aspects of the existence and reality of the individual (Truth 62); these are influenced by countless circumstances, on account of which this knowledge can never be certain. Consequently, Jaspers concluded, we will never be able to formulate a complete theory on the basis of any facts at all nor arrive by means of them at absolute certainty (Ph1: 91). In this context, Jaspers emphasized the need for a motive, interest, or real desire on the part of scientists (Truth 303), which points to the relevancy of the facts they are dealing with to science (Ph1: 124-25).[24] From this aspect, the facts upon which science rests do not have a pure meaning of their own, but only as a component in the reflexive process of scientists' reason. In other words, the standing of objectivity in science is dependent on scientists' finding the facts relevant to the goals that they themselves have defined as being of value. Furthermore, since the scientific method itself is a product of the subject's mind, it constitutes an external element with great influence on the meaning given to the data with which science deals. Without theory to guide us, it is no longer possible to talk about knowledge, but only about "a movement of images lacking a goal" (Truth 346).[25] Method, then, determines the framework in which certain facts are to be examined, and the meaning given to them is also influenced by it.

---

[24] See also Truth 305-06; Ph1: 86-87,90-91,104-05,121. Samay contends that the term *Denken* that Jaspers uses extensively is a generic term, unlike the terms *Wissen* or *Erkennen*, which are specific. In his opinion, this fact reflects the conception, according to which the will that constitutes the reality of knowledge is not concerned with knowing, but with thinking that does not stop only at objects. From this it follows that beyond the objective goal of knowing there are existential or metaphysical goals connected with thinking itself, see Samay, 287 n. 54. This approach of Jaspers is opposite to Popper's conception, in which the consciously reasoning subject has no place in science. In this matter, see Koterski, 152 n. 29.

[25] For more on this subject, see Walter J. Ong, *The Presence of the World: Some Prolegomena for Cultural and Religious History* (New York: Simon & Schuster, 1967).

However, even though the method is a subjective component in science, at the same time it serves as a brake that prevents subjectivity from totally overwhelming it (Ph1: 87). Just as the method draws the line between the facts that will be investigated and those that will not be, it limits the framework of discussion in which scientists are free to move about and, in consequence, also the range of meanings they can give to their objects. Furthermore, the restrictions that method imposes upon scientists and upon the scientific discourse in general reflect more extensive processes to which scientists themselves are subject. Jaspers contended that the individual's central standing is not nourished only by the reflexive processes one undergoes in the framework of doing science. Actually, scholarly traditions are founded upon epistemological structures that are diffused within a society in which scientists live (VuE 26), and the science they do manifests their attitude towards a world of which they themselves are a part (Ph1: 83-84). This understanding makes it impossible, in Jaspers's opinion, to regard modern scientific theories as personal creations,[26] obliging us to see them as part of a larger matrix.[27] One should add to these restrictions unchanging factors such as concepts and conventions of judgment, the centrality of which to scientific activity Jaspers emphasized on more than one occasion (Truth 274-77). He determined that the meaning of science is the conquest of existence in an independent manner with respect to the reasoner or subjectivity (Ph1: 85) and that the a-temporality of thinking serves as a "vantage point" or "foothold" for the motion in science (Truth 305). The conception of the viewpoint of science arising from these statements is anchored in objective elements, which are in themselves stable and independent of the particular viewpoint of the reasoner. All the same, their actual realization brings subjective elements into the arena of scientific activity, the presence of which is unavoidable due to the fact that science is conducted by human beings. From this aspect, the "reciprocal position" constitutes a dialectical position, which is anchored in the complex relations between facts and theories in doing science. This dialectic allocates a real place for subjectivity, but at the same time subjectivity is itself qualified and influenced by external elements.

The undermining of the absolute conception of science, which arises from the study of these contentions, draws attention to the speculative and conditional dimension of doing science. This laid the basis for another conception, in which the respective viewpoints of science and philosophy complement one another. Jaspers contended that in its genuine sense science, as knowledge of the paths that lead to conscious reason and at the same time an acknowledgment of the relative character of its contentions (Philosophy of Existenz 9; IdU 12, 27), can serve as a prior assumption and condition of philosophy.[28] Although scientists may try by means of knowledge and research to liberate themselves from their world, they always find themselves occupying a particular viewpoint from which they can escape only by occupying a different one. In other words, being anchored in a particular subjective viewpoint is the only absolute element in scientific activity

---

[26] *Die Geistige Situation Der Zeit* (Berlin-Leipzig: de Gruyter, 1931) 160-61.
[27] See also Truth 26; IdU 23.
[28] *Einführung in die Philosophie, Zwölf Radiovorträge* (München: Piper, 1950), 142; Report 252. In another place, Jaspers emphasized that this statement applies to modern science as well, despite his well-known critique of it. See Report 249.

(Ph1: 104-05). All the same, even though science deals with limited objects, it is motivated by a counter-inclination that rebels against the formal restrictions imposed by the framework of object-subject relations, which can only provide relative knowledge. The impulse "to push at the limits" (Ph1: 145-16) is meant to overcome this relativity, the source of which is at one and the same time both the particularity of the subjective viewpoint and the formality of scientific reason. This clarifies the possible contribution of the scientific viewpoint to obtaining original and unconditional knowledge about "Being" (Ph1: 322-23), as a totality that contains all relative and particular understandings (IdU 24, 28). This is exactly where the viewpoint of science meets that of philosophy, which was also described as directed towards Being and motivated by an original and unconditional urge to know (WU 16-17). Furthermore, for both science and philosophy, this common aim towards which they are directed manifests a truth that cannot be arrived at only within their own limits (VuE 26).[29] The "reciprocal position," then, is anchored in the view that science and philosophy are directed towards "Being" as a totality extending beyond the relative limits of object-subject relations, but that at the same time harbors the understanding that they are mutually dependent on each other to achieve this goal.

However, the complement required for science differs from the one required for philosophy. No science, contended Jaspers, following Kant and Weber, can be based on itself alone; every science needs ideals to constitute itself as an independent discipline, determine its goals, and define the complete context of its objects (Ph1: xxv).[30] These ideals are provided to science by philosophy (IdU 22), not just by means of the abstract contents it deals with but by its very exteriority to the various particular sciences (Philosophy of Existenz 8).[31] According to Jaspers, the anchor that the scientific viewpoint finds in philosophy makes it possible to identify the source of knowledge with the desire for truth (VuW 25) in the sense of searching for a totality extending beyond any particular achievement. Furthermore, the fact that science itself is directed towards an achievement that is inaccessible to the method, which is applied in the investigation of objects, makes it possible to identify the value of science with the value of truth (Ph1: 141). On the other hand, philosophy also benefits from its dialogue with science, for it does not deny the reality that can be grasped by reason or the scientific grip on veracity that imposes itself on the human mind (IdU 29). Much as Jaspers grasped philosophy as dealing with ideals and abstractions that are not always amenable to objective consolidation, he emphasized the contrast between it and irrationality, sentimentality, or what he termed "dereliction of thought" (Ph1: xxv). Hence it was possible to define scientificness itself as a condition for the rationality and veracity of philosophy (Ph1: xxvi).

---

[29] In another place, Jaspers expanded upon the conception of science as an "open account." See his essay "Wahrheit und Wissenschaft" (1960), in PA 67-72.
[30] For this contention see also Philosophy of Existenz, 8; IdU 18; VuW 26; Ph1: xlii; Report 252.
[31] Regarding the ideals that philosophy provides to science, see also IdU 28; Ph1: 138-39, 322. Regarding philosophy's exteriority to science, see also Ph1: xxv: IdU 18, 28; VuW 2.

The Context of the "Reciprocal Position"

The extension of the limits of the respective viewpoints of science and philosophy was largely accomplished in Jaspers's conception of Being. The objective viewpoint—presented as concealing *Existenz* and as opposed to the possibility of clarifying it—was presented, in those contexts where he discussed Being, as one of the means for attaining philosophical understanding. Thus, for instance, he contended that mere "existence in time" [*Zeitdasein*], with the unmediated experiences it entails, does not anchor man in Being but only in consciousness as an active elucidating attitude (Truth 1, 308f). Furthermore, in contrast to his contentions regarding *Existenz*, in the context of which he dealt with Being, Jaspers contended that the concrete reality in which we live does not constitute an actuality on its own but only when we come to terms with it (Truth 30-31).[32] The need to arrive at an understanding of Being, beyond the unmediated and evident experience of it, is what makes the objective viewpoint that is anchored in conscious reason relevant to philosophy. Nevertheless, this requirement does not transform reflexive knowledge as such into an exhaustive expression of Being, especially not its transcendent dimensions, which are central to Jaspers's conception of Being.[33] However, the effort to anchor philosophizing about Being in an awareness of the consciously reasoning aspects involved in it, makes the discussion of conscious reason an inseparable part of the philosophical explication of Being itself.

The change in attitude towards the objective viewpoint of conscious reason is plainly evident in the concepts of "Encompassing" [*Umgreifende*] and "Cipher" [*Chiffer*], two pillars of Jaspers's conception of Being. As in his discussion of *Existenz*, so too in his conception of Being Jaspers did not back away from his understanding of conscious reason as relative and limited. Nevertheless, when his thinking was directed towards the philosophical explication of "Being," this conception of conscious reason did not prevent him from assigning to both it and objectivity a role in the philosophical explication of "Being." This change in Jaspers's attitude towards the viewpoint of conscious reason reflects the overcoming of the view that characterized his philosophy of Existenz, according to which philosophizing is supposed to arrive at a total understanding of the sole object towards which it is directed. Furthermore, even the object of philosophizing itself—in this context, "Being"—is grasped as accessible to more than one viewpoint. In other words, the change in Jaspers's attitude towards the objectivity of conscious reason reflected at the same time a different understanding of the method as well as the object of philosophizing.

These insights were manifested in the conception of the "Encompassing," which embraces the multiplicity of elements [*Weisen*], including conscious

---

[32] The transformation of the unmediated experience to knowledge is conducted by "Philosophical Logic" see Truth 3-6. About this term, see also Ernst Mayer, "Philosophie und Philosophische Logik bei Karl Jaspers" in *Offener Horizont*, 64f; James Collins, "Karl Jaspers's Philosophical Logic," *The New Scholasticism*, 23 (1959) 416f.

[33] Jaspers has mainly exposed the transcendental dimension of "Being" in "Metaphsyik" [Ph3].

reason.[34] This conception was anchored in the understanding that, just as conscious reason acts upon a multiplicity of objects, so too the point of departure for elucidating Being lies in the multiplicity of its discoveries. Here the multiplicity reflects not only the changing face of consciousness with reference to Being (Truth 703), which by its nature as consciousness is nourished by different objects (Truth 36). It also manifests an essential characteristic of Being itself, which he describes as the state of "splitting" [*Zerrissenheit*] (Truth 703) and as a "Being of rupture" [*Aufgebrochensein*] that is unable to "close" itself (Truth 706).[35] From this aspect, there is a correspondence between the diversity of consciousness, the multiplicity of sources for the understanding of Being, and the variety of manifestations of "Being" itself in reality. In his discussion of "Being," then, Jaspers expresses a complicated attitude towards conscious reason. He assumes its possible contribution to a philosophical understanding of Being, but insists that Being could not be exhausted by the objective viewpoint of conscious reason. This concept enables Jaspers to avoid constituting an absolute philosophical conception, wherein Being is identified with its reflection.

Furthermore, in the absence of a demand to identify thought with Being, Jaspers's thinking is devoid of any demand to exhaust Being by means of objective thought or philosophizing. Thus he is able to find a place even for the objective viewpoint of conscious reason in the framework of his conception of Being, even though he recognizes its limitations.[36] Against this background, it is possible to highlight the essential difference between the attitude towards conscious reason, in the framework of Jaspers's discussion of *Existenz*, and the one in his philosophizing directed towards Being. Conscious reason's entrance into the framework of *Existenz* is accompanied by tension, which prompts Jaspers to examine the possibility of separating it from the world. In his conception of Being, on the other hand, he is able to reveal multiplicity as an infrastructure common to both "conscious reason" and "Being."[37]

Jaspers's positive attitude towards the objective viewpoint is also evident in his conception of "Cipher." At the heart of this conception lies the idea that immanent reality constitutes a symbol or cipher of being itself and of transcendence as well.[38] In other words, immanence, as the concrete reality of the

---

[34] For the discussion of the elements of the "Encompassing" see VuE 38-50; Truth 53-122. The "Encompassing of the conscious reason" is widely explored in Truth 223-49. For the whole concept of the "Encompassing," see Gerhard Knauss, "The Concept of the 'Encompassing' in Jaspers's Philosophy" in Schilpp, 141-75.

[35] See also Truth 261, 873, 956. Jaspers used the term *Zerrissenheit* also in his discussion on the concepts of *Welt* (Ph1: 64f, 78f, 104f, 218f) and *Dasein* (Ph2: 249f).

[36] For a different interpretation, see Urs Richli, *Transzendental Reflexion und sittliche Entscheidung, Zum Problem der Selbsterkenntnis der Metaphysik bei Jaspers und Kant* (Bonn: Bouvier Verlag, 1967) 134f.

[37] In the literature a different interpretation appears that claims that Jaspers's concept of Being is opposed to the very idea of Objectivity and includes this concept in his Philosophy of *Existenz*. See Samay, 48f, 58f; Hans Mader, "Das Seindenken bei Karl Jaspers," *Wissenschaft and Weltbild* 10 (1957) 58f.

[38] Usually Jaspers used the terms Symbol and Chiffer as synonyms. See Hoffman, 108; Johannes Thyssen, 'The Concept of 'Foundering' in Jaspers's Philosophy' in Schilpp, 310; Aloys Klein, *Glaube and Mythos. Eine kritische, religionsphilosophisch-theologische*

world and as man's actual consciousness regarding this world and himself, contains the possibility of arriving at a clarification of transcendence due to its metaphysical depth (Truth 1031-32). The importance of the objective viewpoint for clarifying the metaphysical depth of immanent reality stems first and foremost from the fact that objectivity is what permits accessibility to human consciousness as worldly being. In his words: "[Since] *Existenz* appears to itself in existence, so what is exists for it only in the forms of consciousness; therefore, for *Existenz* connected with existence, what is transcendent also takes on the form of objectivity" (Ph3: 6). Beyond that, the conception of immanence as a cipher of transcendence cannot ignore the viewpoint of formal conscious reason towards immanent reality, since this viewpoint is accessible to the objective dimensions of this reality. Even though understanding reality as a cipher of transcendence constitutes a metaphysical conception, it appears that its anchoring in immanent reality obliges us to examine immanence from other viewpoints as well. In truth, the objective understanding of immanence does not merely complement its metaphysical understanding but is depicted by Jaspers as its cornerstone. In his words: "Conscious reason in general with its framework... is the chassis of existence, without which there is no understanding and no continuity of certainty" (Ph3: 185). Thus, the establishment of the status of immanence in Jaspers's conception of being not only permits access to human consciousness in existence, but also prevents any mystification of the philosophical conception of Being:

> Immersion in symbols is not the mystical immersion, the entrance into non-objectiveness of transcendence by way of an objectless and thus incommunicable union. Rather, as I hear the symbolic language, file phenomenon of transcendence is articulated for my *Existenz* in the medium of lucid consciousness, with the subject-object dichotomy maintained. Like the elucidation of consciousness in world orientation, elucidation in the symbol proceeds here by way of objectivity. Phenomenal lucidity and communicative depth of possible Existenz find their expression in the richly developed, subdivided, and always vanishing world of symbols. (Ph3: 16-17)

What emerges from these remarks is that the objective viewpoint, which endows immanence with clarity and communicability, has a similar effect on the understanding of Being and Transcendence because they are anchored in immanence. Unlike "mythical wallowing," which is characterized by the blurring of limits at various levels, conscious reason acts according to clear-cut rules; therefore there is room for the dimensions of generality and objectivity in philosophizing towards being. Although the "Cipher" is based on the conception that immanence contains symbolic representations of transcendence and thereby extends beyond the limits of objectivity, Jaspers emphasized the contribution of the objective viewpoint to the clarity and stability of the philosophical understanding of Being. He specifically considered objective reason, which manifests a "universal law" in which man "participates in an impersonal way," as

---

Untersuchung des Mythos-Begriffs bei Karl Jaspers (München: Ferdinand Schöningh, 1973) 88.

something that might facilitate "an unequivocal understanding" of Being. Objective reason serves as the basis for our trust in the order of consciousness and as a "support and comfort" to such an extent that "fear grips us if its collapse appears to be imminent" (Ph3: 184-85). Hence, even if the objective viewpoint is unable to facilitate a complete understanding of Being, it contributes to the framework of philosophizing directed towards its explication. The clarification of the limitation of the objective viewpoint, specifically, is the backdrop against which it became possible for philosophical discussion to be liberated from its search after total representations of its objects. The division of the framework of philosophizing directed towards the explication of Being into many—many objects of philosophizing and many viewpoints in which it is anchored—became a constitutive element of a non-absolute conception of Being. This pulled the rug out from under the "oppositionist position" by laying a foundation for the understanding that the respective viewpoints of "science" and "philosophy" enjoy a reciprocal relationship.

In the "reciprocal position" that arises from the conception of Being presented above through our discussion of "Encompassing" and "Cipher," two factors combined to contradict those that constituted the "oppositionist position," which characterized the discussion of "*Existenz*." These two factors were the constitution of the object of philosophizing with reference to a multiplicity of elements and the search after a common infrastructure for this multiplicity. This laid a twofold basis for a connection between the "reciprocal position" and Jaspers's conception of Being. On one hand, the subjective aspect that characterizes the viewpoint of "science" contributed to a more benign understanding of the objective viewpoint, as reflected by the concepts of "Encompassing" and "Cipher." This subjective dimension prevented any identification of science with general and absolute validity that would not have accorded with Jasper's conception of philosophy's viewpoint. On the other hand, the viewpoint of science's need for supra-temporal, fixed "vantage points" became joined in Jaspers's thinking with recognition of the vital importance of such a dimension in the framework of a philosophical conception of Being too. Not only did the presence of this dimension liberate philosophical discussion from dealing with the representation of particular experiences; it allowed Jaspers to identify the possible contribution of different viewpoints towards Being, including the objective viewpoint of conscious reason. However, these moves did not amount to the constitution of philosophizing directed towards Being only upon the foundation of the objective viewpoint in which science is anchored. As stated above, in neither his conception of "*Existenz*" nor in his view of "Being" did Jaspers accord this viewpoint any preeminence, let alone the standing of totality. However, by its very presence in philosophizing directed towards Being, the objective viewpoint opened up new ways of thinking that only liberation from the rigor of the "oppositionist position" could have made possible. Therefore the "reciprocal position" in Jaspers's conception of Being can be characterized as aimed at bridging between the subjective dimension—one that was developed more fully in his philosophy of *Existenz*—and the objective viewpoint, which was discovered to be vital for elucidating the immanent dimensions of Being, but also for making possible a fully mature philosophical understanding of "*Existenz*" as worldly being.

Summary

The interpretation here suggested for the presence of two different conceptions regarding the relationship between the respective viewpoints of science and philosophy in Jasper's thinking rests upon a twofold anchor: context and development. My interpretation of Jaspers's philosophy is guided by a basic understanding, according to which the main matter occupying Jaspers's thinking fashioned patterns of thought that were also applied in broader contexts. Thus, his conception of selfhood as particular being that is inaccessible to the objective viewpoint reflects the position that the objective viewpoint in which science is anchored is opposite to the one in which philosophy is anchored. On the other hand, the anchoring of the conception of Being in immanence, as "reality" and as "consciousness," served as a basis for the integration of the objective viewpoint of conscious reason in the framework of philosophizing directed towards Being. Needless to say, the attempt to point to the broader contexts to which the two typological positions examined above refer does not constitute a contention that Jaspers himself posited a connection between these positions and his conceptions regarding *Existenz* and Being. I am contending that the relation between the oppositionist contention and the conception of *Existenz* and between the reciprocal contention and the conception of Being, respectively, is implicit, and as such serves as basis for interpretation.

However much the connections—between the "oppositionist position and the conception of Existenz and between the "reciprocal position" and the framework of philosophizing directed towards Being, respectively—may give a more comprehensive meaning to these positions, it leaves moot the question regarding the relation between the two contentions. In truth, the answer to this question derives from the relation between the two principal frameworks of philosophizing, and as such it pertains to an overall understanding of Jaspers's philosophical work. My main contention is that the two principal objects of philosophizing around which Jasper's philosophy took shape, *Existenz* and Being, did not give rise to two independent contexts isolated from one another but reflected a process of development. The emergence of the conception of Existenz as solipsistic being, due among other things to its isolation from the objective viewpoint, led to a crisis that obliged Jaspers to extend the framework of philosophizing beyond the limits of the discussion of *Existenz*. In the following, Jaspers tangibly expressed this crisis:

> To me as Existenz, absolute independence is indeed my true unconditionality in temporal existence, but it also drives me to despair. I am aware that as flatly self-based I would have to sink into the void. For my self-realization I depend on a fulfillment that comes to me. I am not myself if I happen to default; I relate to myself as if selfhood were bestowed upon me. [*Existenz*] verifies its possibility, only with the knowledge that it rest upon transcendence (Ph3: 4).

In defining Transcendence as something "that steps up to meet Existenz, as that which fulfills it," Jaspers expressed the bursting of the limits of the discussion of "Existenz" in the direction of Being that is external to it. Without constituting any position towards such being, Existenz is doomed to sink into emptiness and despair. The broader philosophical processes that made this development possible—only the highlights of which this article has alluded to—enabled Jaspers to shift the focus of discussion from *Existenz* in favor of the development of a philosophical conception of Being in which Transcendence as well could be elucidated. This also made it possible for the objective viewpoint to be drawn into the framework of Jaspers's discussion, without leading to the identification of his attitude towards Being and Transcendence with the one typical of science's approach to its objects. Thus, in discussing *Existenz* Jaspers was mainly concerned with buttressing its absolute—in effect, singular—standing in philosophizing; but in discussing Being he found room also for the objective viewpoint, even the particular one of science. It was not only the maturity of Jaspers's philosophical thinking that made it possible to anchor his discussion of Being in a multiplicity of viewpoints and objects of philosophizing; even the conception of selfhood would appear to be in accord. This is because the "oppositionist position," evident in Jaspers's conception of *Existenz*, manifested a relation between two elements grasped as absolute, to which the variegation of multiplicity was quite alien; but in the absence of a struggle for absolute supremacy or totality, no room was left for it. From this aspect, the conception of the viewpoints of science and philosophy as engaged in a relationship of dependence and reciprocity involved not just an extension of the framework of philosophizing, but making it more flexible as well. This course, which was demonstrated by means of the concepts of "Encompassing" and "Cipher," enabled Jaspers to anchor his conception of Being in several viewpoints without feeling obliged to determine their hierarchy specifically seeing them as different parts of a single philosophical course.

Transcendence and Dissatisfaction in Jaspers' Idea of the Self

Abstract

This paper deals with the idea of the search for self, mainly in the thinking of Karl Jaspers. The discussion will focus on the very nature of this search and the power that motivates it. For this purpose, it will employ a phenomenological viewpoint that will follow Jaspers' course from its first point of departure, in which the self-appeared. As an object of observation, up to the point where the self-acquired the status of the subject, i.e., appeared as a personal and existential issue. The positively achieved insights about the self and the frustrations involved in this search will be clarified systematically. The author argues that Jaspers' search was inspired by a constant experience of dissatisfaction, which directed the self to transcend every present understanding of the self and to look for an improved one. Lastly, the search for the self will appear as leading to another search, i.e. that for Being and transcendence.

Preface

The famous instruction of the Oracle at Delphi, "Know thyself", presupposes, at least seemingly, two things: the existence of the self and the possibility of knowing it. Whether these two are correct or not, they have persistently challenged philosophers ever since. Applying to Karl Jaspers' thinking, this paper will put to the test the possibility of coming to terms with both the existence of the self - what one might name the reality of the self or the self as a substance[1] - and the knowing of the self. These two viewpoints about the self are considered here as mutually related. The self that is regarded as a substance and the self that is treated as an object of knowledge, are one and the same. Yet, the self as an object of Knowledge is different from other objects of knowledge, due to its

---

[1] For an historical account of the philosophical question whether selves are substances, see: Sydney Shoemaker, *Self-Knowledge and Self Identity*. Ithaca and London 1963, 41-80.

being that by which object can be known and present.² Furthermore, the self is a being that knows itself as knower, or can achieve "self-knowledge".

The present discussion will focus especially on one's Knowledge of oneself, which is differentiated from general knowledge of the "person" that does not refer in particular to any individual. However, the fact that the search for "self-knowledge" is tied with the search for the existence of the self indicates that such self-knowledge has an objective dimension and hence might be of value not only for the person who achieves it but also for other selves or even for the understanding of the human self as such.³ In fact, this discussion will strive to achieve an understanding of self-knowledge as such, except that this understanding cannot stand by itself but must refer to an individual. In any event, while one's self-knowledge can change and develop throughout one's life, the general understanding of it must show the persistence of the self as the existence or the reality of one and the same thing at different times.⁴ Finally, the self is but the joining of the individual features of self-knowledge together with the constant or objective dimension of one's existence.

The central thesis to be scrutinized below is Jaspers' conviction that there exists in human being something constant which can be called self and to which one can attribute the individual ability of achieving self-knowledge. Yet the fact that Jaspers persistently stressed the particular way in which one's self takes place, seemed problematic to many of his commentators because no epistemological account concerning the way one can achieve self-knowledge exists in his writings; an account which is needed especially whenever the issue under discussion is a particular one. Using the above terminology, one can deduce from the existing literature the following explanation: Jaspers thought he could avoid the epistemological problem, since he did not deal with the self as a knower but as a self-knower. Since the knowledge of the self, or of the self as an object, is different from any other kind of knowledge, the whole discourse remains exclusively rooted in particularity, and hence cannot be observed by an epistemological viewpoint.⁵

---

² This understanding is scrutinized in Seebohm's commentary of Husserl's Phenomenology, to whom the discussion will relate later. See: Thomas Seebohm, *The Other in Field of Consciousness, Essay in the memory of Aaron Gurwitsch*. Lester Embree (Ed.), Washington, D.C., 1984, 292 f.

³ On the problem of reality in Jaspers' thinking, see: Ronny Miron, "Towards Reality: The Development of the Philosophical Attitude to Reality in Karl Jaspers' Thought", *Journal of the British Society for Phenomenology*, 37/2, 2006, 152-172. Reprinted in this collection as Miron, 2006a.

⁴ For the objective aspect of the self from the perspective of problem of identity, see: Thomas Reid, *Essay on the Intellectual Power of Man*, London 1941, 205 f.; Butler, "Of Personal Identity". In: *The Works of Bishop Butler*, J.H. Bernhard (ed.), London 1900, 281 (quoted from Shoemaker 8, note 7).

⁵ The particular language characteristic of Jaspers has often appeared as an explanation for his marginality in the philosophical discourse and even for the failure to understand his ideas. On Jaspers' marginality, See: Charles Wallraff, "Jaspers in English: A Failure in Communication". In : *Philosophy and Phenomenological Research* 37 (1977), 537-548; Fritz-Joachim von Rinteln, *Beyond Existentialism*, London 1961, 204; Fritz Heinemann, *Existenzphilosophie—lebendig oder tot?* Stuttgart 1951, 65, 71. On Jaspers' particular way

Nevertheless, this paper will suggest a different view of Jaspers' idea of the self. In my opinion, Jaspers did not simply stay away from epistemological reasoning, but in the first place was concerned with creating an appropriate context in which the self could be safe, especially from damaging and narrow perspectives of it. Accordingly, we find in the vast corpus of his writings a continuous effort to enlarge the sphere in which the self takes place, as well as a growing awareness of that process itself. In each of the different contexts, different meanings were bestowed upon the existence of the self and upon its self-knowledge. The dynamic of enlarging the sphere within which the self is elucidated will be regarded also through the perspective of the classical problem of transcendence, i.e., the possibility of breaking out of immanence and constituting a conscious relation to what lies beyond it. Though the attempt to transcend immanence frequently evoked epistemological problems, these did not stand at the core of Jaspers' metaphysical search because already before he was satisfied with the context within which the self could be elucidated, his thinking reached a crisis that finally led to putting aside, though not relinquishing, the effort to achieve an encompassing understanding of the self. From this perspective one can contend that Jaspers' search for the self-remained unaccomplished, or even failed. Nonetheless, that cannot diminish the value of the search after the self that is suggested in his writing, which consists of the specific ethos of seeking perfection and the relatively rare integrity that admitted its own deficiencies and finally its impasse.

The present discussion will focus, then, on the very nature of the search for the self and the power that motivates it. For this purpose, it will follow Jaspers' course from its radical point of departure, in which the self-appeared as an object of observation, up to the point where the self-acquired the status of a subject, i.e., appeared as a personal and existential issue. The positively achieved insights about the self and the involved frustrations will be clarified systematically. I shall argue that Jaspers' search - whose stages marked by using different terms to denote the self, i.e., psyche, subjectivity, Existenz - was inspired by a constant experience of dissatisfaction. This experience was expressed in Jaspers' thinking as revealing a profound truth about one's self-understanding as an inexhaustible, and thus never ending, search. The dynamic of dissatisfaction, which actually covers Jaspers' thinking as a whole, reveals a resemblance to Hegel's way of philosophizing in Phenomenology of spirit. Like Hegel, Jaspers experienced dissatisfaction as evidence of the inadequacy of the conception out of which it was evoked, but at the same time he found in it a clue to an improved conception that could lead to such. That is to say, that every stage in the development of their ideas was negated by the following stage, within which it was preserved in a different form. These dialectics of approval and negation will be regarded also via the perspective of the concepts of immanence and transcendence. This occurs in two ways: the negated understanding of the self is either what is identified with the immanent aspect of its being (one's body and consciousness), whereby according to the approved understanding, the being of the self cannot be embodied in. any physical aspect and therefore is regarded as transcendent to

---

of reasoning, see: Kurt Hoffman, *The Basic Concept of Jaspers' Philosophy*. In: Paul Arthur Schilpp (ed.): *The Philosophy of Karl Jaspers*, New York 1957, 95-113, 95 ff.

one's immanent being. Alternatively, the negated understanding is that which was identified as belonging to the former stage in the development of Jaspers' idea of the self, hence this understanding is left behind in virtue of the later and riper one. Here immanent is the current understanding of the self, whereas transcendent is the understanding that has already been negated or the understanding which has not yet come into to view in. the process of explication. While in the first way the concepts of immanence and transcendence referred to aspects of the being of the self, in the second they refer to the process in which the idea of self-reveals itself and becomes known to its observer. One way or another, what is called above dissatisfaction will be revealed as a consistent element that did not let Jaspers rest upon the concept of self-achieved at each stage and that motivated him. again' and again to look for a better viewpoint that would uncover the subject being in its fullness and uniqueness as a being that consistently seeks out better self-understanding. The discussion will seek, then, to illuminate the inspirational function of the experience of dissatisfaction in generating deep modifications in jaspers' understanding of the self.[6]

The Self of the Mentally Ill Person

Jaspers' first attempt to consolidate a viewpoint that could facilitate accessibility to the self-appeared in his first book *General Psychopathology* (1913). In the following words, he indicated his interest in what he then called "Psyche".[7]

> "We want to feel, understand, and think what really happens in human beings' psyche. The general desire [*Drang*] for reality, means in psychopathology the desire for real psychic life which we then want to recognize in contexts only partly accessible to sensibly discernible as objects are in natural sciences [...] without the ability and the desire to observe the psychic and to set it before our eyes in its fullness it is

---

[6] Such understanding of Hegel's Phenomenology of Spirit is well implemented in Laurer's interpretation. Yet in his interpretation, the dissatisfaction appears mainly as an epistemological mechanism, by which an improved knowledge about the reality of objects can be achieved, while its contribution to the explication of the self remains relatively marginal. See: S.J. Lauer Quentine, *A Reading in Hegel's Phenomenology of Spirit*, New York, 1976, 4. For a different and more harmonizing interpretation of Hegel, see: Jon Stewart, *The Unity of Hegel's "Phenomenology of Spirit"*, *A Systematical Interpretation*, Evanston, Illinois, 2000, 1-3.

[7] This approach first appeared in Jaspers' early articles (1910-1913). The book *General Psychopathology* that appeared in nine editions and two versions: the first (1913) was narrow (henceforth Psychopathology1), and the enlarged version that appeared as the fourth edition (1942) after his main philosophical works were published (henceforth Psychopathology4). The basic insights concerning the self, which appeared in the first edition, found their explicit continuation and exploration within the enlarged version. Yet, in addition to the original sections, new ones, which were permeated by his mature philosophical ideas, were added to the enlarged version.

impossible to occupy oneself with psychopathology". [8] (Psychopathology1, 12)[9]

Reading these words, one cannot miss Jaspers' conviction that such a thing as "psyche" really exists. Likewise, his usage of neutral terms as "Reality", "Human being", "Psychic life", clearly expressed the priority he bestowed upon the humaneness of the mentally ill person despite his abnormal symptoms. This approach fits Jaspers' description of the work of the psychiatrist as one who experiences personal interaction with his patient and directs his attention to the "human being in his singularity and completeness" (Psychopathology1, 1). Accordingly, Jaspers criticized the scientific approach of the psychopathologist who regards such symptoms as a mirror of the reasons for the disease and therefore concentrated on "identifying and recognizing, characterizing and analyzing not the single person but the General" (Psychopathology1, 1).

Yet, the awareness that natural sciences are limited in approaching the mentally ill person does not mean that Jaspers dismissed the scientific approach as such.[10] Nevertheless, for him the guide to the understanding of mental diseases should be the fact that the physical symptoms and the mental or emotional ones, appear together, and there is no way to separate between the two; especially not by using the scientific method of psychopathology which, according to him, could not address the mysterious continuity between the physical and the mental

---

[8] Accordingly, Jaspers demanded a close examination of the concrete situation by which the sick person is surrounded (for instance, his personal abilities, social support, etc.). Jaspers was clearly influenced at the present point by Dilthey's idea of Understanding. See: Dilthey, *Der Aufbau der geschichtlichen Welt in den Geisteswissenschaften*, Leipzig 1927; Dilthey, "The Understanding of the Other Person and their expressions of life". In: *Descriptive Psychology and Historical Understanding*, R.M. Zaner and K.L Heiger (trans.), The Hague, 1977 (1927), 127-147; Chris Walker, "Karl Jaspers and Edmund Husserl III. Jaspers as a Kantian Phenomenologist". In: *Philosophy, Psychiatry and Psychology* 2/1 (1995), 65-82; Chris Walker, "Karl Jaspers and Edmund Husserl IV. Phenomenology as Empathic Understanding". In: *Philosophy, Psychiatry and Psychology* 2/3 (1995), 247-266; Fritz K. Ringer, *The Decline of the German Mandarins. The German Academic Community 1890-1933*, Cambridge Mass., 1969, 351 f.; Herbert Schnädelbach, *Philosophy in Germany 1831-1933*, Cambridge 1984, 54 f.

[9] The following works of Jaspers are referred to during the paper (abbreviations):
- "Die Phänomenologische Forschungsrichtung in der Psychopathologie". In: *Zeitschrift für die gesamte Neurologie und Psychiatrie* 9 (1912), 391-408 (Phen.).
- *Allgemeine Psychopathologie. Ein Leitfaden Für Studierende, Arzte und Psychologen*. Berlin, 1913. (Psychopathology1); Berlin-Heidelberg [8]1942 (1965) (Pyschopathology4).
- *Die Geistige Situation der Zeit*. Berlin-Leipzig 1931 (Spiritual Situation).
- *Philosophie* (1-3). Heidelberg 1994 (1932): *Philosophische Weltorientierung* (Ph1); *Existenzerhellung* (Ph2); *Metaphysik* (Ph3).
- *Philosophie und Welt. Reden und Aufsatze*. München 1958 (PW).
- *Psychologie der Weltanschauungen*. Heidelberg 1985 (1919) (Psychology).
- *Rechenschaft und Ausblick. Reden und Aufsatze*. Tübingen 1958 (Report).
- *Vernunft und Widervernunft in Unserer Zeit. Drei Gastvorlesungen*. München 1950. (VuW)
- *Von der Wahrheit*. München 1991 (1947) (Truth).

[10] Jaspers himself paid attention to the physical aspects of the disease, which he termed as "objective psychopathology", see: Psychopathology1, 94-106.

(Psychopathology1, 9). By defining the craft of the psychiatrist as "expertise" (*Kennerschaft*) and "Vocation" (*Beruf*) (Psychopathology1, 1), Jaspers intended tended to add to psychopathology a personal and unique dimension that might be capable of meeting the individual "singularity" (*Einzeinheit*) of the mentally ill person (Phen. 408).[11] Unlike the physical symptoms, this aspect cannot be exhausted by any intelligible and general concept (Psychopathology1, 1 f.).[12] Furthermore, Jaspers admitted no unitary concept of illness (Psychopathology1, 3; Psychopathology4, 651 f.), so even from the physical aspect one cannot get a complete grip on the mentally ill person.[13]

One cannot separate between Jaspers' understanding of the self in this context and his criticism of the scientific approach, which at that time was deeply influenced by positivism.[14] Yet, the critical observation itself did not serve him as a base for achieving a positive understanding of the self. It appears that the absence of any affirmative contentions about the self, at the present stage of his thinking, was more deliberate than accidental. It is very likely that Jaspers refrained from posing anything of content about the self, for he was afraid that content as such would fall into generalizations that would fail to address the particularity of the subject being. To be more precise, Jaspers did not contend that subjectivity could not have any content that could give expression to it, as Sartre

---

[11] Jaspers used the German term *Beruf* (vocation) to denote the profession of the psychiatrist. This point reveals the influence of Max Weber's ideas upon Jaspers' — an influence he always admitted. See: Weber, "Wissenschaft als Beruf" (1919). In: *Gesammelte Aufsatze zur Wissenschaftslehre*. Tübingen 1922, 524-555; Weber, *The Protestant Ethic and the Spirit of Capitalism*, New York 1958, 79-92.

[12] Jaspers distinguished between the "limitations" (*Beschfankungen*) within which the scientific approach operates and the "boundary" (*Grenze*) that depicts the irreducibility of the human being's individuality which one cannot overcome by any systematic approach. Jaspers' use of the idea of boundary in this context was elaborated later in his philosophical writings in which he presented two concepts of border: "contextual borders" (*jeweilige Grenzen*) and "principle borders" (*prinzipielle Grenzen*) (Ph1, 45). This distinction is parallel to Kant's concepts, which differentiated between *Grenze* and *Schranke*. See: Kant, *Prolegomena to any Future Metaphysics* (Beryl Logan, ed.), London & New York, 1966, 111. On the influence of Kant on Jaspers, see: Chris Walker, "Karl Jaspers as a Kantian Psychopathologist II. The Concept of Form and Content in Jaspers' Psychopathology". In: *History of Psychiatry* 4 (1993), 321-348; Chris Walker, "Karl Jaspers as a Kantian Psychopathologist III. The Concept of Form in Georg Simmel's Social Theory: A Comparison with Jaspers". In: *History of Psychiatry* 5 (1994), 37-70; Walker, "Karl Jaspers and Edmund Husserl III".

[13] See especially the chapter "Concepts of health and illness" (Psychopathology4, 651-661).

[14] Jaspers entitled the positivistic approach in psychiatry as "prejudice" and the understanding of mental illness as brain disease he named "brain mythology" (Psychopathology1, 8). It seems that his main criticism was directed at Griesinger and his followers, see: Wilhelm Griesinger, *Pathologie und Therapie der Psychischen Krankheiten*, Braunschweig [4]1786. See also Jaspers' criticism of psychoanalysis which is actually complementary to that of the scientific approach. VuW, 9-29; Spiritual, Situation, 137 f.; Report, 260-271; Kurt Kolle, "Jaspers as Psychopathologist", In: Paul Arthur Schilpp (ed.), *The Philosophy of Karl Jaspers*, New York 1957, 437-466.

intended in his idea of a self "without speech" (*sans paroles*).[15] Otherwise, he could not even have been able to point to the very uniqueness and particularity of the subject being. It transpires, then, that Jaspers not only rejected the bare attempt of achieving content about the self; he especially criticized the impersonality characteristic of the attempt to know objects of any kind, which he saw as lacking the crucial involvement without which subjectivity is dismissed. Therefore, being faithful to his primordial understanding of subjectivity, Jaspers himself avoided from saying anything positive about it, except for pointing again and again to its uniqueness and particularity - features which actually say nothing of content about the self.

In my opinion, the understanding according to which one's self is beyond any possible observation and rational access is merely the presupposition of the transcendence of the self, which refers to its very existing being. Though the term of transcendence did not appear in Jaspers' writing from this stage, he nevertheless employed a unique meaning of it. On the one hand, transcendence signifies here the specific meaning that Jaspers attributed to the self as an idea. It is reflected first and foremost in the association of the psyche with one's unique and idiosyncratic personality, which extends beyond the individual's physical features.[16] This distinction can be elicited from Jaspers' statement that as the investigation of the physiological symptoms is progressing, the mental elements that are linked to it evade examination. Additionally, the inquiring into the mental symptoms finally reaches a certain point when one can no longer find any accompanying physical aspect (Psychopathology1, 5).[17] In other words, the transcendence of the Self appears as equal to the independence of the mental aspects of the mental illness from the physical ones, or as reflecting the inaccessibility accessibility of the mental aspects of it to the scientific approach. On the other hand, the discussed idea of transcendence refers to the very ontological entity of the self as a concrete being. Ostensibly, the ontological aspect of transcendence is in conflicts with that of accessibility, i.e., how one can argue for the existence of self and at the same time for its inaccessibility? At the present stage of the explication, it was still impossible to see how one can extricate himself from this contradiction. Yet it is clear that in Jaspers' reflection on the self, the inaccessibility of the self was associated with its transcendence, claiming that for the being of the self is transcendent (mainly to empirical observation), the inaccessibility revealed as the very definition of the self as an entity.

---

[15] Sartre explored this concept of the self both in *The Transcendence of the Ego* and in *Being and Nothingness*. On Sartre's concept of the self, see: Hugh J. Silverman, "Sartre's Words on the Self". In: Hugh J. Silverman, Frederick A. Elliston (eds.): *Jean-Paul Sartre: A Contemporary Approach to his Philosophy*. Pittsburgh 1980, 85-104; Thomas W. Busch. *The Power of Consciousness and the Force of Circumstances*, Indiana 1990, 1-17.

[16] There is a resemblance between Jaspers' understanding of the self of the mentally ill person and the idea of the hidden self in K. G. Jung's writings. See: Jung: *Persönlichkeit und Übertragung. Grundwerke 3*. Zürich und Düsseldorf, 1966.

[17] This idea is acknowledged as a landmark in the process of integrating the phenomenological method into the field of psychiatry and psychopathology, see: Herbert Spiegelberg, *Phenomenology in Psychology and Psychiatry*, Evanston, 1972, xxxiv-xxxv.

In any event, the ontological meaning of transcendence excludes the possibility of associating it with one's consciousness or self-consciousness – terms which were not mentioned in these writings at all. To be precise, consciousness as realm of rationality and especially of representation cannot bear witness to the self, for it is transcendent of any kind of content. Therefore Jaspers' distinction between one's subjectivity or psyche and one's physicality to which it is transcendent, did not agree with Husserl's split between the "empirical I" and the "transcendental I".[18] Seemingly, the meaning of "transcendental", i.e., going beyond, could have fitted Jaspers' idea of the self in this context which was conceived as beyond one's physical and empiric manifestations. Yet, for Husserl the "I" is transcendental because it reaches beyond itself and insofar as it is involved in cognition of contents.[19] In other words, whereas Husserl linked between the self and the immanent consciousness as such - i.e., its intentional ability that opens for the "I" the world of consciousness and thus constitutes it as transcendental - Jaspers strived to save the self from any encounter with contents produced by consciousness. To be precise, it is especially the function of generalizing characteristic to consciousness that motivated him to strive for separating the understanding of the self of the mentally ill person from firm contents, which due to his training were usually based on observation of abnormal physical symptoms. It transpires, then, that the dominance of Jaspers' criticism of the scientific approach, which was committed to achieving generalizations about mental diseases, in consolidating his stance regarding the mentally ill person that blocked his view not only from other features of consciousness than that of generalizing, but also from the very possibility of saying anything of content about the self.

Finally, from Jaspers' mostly implicit notes about the mentally ill person one can elicit two aspects of his/her being: a limited or partial one and an infinite one. The first is reflected in the narrow view of the science of Psychopathology that focuses mainly on symptoms whose source is physical, whereas the second is mainly an intuition according to which one's subjective being is an elusive and infinite entity which cannot be reached by the fixed tools suggested by science. Only the second can relate to the idea of the self. Paradoxically, the limited side of the being of the mentally ill person can find many words to express itself which are originated in the objective language of science, while the infinite one remains vague and speechless due to the common difficulty to express uniqueness by general words. One way or another, these sides were for Jaspers two sides of the same coin, for the limitation of what can be stated about the mentally ill person arises from the awareness of infinity of the person's being, and vice versa,

---

[18] According to Husserl, both concepts of ego are constituted in consciousness. See: *Ideas Pertaining to a Pure Phenomenology and to a Phenomenological Philosophy*, Rojcewicz and A. Schuwer (trans.) 1989, 109, 119 f. For the discussion of these concepts, see for example: David Carr, *The Paradox of Subjectivity*, New York & Oxford 1999, 67-97.

[19] Marbach's interpretation of Husserl's idea of "transcendental I" stressed its function as an agent of contents and truth, see: Eduard Marbach, *Das Problem des Ich in der Phänomenologie Husserls*, The Hague 1974, 44 ff. This view appeared also in a reading suggested by Sokolowski. For an ontological interpretation of Husserl's Phenomenology and particularly his understanding of subjectivity, see, Lauer: *Phenomenology - its Genesis and its Prospect*, New York 1955, 81 ff.

it is exactly this awareness that cannot but allow us to restrict ourselves to the limited aspect of the single phenomenon which we observe. So the negative side of Jaspers' criticism of the science of Psychopathology meets its affirmative side, which he directed towards the mentally ill person as human being.

What is interesting about Jaspers' view in this context is that the unsatisfying part of his concept was not connected with the vagueness that characterized his concept of the psyche - for he conceived this feature as essential to it. Instead, the experience of dissatisfaction concerns the scientific approach, due to its focus on the physiological dimensions of mental illness; these appeared to him as concealing the emotional ones, in which a clue might be found to the self of the mentally ill person, i.e., the real key to the understanding of his illness. The fact that the experience of dissatisfaction referred to the scientific method and not to the self is understandable, for the formation of the self as transcendent blocked it from any experience, including that of dissatisfaction. It is precisely the void that was left from the closing of the self from any touch that could leave for Jaspers the space free for digging into the deficiency of the scientific method. One can add that the conditionality characteristic to science, which subjects it to alterations according to new findings or contemporary theories and methods, even deepens the dissatisfaction from it, because of its incapability of meeting Jaspers' very idea of the self as independent of any immanent factors.[20] Lastly, the meaning of the transcendence of the self-referred at the present stage to all that falls outside the limitations of the scientific understanding of the psychopathology

Nevertheless, already in the unsatisfying part, one can find an indication of the next step, which Jaspers took in order to achieve a more explicit understanding of the self, i.e., the psychological perspective into the self, which from the outset assumed the individual differences between human beings. Jaspers the psychiatrist spoke of the need to employ in. psychiatry a psychological approach. He stated that the fact that in certain cases psychology — which is basically addressed to normal people — cannot be implemented practically by psychiatrists, should serve as a goad for Psychopathology to explore its own psychology to complete the unique elements that are irrelevant to normal people (Psychopathology1, 3f.).[21] Consequently, the distinction between normal phenomena and abnormal ones will always be at most presumable and thus remain vague. The gathering of the individual differences between mentally ill people and the lack of a unitary concept of illness compels us to carry out an "unlimited search" for methods and new viewpoints (Psychopathology4, 460) together with an empathic attitude that can be alert to the uniqueness in which the mental illness occurs to a single concrete personality.[22] All these means will

---

[20] Jaspers' position can be viewed also via the historical context of the so called "methods controversy". See: Walker: Karl Jaspers and Edmund Husserl IV.

[21] Jaspers pointed on initiations that took this challenge, see: Psychopathology4, note 1.

[22] Among the required qualifications, required from the psychiatrist, Jaspers counted the following: "empathy" (*Einfühlen*), "participation" (*Miterleben*), and "inner understanding" (*Hineinverstehen*) (Phen, 391). About empathy see: Herbert Spiegelberg, *Phenomenology in Psychology and Psychiatry*, Evanston 1972, 186; Walker, Karl Jaspers and Edmund Husserl IV; Wiggins, O. P, M.A. Schwarts, M. Spitzer, "Phenomenological / Descriptive Psychiatry: The Methods of Edmond Husserl and Karl Jaspers". In: Spitzer, Manfred,

hopefully meet the same early urge to find a door to the infinite being of the person afflicted with a mental illness (Psychopathology1, 2).

The indication of the next steps to be taken is even more far-reaching. Already in the first edition of *General Psychopathology*, long before he manifested his interest in philosophy, Jaspers referred to the need of philosophy, and what he denoted then as "thoughts of a realm of spirit" (Psychopathology1, 12), that might be of use for testing and criticizing the presuppositions of Psychopathology as well as for the exploration and designing of its methodological instruments themselves (Psychopathology1, 6f.). Despite the vagueness characteristic of the above statements of Jaspers, they clearly indicated his striving for new perspective, wider and different from the scientific one, out of which it will be possible to view the human being as an infinite entity. Finally, both the emphasis on the singularity of the mentally ill person and the wish to anchor the curing of this illness in an apriori understanding of human beings as such, independent of any contemporary conventions of research and healing, led Jaspers outside the realm of psychopathology

True, Jaspers' early insight as a psychiatrist, according to which there was a subjective existence that referred to human beings as such that cannot be exhausted by rational, lasted throughout all his writings. Nevertheless, after he quit the scientific discourse, he could no longer be satisfied with the absence of real knowledge about the self. Furthermore, while as a scientist and psychiatrist the problem which was at stake for Jaspers was "how to achieve knowledge about the self?" - knowledge that can be used for investigation and practical needs - from that point on the problem turned out to be how one can be able to achieve self-knowledge or self-understanding. In other words, the idea of the self is about to shift from the status of an object to that of a subject. Since the relations between immanence and transcendence changed entirely as a result of that shift, Jaspers' thinking needed to provide an account also about the aspect of self-consciousness. Nonetheless, his criticism of the scientific approach later revealed as including the very main motive characteristic to his philosophical concept of the self: exactly as the science of psychopathology cannot offer a complete understanding of the mentally ill person and hence of his illness, so philosophy is also restricted to our conceptual abilities and therefore cannot uncover the wholeness of one's particular being.

The Self of the Normal Person

Jaspers' idea of the self-reached its second stage of development in *Psychology of Worldviews* (henceforth: Psychology) as he achieved a psychological perspective. Though normality was regarded before as a suitable perspective for viewing the pathological phenomenon (Psychopathology1, 3), within the present stage a conscious path to the self was established, called "Psychology of Worldviews". Additionally, the term of subjectivity replaced that of psyche and the former insistence upon the inaccessibility of the self was substituted in Psychology by a

---

Uehlein, Friedrich, Schwarts, Michael, A, (eds.), *Phenomenology, Language & Schizophrenia*, New York-Berlin, 1992, 46-69, 56 f.

more systematic viewpoint, which was directed to the explication of the particular being of the self.

The term "Worldview" (*Weltanschauung*) historically means in western culture the sum of knowledge, norms and values that one can be granted by his culture, as well as by being a universal agent.[23] Yet, Jaspers tied this term to the subjective individual, without referring to the general and cultural dimensions, which are fundamentally reflected in it. He contended that knowledge (*Wissen*) of the world or even information about oneself, of which worldviews typically consist, do not signify what is important about them but rather the content regarding the different faces of subjectivity itself. This subjectivity appeared in this context as an experiencing being that can arrange its experiences via rational objectifications (Psychology, 1). Jaspers focused especially on the explication of the experiences and analyzed the meaning bestowed upon it by the subject.

> We do not look for the frequent neither the average [...] we seek the particular patterns even if these are entirely rare. Our field [...is] what we perceive in the historical and internal experience [...] even when it is once in a life time. (Psychology, 14).[24]

The prominent emphasis on the particularity of worldviews indicates that Jaspers conceived one's personal worldview as an ontological representation of one's self. The objectifications out of which the personal worldview is established did not occupy his interest, but specifically their function as "means for self-understanding" (Psychology, iiix) or as an instrument for self-reflection (Psychology, 5). Not only he did not separate between the subjective experience and its objectification, he did not even deduce out of it epistemological consequences. That is to say, he was looking for what was meaningful in the experience of the subjectivity, or what one might consider as meaningful in his own experience.

What remained from Jaspers' early idea of the self in the psychopathological context is then clear: the self is a particular being that cannot be reached by universal concepts and therefore cannot be generalized. In other words, the same urge "to feel [...] what really happens in human beings' psyche" (Psychopathology1, 12) of mentally ill people, achieved its continuation and an even more complete realization in *Psychology* by observing the particular dimensions of personal worldviews. Exactly as in the discussion of mental illness, Jaspers focused his interest on the person who experiences illness more that on his/her disease, so in *Psychology* his attention was aimed at the self-reflected in his worldview more than at the worldview itself.

Nevertheless, the persistence of the interest in the subjective being was not a barrier to the introduction of changes into to Jaspers' understanding of the self. One of the most remarkable modifications in Jaspers' understanding of the self

---

[23] The term *Weltanschauung* first appeared in the context of Kant's writings, see: H.G. Meier, *Weltanschauung. Studien zur Geschichte eines Begriffs*, Münster, 1970; Paul Watzlawick, *Die erfimdene Wirldichkeit*, München/Zürich, 1981.

[24] It is important to note that Jaspers dealt also with the typical and the general in the worldviews as such (Psychology, 4f.), but this direction was relatively marginal compared with the discussion of their particular features.

refers to the component of transcendence, which was previously ascribed to it, but at the present stage it almost disappeared or at least went through a profound decline. This change might be regarded not only as a likely effect of the fact that the discussion of the subjective being ceased to be a deviation from the context in which it appeared, but especially as a consequence of abandoning the feature of inaccessibility concerning the self. Consequently, in *Psychology* not only did the self-become central in Jaspers' discussion; via the perspective of one's worldview the self-appeared as more perceptible. To be more precise, the self-appeared as an immanent constituent that externalizes itself on one's own worldview. Hence, the former unbridgeable gap between the understanding of the self as a concrete being and its inaccessible transcendence was replaced with its opposite: an accordance between the self as a concrete being and its accessibility to an immanent understanding via the objectifications of one's personal experiences.

Furthermore, there is a clear connection between the decline of self's transcendence and the appearance of a totally new characteristic of the self, i.e., consciousness. Consciousness as an immanent element can be seen as a completion that decline itself. In *Psychology*, the self is merely the way one organizes his experience and consolidates out of it a self-understanding. Unlike the inability to have a real clue about the self-knowledge of the mentally ill person, in *Psychology* subjectivity was depicted as the activity of conferring meaning upon its own experience; activity which is mirrored in the very act of objectification itself. In other words, whereas as a psychiatrist Jaspers mainly referred to his own interest in the self, in *Psychology*, in addition to that he analyzed the interest of human beings in self-understanding and by that conferred upon it a general view, i.e., such which before he unreservedly refused.

Finally, in *Psychology*, real achievements concerning the understanding of the self-came about and the early dissatisfaction with the scientific framework was left behind. These cannot be elaborated here, however the most important contribution of *Psychology* is the exposition of the self as an explicable being that replaced the former enigmatic one. Concerning the analysis that linked the feature of inaccessibility with the experience of dissatisfaction, one can regard the stage of *Psychology* as offering a reasonable solution to it. Hence it should not be surprising that in the present context one does not find an explicit expression of dissatisfaction. Consequently, the being of self was treated as immanent, its transcendence was substituted with its transcendentalism and thus contents about the self could be accumulated. Nevertheless, as will become clear later on, perceivable frustrations still remained and therefore progress was necessary.

The Worldly Self

Despite the word "world" inherent in the term "Worldview", no being external to the self was taken into account in Jaspers' discussion of it in *Psychology*, but only the internal process of the individual's bestowing meaning upon his/her own experience. The isolation of the self from its external environment reflected the tendency towards solipsism in Jaspers' early thinking. To be sure, Jaspers did not conceive of the human consciousness as the only source for certitude, and certainly not as detached from the world. Differently from Leibniz' solipsism which relied on metaphysical infrastructure or from that of Descartes, which was basically methodical, in Jaspers' case the solipsism reflected his very early desire to focus on the subjective being in its singularity and particularity on the one hand and his lacking useful tools to illuminate the self in its full context on the other hand. This interpretation of Jaspers' solipsism that points to its moderate shape in the context of his early writings, will later serve as an explanation for Jaspers' overcoming it in. his philosophical writings to which the discussion shall now turn.

In *Philosophical World Orientation* Jaspers posed the "world" (*Welt*) and the "Formal-Consciousness" (*Bewußtsein-überhaupt*) as two perspectives out of which the self — termed in this context "Existenz" — would be elucidated. These terms served first and foremost as a basis for the establishing of Jaspers' concept of Being (*Sein*), which gradually achieved the centrality that was formerly granted to subjectivity. However, the employing of the idea of world and that of Formal-Consciousness as general viewpoints in the same context in which the subjective being was also discussed indicated a change in. Jaspers' understanding of the self. Unlike the superiority, which was conferred to one's own self-understanding in *Psychology*, in this context Jaspers stated: "In no way of making existence conscious, I exist at the foundation [*am Grunde*] [of myself]" (Ph1, 12). That is to say that the self is not revealed solely within ones' self-consciousness, and hence the self-relatedness of one's self cannot exhaust his/her very being. This is exactly the reason why Jaspers integrated two perspectives external to the self, i.e., that of the world and that of Formal-Consciousness into to his philosophical elucidation of the self as Existenz. As will become clear below, this perspective, then adopted by Jaspers the philosopher, undermined the solipsistic tendency characteristic to his early writings and thus served as a cornerstone in consolidating the understanding of the self as a worldly being.

Existenz, according to Jaspers, is anchored in the world's existence (*Dasein*) by its "situation-being" (*Situationsein*), which consists of the freedom to fulfill one's possibilities and the inescapable necessity stemming from reality's factuality (Ph1, 1).[25] The idea of "Situation-being" reduces the meaning of the world to the personal perspective of Existenz and uncovers a profound truth about the way Existenz experiences the world, i.e., a person by no means experiences the entirety of the world, but only some of its dimensions in which s/he is directly involved. The prominent importance of the new perspective is that not only there is still room for the uniqueness of the self as a particular being, stemming from one's personal freedom to take up specific possibilities, but by the light of the situations in which Existenz is involved, the idea of self is granted by a totally new feature, i.e., a conscious context. Such a context is recognized as crucial for the illumination of Existenz, so much that "Situation" became the starting point and the target [*Ziel*], because nothing else is real and present" (Ph1, 69). The establishing of the idea of Existenz retains, then, at the same time the particularity

---

[25] The first version of the idea of "situation" appeared in Spiritual Situation, 23. Jaspers continued to explore this term within the context of his famous concept of "Ultimate Situations" (*Grenzsituationen*).
See especially its late version that appeared in Ph2, 201 f. (the earlier appeared in: Psychology, 229 f.). See also: William D. Blattner, "Heidegger's Debt to Jaspers' Concept of Limit-Situation". In: Olson, Alan. M, (ed.): *Heidegger & Jaspers*, Philadelphia 1994, 153-165.

of the subjective meaning, but in addition to that, the awareness of situation that it is surrounded by a world. Consequently, the idea of Existenz marks the shift to the understanding of the self as a worldly being.

This is exactly the point in which solipsism, even as a slight inclination, became impossible or at list hard to maintain. This change not only modified Jaspers' immanent understanding of the self, for according to Jaspers "I cannot grasp my situation without proceeding to conceive the world" (Ph1, 69). Moreover, this change pointed to new horizons, which are transcendent both to Existenz itself and to the situation-being by which it is encircled. Jaspers states that Existenz' awareness of itself as experiencing the world only within particular situations, cannot satisfy one's urge to have an idea about the "world" as a reality which is independent of the subjective consciousness relating to it.[26] Thus the philosophical explication of the self cannot be exhausted by following Existenz' experience of the situations in which it is involved. Such explication is compelled to contain within itself the "world's thinking" and the "world's reality" (Ph1, 69), i.e., a general understanding of the world's reality which is not subordinated to one's personal view of it. Finally, two concepts of the world are included within the philosophical understanding of the self: the "world" as "existence that finds itself as [...] non-I [*Nichtich*]" and the "world" as the "other" accessible for investigation, which is revealed as a single thing and universally applicable (Ph1, 63). Whereas the former is narrow and solely determined by the limits of one's "situation-being", the latter is much wider, and its full meaning exceeds the borders of the being of the self. As a result of this, not only does the self-cease to stand as a single object in Jaspers' discussion. Moreover, the idea of the self appears from now on as pointing to the world as a transcendent horizon to which the self relates as an immanent being. Thus, the understanding of the transcendence of the self also changed. Henceforth transcendence did not denote anymore the uniqueness and particularity of the self that exceeds one's empirical being or the observer's position towards the self, but the ontological reality of the world by which the self is surrounded.

Jaspers' attempt to widen his perspective on the self can be seen also from his discussion of the question whether the Formal-Consciousness can be used for explicating Existenz. Actually, what was at stake was whether in addition to Existenz' particular dimensions there exists additional faces of it that can be accessible to the objective viewpoint of Formal-Consciousness as well. Basically Jaspers' answer to this question was negative, contending that "Existenz was not an object but being that relate to its possibilities, [and therefore] it does not exist for Formal-Consciousness as such" (Ph1, 14).[27] It is exactly the potentiality of

---

[26] Most of Jaspers' commentators ignored the independence of his interest in the reality and objectivity of the world, and interpreted this interest as integral part of his idea of Existenz. See: Thomas Räber, *Das Dasein in der "Philosophie" von Karl Jaspers. Eine Untersuchung im Hinblick auf die Einheit und die Realität der Welt im existenziellen Denken*, Bern 1955, 30 f., 69 f., 133 f.; Alan M. Olson, *Transcendence and Hermeneutics. An Interpretation of the Philosophy of Karl Jaspers*, Boston/London 1979, 10-12; Werner Schneiders, *Karl Jaspers in der Kritik*, Bonn 1965, 167. For a different view see: Miron, 2006a.

[27] The limitations of "Formal Consciousness" for the elucidation of Existenz were discussed by a few of Jaspers' commentators, see: Elisabeth Young-Bruehl, *Freedom and*

Existenz, namely the possibilities belonging to Existenz, which were still not fulfilled, that were recognized as inaccessible to Formal-Consciousness. This understanding was anchored in Jaspers' distinction between the ability to become known (*Erkennbarkeit*), which is referable to objects, and the ability to be elucidated (*Erhellbarkeit*), pertaining to Existenz (Ph1, 17 f.).[28] Knowing and elucidating appear then as two different functions of consciousness: whereas the first reaches out to its objects, the second lets them uncover themselves without trying to adjust them to any ready-made pattern.[29] In any event, "Existenz finds itself [...] in the world, without coming to be recognizable [*erkennbar*] as mundane [*Weltsein*]" (Ph1, 17).

It is clear that Jaspers' present understanding of Formal-Consciousness, which partly continued the one that appeared previously, made it impossible for him to bestow upon it a positive function in his philosophy of Existenz. Yet, this fact does not testify to the being of Existenz outside immanence or to Jaspers' withdrawal to his early concept of the self as a totally particular being, which acknowledges no externality as relevant to one's self-understanding. The discussion of the drawbacks of formal-Consciousness is nothing but an additional means of concentrating on Existenz' uniqueness and particularity.[30] Therefore, one can see the understanding of Existenz as inaccessible to Formal-Consciousness as a continuation of Jaspers' early criticism of the positivism in science. To the extent that one is taking into account the philosophical stage of Jaspers' elucidation of the self, it is possible to understand the very confrontation with Formal-Consciousness's viewpoint as an indication of Jaspers' reservation from extreme idealistic and romantic approaches in philosophy that did not acknowledge the possible applicability of Formal-Consciousness to philosophizing. Hence, though the perspective of Formal-Consciousness cannot

---

Karl Jaspers' Philosophy, New Haven, London 1981, 5-9; Heinemann, *Existenzphilosophie*, 61-83; Olson, *Transcendence and Hermeneutics*, 1979, 45 ff. Jaspers changed his attitude to Formal Consciousness in the context, which was aimed at the explication of "Being" (*Umgreifendes*). Then, Formal Consciousness was not identified as dealing solely with object, see: Truth, 225 ff.

[28] For a wider perspective on this distinction, see: Miron, "From Opposition to Reciprocity — Karl Jaspers on Science, Philosophy and What Lies Between Them". In: *International Philosophical Quarterly* 44/2 (2004), 147-163. Reprinted in this collection as Miron, 2004c.

[29] Jaspers' deliberate usage of the relatively rare verb "elucidate" (*Erhellen*) and not the verb "explain" (*Erklären/Erläutern*) or "illuminate" (*Erleuchten*) intended to demonstrate the uniqueness of Existenz, see: Gabriel Marcel, "Grundsituation und Grenzsituationen" (1932/1933). In: Hans Saner (ed.): *Karl Jaspers in der Diskussion*, München 1973, 160.

[30] The gap between the being of Existenz and what can be indicated by the objective viewpoint of Formal-Consciousness, is well reflected in the different interpretations to Jaspers' concept of Existenz, i.e., as a relative and irrational being (Otto Friedrich Bollnow, "Existenzerhellung und philosophische Anthropologie". In: *Bulletin für Deutsche Philosophie* 12/2 (1938-1939), 136-139, 157; Bollnow, *Existenzphilosophie*, Stuttgart 1960 (1942), 11 f.; Joseph Lenz, *Der moderne deutsche und französische Existentialismus*, Trier 1951, 32 f.), as an idealistic being (Leo Gabriel, *Existenzphilosophie von Kierkegaard bis Sartre*, Wien 1951, 20; Stegmüller, *Hauptströmungen der Gegenwartsphilosophie*. Stuttgart 1960, 233 f.), and as opposed to any scientific understanding (Jürgen von Kempski, "Philosophie als Anruf". In: *Brechungen. Kritischer Versuch zur Philosophie der Gegenwart*, Hamburg 1964, 235 f.).

be the only tool of the philosopher who seeks the self, unlike those approaches, Jaspers acknowledged the possible contribution of the objective viewpoint to his philosophizing, at least as a negative teaching way.

The challenge of the philosophy of Existenz, in which the self-conceived as a worldly being, is then twofold: it aimed to find a way to anchor self in world's reality; namely, that its self-understanding would not be detached from the world as the context of possibilities for its self-fulfilling. No less than that, the philosophy of Existenz was directed to maintain the singular uniqueness of the self-compared with other objects that appear in the same world in which it finds its being. The relations between these two are well depicted by Jaspers' contention according to which "possible Existenz separates itself from the world in order that afterwards it genuinely enters into the world" (Ph2, 4). That is to say that the idea of the self as a worldly being does not contradict its conception as a particular being, but rather agrees with it. Furthermore, objective thinking appears as possibly useful for analyzing concrete situations in order to deduce from them latent possibilities for its self-fulfillment. To be precise, Jaspers did not argue that fulfilling one's own possibilities could be deduced from objective or logical understanding of world's reality. Though the world's possibilities can become known to Existenz also by objective consciousness, it is the only one to regard one as belonging to itself. Hence the whole meaning bestowed upon the reality of the world is necessarily subjective.

> What I am offered as being in this train of thought, in reply to my question what am I, is a schematization of my objective existence (*Dasein*). I find myself in the schema, but each time I make the experience that it does not fit entirely. *None of these objectivations will achieve an absolute identity with myself* I go beyond such schemata; in. them I would be bound to lose myself. (Ph2, 32)[31]

Jaspers' understanding of the immanent dimension of the self — be it the Formal-Consciousness or the objective reality by which it is surrounded — achieves its full meaning at the present point. On the one hand, Existenz is conceived as an outcome of self-constitution, but at the same time it is understood as a being that finds itself already in. the world. Existential freedom is located exactly between these two; although forced by conditions indifferent to its wishes and needs, Existenz has the ability consciously to transcend concrete situations and to avoid identification with anything external to it. Thus Existenz incessantly seeks after new possibilities in the world that appears to it as concealing within it a possibility for a more complete self-fulfillment. Indeed, Existenz may abandon a concrete option in favor of a speculative one that at a certain point seems better than the one formerly chosen. This does not mean that Existenz is motivated by a caprice or irrational mood, but expresses the dynamic of Existenz' experience of life and world, i.e., a constant movement between actuality and possibility is therefore characteristic to Existenz as long as it strives to live in the world as such (Ph2, 21). However, since Existenz is located in the same world towards which

---

[31] Emphasis in original.

Formal-Consciousness is directed it must employ the objective viewpoint while seeking out self-understanding.

The need to employ the Formal-Consciousness in the explication of the self as a worldly being excludes the possibility of seeing this kind of awareness as the present cause of dissatisfaction. Moreover, though the very relating to Formal-Consciousness appeared firstly within the elucidation of Existenz, the dialectic that was introduced by this to Jaspers' understanding of the self-ended up bringing to the extreme the same original emphasis on its particularity and uniqueness. Allegedly, the philosophical stage can rightly be seen as fulfilling Jaspers' original insights about the self and even as overcoming what formerly appeared a source for dissatisfaction. Yet, Jaspers' concluding words to the path he took while elucidation of Existenz, leave no doubt that this is not the case.

> To me as Existenz absolute independence is indeed my true unconditionality in temporal existence, but it also drives me to despair. I am aware that as flatly self-based I would have to sink into the void. For my self-realization I depend on a fulfillment that comes to me. I am not myself if I happen to default; I relate to myself as if selfhood were bestowed upon me. S/he [Existenz] verifies its possibility, only with the knowledge that it rests upon transcendence. (Ph1, 4)

These words point to the roots of the crisis that occurred in Jaspers' philosophy of Existenz, and at the same time indicate the direction whose solution was to be found. The understanding of the self as in. dependent of any externality, i.e., Jaspers' early conception of the self, turned out to a source of despair. Yet, what seems to me even more significant than the present awareness of the problematic character of the understanding of the self as an independent being – a point that concerns the content of Jaspers' idea of the self - is the very unequivocal awareness of the experience of dissatisfaction itself.

In other words, what had been implicit up to this stage, and was revealed only by the suggested critical interpretation, is proclaimed now by Jaspers himself. Uncovering the awareness of the philosopher of his own experience within philosophizing - an awareness that is basically not a matter of content – sheds light retrospectively on the different position from which the former phases of understanding the self were consolidated.[32] Consequently, the experience of dissatisfaction, which formerly appeared as a transcendental force for achieving each time a better understanding of the self, transpires now as emerging from the very personal being of the philosopher who appears as seeking out not only an improved understanding of the idea of the self but as influential on him personally. The movement reached its culmination where the self ceased to function as an object of search but is revealed as the subject who conducts the search. This development should not be seen as accidental but as predictable from the whole spirit of Jaspers' search for the self, as it expressed a constant approach

---

[32] For a different interpretation of the discussed experience of dissatisfaction, see Hans Kunz, "Critique of Jaspers' Concept of Transcendence". In: Paul Arthur Schilpp (ed.), *The Philosophy of Karl Jaspers*, New York 1957, 499-522, 507-509.

towards a more accurate understanding of it, until the gap between the self as a subject and the self as an object seemed to be abolished.

At the present point, it may be useful to recall Hegel's concept of necessity as an "experience of consciousness" and as "inner movement" of the contents of consciousness which cannot rest until its culmination.[33] However, the goal of the whole move was there from the very beginning, a goal which as a matter of a fact served at the same time as a promise that what is logically acknowledged as necessary will come into being. Yet, concerning Jaspers' search for the self, a reservation from the Hegelian association must be taken. Unlike Hegel, who brought his philosophical voyage, and hence the very experience of dissatisfaction, to its end at the stage of "absolute Knowledge", Jaspers did not yield any promises of this kind. For no ontological account of the being of transcendence - the being that the ability to constitute a conscious attitude was revealed as conditioning one's self-knowledge - was given in any context of Jaspers' writings, thus the experience of dissatisfaction that accompanied his search for the self was not even supposed to vanish. It is not surprising, then, that Jaspers could not find any way out of the present experience of dissatisfaction but turned to new target independent of it, i.e. explicating being and transcendence. In any event, all that was achieved at the current stage, concerning the understanding of the self, is the insight that "where I am really myself I am not myself only" (Ph3, 220) but resting upon the being of transcendence (Ph3, 4). This insight does not mark the end of the discussed search, but a new starting point, or better a more accurate one, i.e., "Existenz is either in relation to transcendence or not at all" (Ph3, 6). Consequently Jaspers' concept of the self reveals the individual as a person who is not "worrying" solely about himself/ herself but is relating to the Being that exists beyond himself/herself, i.e., to transcendence.

The new beginning of the elucidation of the self, which was achieved, not only could pave a new way for a different understanding of it, but also changed retrospectively the understanding of the very aiming at the self as "a way to transcendence" and of "Their elucidation [as] philosophical metaphysics" (Ph3, 3). It is clear that the uncovering of the metaphysical anchor of the being of the self, which led to the understanding of the philosophy of Existenz as metaphysics (Ph1, 27), was facilitated not only thanks to the maturity of Jaspers' understanding of the self, but also embodied its maturity. Finally, Jaspers' shift from the elucidation of the self to that of being and transcendence reflected the change in the self's mode of being: from "being as Existenz" to "being as Existenz in the face of transcendence".

Summary

The fact that Jaspers' early interest in the subject being occupied his mind also in his philosophical writings determined the framework of the present discussions. The analysis of Jaspers' pre-philosophical writings uncovered a solipsistic

---

[33] Georg Wilhelm Friedrich Hegel, *Phenomenology of Spirit*. Miller, A.V. (Trans.), Oxford 1977, 56-57. The same idea of necessity underlies also Hegel's *Science of Logic* (see: *Wissenschaft der Logik*, Lasson, G. (ed.). Vol. 1 1963, 35). See also: Walter Kaufmann, *Hegel*, New York 1965, 371; Lauer, *A Reading in Hegel's "Phenomenology of Spirit"*, 31 f.

understanding of the self, in which no place or legitimacy for any aspect of externality or objectivity pertaining to the subject being. Although in these writings Jaspers did not reject the very existence of externality to self, this was not recognized as a significant element in the understanding of process by which a person establishes his own identity. A change with far-reaching consequences occurred in Jaspers' philosophical writings, in which the reality external to the subject appeared as a meaningful factor, and therefore was acknowledged as crucial to the explication of the self which from then onwards was termed Existenz. The broader philosophical processes that made this development possible, of which this article has alluded only to the highlights, enabled Jaspers to anchor the self in a context which is external to it. This not only revealed a whole realm transcendent to the self, but also the illumination of this sphere acknowledged as crucial to its understanding.

The developmental perspective that was implemented in the interpretation of Jaspers' concept of the self-transpired as fruitful for the concept of self, as well as for understanding the complete mind from which his creation came into being — firstly as a psychiatrist and finally as a philosopher. The reason for employing this methodical approach was not only due to the fact that Jaspers changed the starting points from which he accessed the idea of the self during his writings, but also since the insights that emerged from these viewpoints were remarkably different and even contradictory. As the matter of a fact, the relevance of the discussion of his pre-philosophical writings to the understanding of the philosophical ones, or rather the unity that binds them, became clear only after elucidating the latter. In other words, one cannot reach the depth of the tensions that characterize Jaspers' philosophy of Existenz without the awareness of the solipsistic background that predicated it and the increasing awareness of the experience of dissatisfaction that motivated it. Hence, only now can one understand what Jaspers really meant by his statement in the opening of "The Hundredth Symposium of the German Society for Natural Sciences and Physicians", long after he ceased to practice psychiatry and to conduct research in this field: "The Practice of the Physician is a concrete philosophy."[34]

---

[34] Quoted from: Heinrich Schipperges, "Medizin als konkrete Philosophie". In: Jeanne Hersch, Jan Milic Lochman, Reiner Wiehl (ed.), *Karl Jaspers - Philosoph, Arzt, politischer Denker*, München, Zürich, 1986, 88-111, 88.

Towards Reality: The Development of the Philosophical Attitude to Reality in The thought of Karl Jaspers

The question that motivates this article relates to the nature and meaning of reality presupposed in the idea of the self in Karl Jaspers' thinking, which is the primordial theme on which his whole philosophical work was founded.[1] The understanding of reality, in which the subjective being lives and practices, turned out to be a philosophical problem in Jaspers' thinking, because of the decisive status given in it to a person on constituting its own identity. For Jaspers, the person is to determine the meaning and value of various aspects of the reality external to it. Hence, the idea that reality or even dimensions of it could be independent of the subjective being or could impose anything upon it, did not loom large in the initial stages of his thinking. This fact evokes questions about Jaspers' understanding of reality. These questions are primarily concerned with the scope of that reality and with the way one can come to know it.

Allegedly this problem is relevant to other philosophical systems that were anchored in the idea of the self. Yet, in my opinion Jaspers' case is interesting not only because of the transition that appeared in his writings, from his original interest in the self towards philosophizing about Being, which included an explicit account of external reality. Furthermore, the very fact that this development did not entail abandoning the original interest in the self but kept it

---

[1] Despite its general relevancy to Jaspers' understanding of reality, his idea of the self will not be discussed here beyond the context of the relation of the self or the subjective being to its external reality. Jaspers' mature understanding of the self appeared in the second volume of his *Philosophie*, published 1932, named '*Existenzerhellung*' (from now on referred to as Ph2). For the main interpretations of Jaspers' idea of the self, see: Fritz Heinemann, *Existenzphilosophie - Lebendig oder Tot?*, Stuttgart 1954; Otto Friedrich Bollnow, (1960). *Existenzphilosophie*, Stuttgart 1942; Joseph Lenz, *Der moderne deutsche und französische Existentialismus*, Trier 1951; Kurt Salamun, *Karl Jaspers*, München 1985; Sebastian Samay, *Reason Revisited: The Philosophy of Karl Jaspers*, Dublin 1971; Elisabeth Young-Bruehl, *Freedom and Karl Jaspers' Philosophy*, New Haven 1981. See also Ronny Miron, "Transcendence and Dissatisfaction in Jaspers' idea of the Self" in: *Phänomenologische Forschung*, 2005, 221-224 (reprinted in this collection as Miron, 2005).

within the realm of discussion, while integrating the insights concerning the deficiencies of the understanding into the concept of Being, makes Jaspers' case interesting. Hence, this article seeks to determine whether within Jaspers' understanding of the self an awareness of the problem of reality was achieved and whether the transition of the focus from the self to the idea of Beign proposed a solution to that problem or at least attempted to do so. The purpose of this paper may be seen also as an attempt to determine the scope and meaning of Jaspers' Idealism and to evaluate the way he dealt with one of the most typical problems characteristic of such a philosophical position, i.e. the meaning of the reality external to the self.

The interpretation suggested in this article is based on a phenomenological viewpoint and will be carried out in the following way: first, Jaspers' concept of the self as it appeared in his early writings (1909-1919) will be presented. In these writings, which focused on the self from the perspective of psychiatry and psychology, external reality was hardly mentioned and actually remained implicit, though clearly not denied. The aim of this section is to discover which element of the conception of the self here developed hindered Jaspers, or better still, left him no place to conceive of the relation of the self to external reality. Against this background I will clarify the conception of the subjective being as it stands in the forefront of his interest.

The discussion will then shift to Jaspers' understanding of the reality external to the subject, as well as to Jaspers' concept of Being. This part will relate to Jaspers' philosophical writings from 1932 to 1947, in which the reality external to the subject was denoted by a variety of terms: World (*Welt*), Existence (*Dasein*), Reality (*Wirklichkeit*), the 'Encompassing' (*Umgreifende*), Being (*Sein*), and Transcendence (*Transzendenz*). The modifications that occurred in Jaspers' understanding of the self and their reflection and implementation within the concept of Being will be elucidated. To put it briefly, Jaspers' understanding of the reality external to the subject will be criticized both as a latent dimension in his early idea of the self and as an explicit theme in his philosophical writings.

The interpretation of Jaspers' philosophy as it arises from these considerations differs from more traditional ones in that these generally failed to recognize what I call 'the problem of reality' as an issue that certainly arises in his writings. Many of these do not pay any attention to the concept of Being, but focused mainly on Jaspers' philosophy of Existence (*Existenzphilosophie*).[2] Yet, as it will become clear later on, Jaspers' concept of Existence neither exhausts his idea of the self nor his thinking as a whole. Furthermore, the interpretation

---

[2] See, for example, Samay, op. cit. 66f; Hans Mader, "Das Seindenken bei Karl Jaspers", in: *Wissenschaft und Weltbild*, vol. 10, 1957, 58; Heinemann, op. cit. 78. There is a clear affinity between these interpretations of Jaspers' philosophy of Being and those interpretations that understood his concept of the Self as irrational, as cut off from any externality, and finally as reflecting an extreme individualism. For such interpretations, see Bollnow, op. cit., 11-27, and his "Existenzerhellung und philosophische Anthropologie", in: *Bulletin für deutsche Philosophie*, 12/2, 133-174, 1938-1939; Lenz op. cit., 14, 32; Fritz-Joachim von Rinteln, *Beyond Existentialism*, London 1961, 204ff; Salamun op. cit., 46f; F. Imle, "Jaspers als Existenzphilosoph", in: *Philosophisches Jahrbuch der Görresgesellschaft*, Bd. 49, 1936, 487-504, and "Jaspers als Existenzphilosoph", in: *Philosophisches Jahrbuch der Görresgesellschaft*, Bd. 50, 1937, 86.

proposed here disagrees with those commentators who, though acknowledging the awareness to the external reality in Jaspers' writings, saw it as an integral part of his understanding of the self or even as subordinated to it.[3] Thus I will lay claim both to the existence of a concept of reality in Jaspers' writings and to its independence of, though not severance from, his idea of self.

The Internal Reality of the Subjective Being

Jaspers' interest in the being of the subject is apparent already from the opening to his first book *General Psychopathology*, where he posed that "in the Psychiatric practice" the interest always turns to "the human being in his singularity and totality"[4]. Although he thought that the 'psychic' element contained the key for the understanding of the particular character of a specific mental illness of the concrete personality (Psychopathology1, 12), he contended that the 'singularity' (*Einzelnheit*) with which the human being is imbued[5] restricts the very possibility of making comprehensive and scientific claims about pathological psychic phenomena as such.[6] The description of the psychic element as "foam that floats from the ocean depth" (Psychopathology1, 14) clearly alludes to a hidden reality, deeper than that accessible to psychopathology, which is subjected to the restrictions of rational consciousness.[7]

---

[3] See, for example, Thomas Räber, *Das Dasein in der "Philosophie" von Karl Jaspers*, Bern 1955, 84f and Young-Bruehl op. cit., 19-20

[4] Karl Jaspers, *Allgemeine Psychopathologie*, Berlin 1913, 1 (from now on referred to as Psychopathology1 in the text). In his understanding of the scientific character of psychiatry, Jaspers was influenced by Weber, as he admitted himself. For Weber's concept of science compare his "Wissenschaft als Beruf" in: *Gesammelte Aufsätze zur Wissenschaftlehre*, Tübingen 1922, 534-535 and *The Protestant Ethic and The Spirit of Capitalism*, New York 1958, 79-82. For other interpretations of this influence, see: Heinemann, op. cit., 61-66; and Ernst Moritz Manasse, "Max Weber's Influence on Jaspers", in: P. A. Schilpp, ed. *The Philosophy of Karl Jaspers*, New York 1957, 369-393.

[5] "Die Phänomenologische Forschungsrichtung in Psychopathologie", in: *Zeitschrift für die gesamte Neurologie und Psychiatrie*, 1912, Bd. 9, 391-408, 408.

[6] Jaspers' distinction between the restrictions of science [*Beschränkungen*] and its boundary [*Grenze*], originates in the very fact that it is impossible to achieve an exhaustive understanding of the individual [Ap1, 1-2]. This distinction reflected Kant's influence on Jaspers. See: Immanuel Kant, *Prolegomena to any Future Metaphysics*, London & New York 1996, 11. See also: Chris Walker, "Karl Jaspers as a Kantian Psychopathologist, I: The Philosophical Origins of the Concept of Form and Content", in: *History of Psychiatry*, 1993, Vol. 4, 209-238 and "Karl Jaspers as a Kantian Psychopathologist, II: "The Concept of Form and Content in Jaspers' Psychopathology", in *ibid.*, 321-348; J. Rudolf Gerber, "Karl Jaspers and Kantian Reason", in: *New Scholasticism*, 1969, Vol. 43, 400-423; and Erich Grünert, "Der Einfluss Kants auf Karl Jaspers: Zugang zur Transendenz bei Kant und Karl Jaspers", in: *Freiburger Zeitschrift für Philosophie und Theologie*, 1956, Bd. III, 21-28.

[7] On this point, there is a recognizable affinity between Jaspers' and Jung's concepts of hidden subjectivity. See Jaspers relation to Jung in: *Allgemeine Psychopathologie*, Berlin and Heidelberg, 8th edition, 1965, 277f, 300f, 341. See also: C. G. Jung, *Persönlichkeit und Übertragung*, Zürich und Düsseldorf 1996: and Ronny Miron, "Was Jaspers really a Kantian?", in *Yearbook of the Austrian Karl Jaspers Society*, 2006, 19, 73-106 (reprinted in this collection as Miron, 2006b).

Jaspers' approach towards mental illness, or rather to mentally ill people, differs from the positivistic one, which in psychopathology characteristically focuses on the investigation of the physiological dimensions of mental diseases in order to achieve an objective understanding of them.[8] Unlike this approach, Jaspers' required close contact with the concrete being of the patient.[9] Establishing a contact with "what really happens in a human being's soul" was for Jaspers a fulfillment of "The general urge to reality ... in psychopathology" (Psychopathology1, 12). In other words, the idea of reality that Jaspers had in mind at that time, or better, the one that is to be addressed by the psychiatrist, was identified with the reality of the internal psychic life. Accordingly, the relation to reality – which is external to the mentally ill person and where scientists as well as the healthy people live their lives – was not considered relevant to the understanding of the ill person. Finally, though the external reality was not denied, the internal psychic life appeared as the real reality towards which Jaspers' interest was directed.

After Jaspers ceased practicing psychiatry and conducting research in this field, he discussed the subjective and particular being of the normal human individual more directly and systematically from a psychological perspective.[10] This discussion was at the time dominated by the perspective of 'Worldviews' (*Weltanschauung*) – one of the central concepts of German philosophy. It refers

---

[8] However, Jaspers' criticism of positivism was not accompanied by a denial of the relevance of objective investigation to the understanding of the phenomenon of mental illness. Moreover, Jaspers himself developed an objective terminology of his own [Psychopathology1, 94-144]. Actually, his critique was directed against medical training that did not evaluate a wide understanding of the patient as human being, as a first condition for practicing psychiatry [Psychopathology1, 22]. As an alternative to this approach, Jaspers proposed exploring the appropriate personal qualifications of the psychiatrist. Cf. Ap4, 254 and *Die Phänomenologische Forschungsrichtung*, 391-397. See also: Herbert Spiegelberg, *Phenomenology in Psychology and Psychiatry*, Evanston 1972, and Chris Walker, "Karl Jaspers and Edmund Husserl: Phenomenology as Empathic Understanding", in: *Philosophy, Psychiatry and Psychology*, 1995, Vol. 2, No. 3, 247-266.

[9] Jaspers critically designated the comprehensive theories of psychiatry "prejudices", and, in the same spirit, he called all theories which identified mental diseases as brain diseases 'brain mythologies'. This critique was explored in his articles published between 1910-1913 [see also: *Philosophie und Welt, Reden und Aufsätze*, München 1958, p. 290f, from now on referred to as PW], and was mainly directed at Griesinger (see: Wilhelm Griesinger, *Pathologie und Therapie der Psychischen Krankheiten*, Braunschweig, 4th edition, 1986). For further discussion see: Heinz Häfner, "Einleitung in den Psychiatrischen Teil" in: Jeanne Hersch, Jan Milic Lochman & Reiner Wiehl, [eds.], *Karl Jaspers - Philosoph, Arzt, politischer Denker*, München & Zürich, 1986, 83-87; Werner Janzarik, "Jaspers, Kurt Schneider und die Heidelberger Psychopathologie", in: *ibid.*, 112-126; Joachim-Felix Leonard, (ed.), *Karl Jaspers in seiner Heidelberger Zeit*, Heidelberg 1983; and Ludwig Binswanger, "Karl Jaspers und die Psychiatrie, in: Hans Saner (ed.), *Karl Jaspers in der Diskussion*, München 1973, 21-32.

[10] This perspective was mainly explored in the *Psychology of Worldviews* (*Psychologie der Weltanschuungen*, Heidelberg 1985). It is remarkable that as a psychiatrist he points to the need for a psychological book that will give the pathological viewpoint a wider perspective, anchored in the investigation of the 'normal' person. He considered such a contribution as crucial as physiology; nevertheless he admitted that it could not always help the practice of psychiatrists [Psychopathology1, 4].

to the sum of knowledge, norms and values that one can absorb from one's culture, as well as characterizing the human being as a universal agent. Jaspers tied this term to the subjective individual, without referring to the general cultural dimensions beyond the subjective agent, which are reflected in it. He contended that one's worldview does not generally contain knowledge (*Wissen*) about the world or even about oneself as a person, but rather, different aspects of subjectivity: the experiential part of experience and the human effort to arrange those experiences via rational objectifications (PW, 1). According to Jaspers, one's worldview embodies especially one's subjectivity as a total experience that determines exclusively the meaning bestowed upon different objects one considers as existing (PW, 22-23). Consequently, the reality external to the subject was not a theme that the concept 'worldview' as such was supposed to cope with, since what was important for Jaspers was reality as a creature of one's own spirit and the self-understanding that comes out of it.

The view described above, appearing in the context of psychiatry – namely that dimensions referring to the reality external to the subject were not considered as relevant to the understanding of the self – was then further developed and deepened. In the present context the subjective being was shaped by Jaspers as a totality whose personal experiences fill the whole world that exists for him/her. Moreover, the hierarchy of values and the nature of reality itself are exposed as determined according to meaning bestowed by the person upon these experiences.

Furthermore, one can identify in both contexts an inclination to grant the subjective being a solipsistic character. To be precise, the solipsistic inclination was not crystallized as radical solipsism, as in Berkley's thought, or in the methodical solipsism of Descartes. Jaspers did not see the contents of consciousness as the only embodiment of reality or as the exclusive source for certainty. In other words, Jaspers' solipsistic inclination was not based on the metaphysical foundation characteristic of the extreme solipsistic position, which deprives the external world of reality. In positive terms, Jaspers' solipsism appeared more as a kind of Egoism[11] or indicated the existence of an emotional quality of the self which cannot be manifested to other people and relates to no data of external reality. Hence Jaspers' position can be termed as solipsism, more because of its implications than its ontological or epistemological infrastructure.

One can say that Jaspers' observation of the idea of worldview as a general phenomenon extended to the particular and subjective meanings that one can achieve while seeking self-understanding (PW, 4, 15f). Heidegger, for instance, understood Jaspers' psychological observation as not limited to the experience of the subject but as related to the phenomenon of existence.[12] Yet this discussion remained in the margins of his writings from the first period. As to Heidegger's interpretation, it seems to reflect first and foremost his own interest in Being, which he explored later on in *Being and Time*. I contend then that in this context Jaspers simply revealed no interest in the existence of an external world.

---

[11] See C. D. Rollins, "Solipsism" in: Edwards, ed., *The Encyclopedia of Philosophy*, vol. 7, New York 1967, 487-491, 487f.

[12] Martin Heidegger, "Anmerkungen zu Karl Jaspers' *Psychologie der Weltanschauungen*", 1920, 70-100. The same can be said about Jaspers' discussion concerning the physical dimensions of mental disease, named as 'objective symptoms' of pathology, which are typical and not personal; see Psychopathology1, 94f.

Therefore, Jaspers' solipsism was mainly a result of his primordial interest in the subjective being, as well as evidence of the very fact that he lacked the means to explore an inclusive concept of selfhood, not limited to the subjective and particular dimensions of one's personality. It is possible to explain Jaspers' focus on subjectivity, in these writings from the first period, by the very fact that psychic pathology can be manifested in falsification of reality, as well as through the idea that psychological analysis does not necessarily require reference to external reality. In any case, it is clear that the subjective being engaged Jaspers' interest at that time in a way that left no room for exploring an attitude towards the external reality in which this being is anchored.

Nevertheless, the understanding of Jaspers' early concept of the subjective being is crucial and indispensable for considering the change that enabled him to confront the problem of reality in his philosophical writings. In my opinion, it is especially the awareness of the problematic nature of the solipsistic tendency that characterized his early idea of self, which functioned as a transcendental condition for Jaspers' philosophical attitude towards external reality. As will become clear below, Jaspers began to realize that the solipsistic concept of the self was inadequate or restrictive for an understanding of the subjective being, and hence should be abandoned. This insight that was to be fulfilled in Jaspers' idea of Existence, at the same time enabled him to consolidate an explicit concept of reality. This development was closely linked to the increasing distance from his early solipsistic inclination, so that every stage of this exploration was at the same time a stage in the process of overcoming that inclination itself.

The Reality in Which Existence Takes Place

What was for Heidegger an *a priori* basis for the explication of the human being (*Dasein*), i.e. being-in-the-world, which made the elucidation of world's reality an integral part of human existence, was for Jaspers the consequence of a quite a long way he had already taken in realizing his original interest in the subjective being.[13] In other words Jaspers' thinking started from an earlier or rather more radical point than Heidegger's, and hence it included the disillusionment with the introspective approach where psychological and extreme kinds of idealistic ways of thinking meet. Yes, it is important to point out that Jaspers' radicalism in this context is limited, or that his solipsism was relatively easy to overcome, precisely because this solipsism was not supported by the Cartesian idea, according to which the existing self is bound to its thinking or cogitations, but a growing awareness of the need to enlarge the perspective of self-awareness, which itself paved the way for dealing with the problem of reality.

Jaspers' first acknowledgment of the relevance of the reality external to the understanding of the self-marks the beginning of the philosophical period in his writings. By contending that "philosophizing starts with our situation",[14] Jaspers posed the concrete reality, in which people live and practice, as the framework

---

[13] For Heidegger's path from the *cogito sum* to Dasein, see: John N. Deely, *The Tradition via Heidegger*, The Hague 1971, 43-61.

[14] Jaspers, 'Philosophische Weltorientirung', vol. 1 of *Philosophie*, Heidelberg 1994, 1, from now on referred to as Ph1.

where the philosophical discourse is to be conducted. Hence philosophizing about the self cannot be exhausted by one's personal and subjective representation, but indispensably needs to include within itself an explicit concept of the external reality. This meaningful change was accompanied by a more systematic style of expression, as well as a new terminology that substituted the early terms 'psychic', 'self' and 'subjectivity' with the term 'existence', which was characterized by a clear philosophical connotation.

The new viewpoint of the subjective being as existing in a concrete reality, contained the potential undermining of his early solipsistic stance.[15] Henceforth, Jaspers presented the philosophical elucidation of existence as an integral part of the exploration of 'philosophical world orientation'. This means that the explication of the reality external to the subject became crucial for the establishment of a philosophical concept of the self. Moreover, treating the subjective being as existing in a concrete reality opened new horizons for Jaspers' thinking, which enabled him later to develop a comprehensive conception of the reality that exists independently beyond the subject – including the notions of immanence and transcendence. So, in the second period of Jaspers' writings, a fundamental infrastructure for the explicit handling of the problem of reality was established.

Nonetheless, these modifications in Jaspers' thought were not sufficient to detach the dependence of the problem of reality from the context of elucidation of existence. In his words: "Being will not be elucidated via analysis of existence (*Daseinsanalyse*) but by elucidation of Existence (*Existenzerhellung*)" (Ph1, 12). That is to say, the boundaries of the discussed reality were determined at the present stage according to their relevance to the understanding of Existence. This limited reality recognized by Existence as its own, Jaspers called 'situation-being' (*Situationsein*). This original term expressed the freedom of Existence, i.e., the possibilities engrained in the environment through which one can achieve self-fulfillment, as well as the existence of limitations stemming from reality's factuality, such that cannot be changed by a person but is indiscriminately imposed on him/her.[16] Finally, the term of 'Situation-being' was the one around which the understanding of Existence was consolidated as a worldly being.

Considering the background of Jaspers' early solipsistic inclination, it is clear that unique term of 'Situation-being' was very helpful in integrating the new element of concrete reality into his concept of the subjective being. While the general term 'world' (*Welt*) could have demanded a more comprehensive account, not necessarily tied to what could serve the needs of Existence to understand itself, the term 'Situation-being' remained close to the understanding of Existence as a being that establishes itself out of freedom. That is to say that even after

---

[15] Jaspers later referred to his *Psychology* as "a hasty book of my youth' [*Rechenschaft und Ausblick*, Tübingen 1958, 392f].

[16] See Ph1, p. 1. Jaspers discussed these possibilities in: Ph2, 9, 18, 134f. A first version of the concept of 'situation' appeared in: *Die Geistige Situation Der Zeit*, Berlin, Leipzig 1931, 23. Jaspers continued to explore this term in the context of his famous concept of the 'Limit Situation' [*Grenzsituationen*]. See especially the later version that appeared in: Ph2, 201f [the earlier appeared in: PW, 229f]. See also: William D. Blattner, "Heidegger's Debt to Jaspers' Concept of Limit-Situation", in: Alan M. Olson, [ed.] *Heidegger & Jaspers*, Philadelphia 1994, 153-165.

Existence was understood as anchored in the concrete reality of the world, Jaspers did not abandon his original wish to put it in the center of his interests, and the reduction of the term 'world' to 'Situation-being' was designated specifically to facilitate that very centrality. This interpretation of the term 'Situation-being' reveals, then, the inner dynamics of, or the transcendental conditions for, his elucidation of the problem of reality: it could not threaten the centrality bestowed upon the original interest in the subject being, but had rather to be understood as crucial to that very interest itself. However, in light of these considerations, a profound truth about the nature of our experience of the world is revealed: a person by no means experiences the entirety of the world, but only some of its dimensions in which it is directly involved. This point is uniquely crystallized in what Jaspers termed 'Situation-being'.

Undoubtedly the understanding of Existence as a worldly being opened for Jaspers new horizons that drew his thinking nearer to the idea of external reality. Yet, it seems that the restriction of the idea reality to the sphere of 'Situation-being' could not be sufficient for his growing interest in an idea of reality, or better, to the acknowledgment of the need of such a reality, that would be independent of Existence's self-understanding. Henceforth, the general terms of 'world' and "world's reality" were integrated and the requirement arose to achieve an understanding of the "world's thinking", supposed to provide a broader and more general understanding of reality compared to that in which Existence takes place. Hence, though the idea of 'situation-being' was recognized as "the starting point and the aim (*Ziel*), because nothing else is real and present" (Ph1, 69), it transpired to Jaspers that

> the situation itself becomes clear to me only when I think with reference to the objective being of the world – a being that, time and again, I must conceive as existing only to void it (*aufheben*). I can neither grasp my situation without proceeding to conceive the world, nor grasp the world without a constant return to my situation, the only testing ground for the reality of my thoughts. Inescapably, the situation is my mode of real existence (*Dasein*)... [however] this mobility is not absolute. There remains a tie (*Bindung*) to [my] finite existence and to [my] past habit and usage (Ph1, 69).

These words reveal the complexity that underlies the awareness of the restrictedness of human beings' experience of 'situation': although this awareness is perceived as helping Existence to specify more clearly the expanse in which it finds its existence (*Dasein*), a person nonetheless cannot silence the urge to contemplate the reality as independent from his or her own being and thinking. This is the point where the philosophical insight, according to which only a general and objective comprehension of the 'world' can grant Existence a better understanding of the reality in which it takes part, matured. In other words, the consolidation of an independent "world's thinking" transpired as no less essential than the elucidation of 'Situation-being' for Existence's self-awareness.

Accordingly, Jaspers derived two 'world' concepts from this insight: the 'world' as the 'other', accessible for investigation, which is revealed as a single thing and universally applicable, and the 'world' as "existence that finds itself as... non-I (*Nichtich*)" (Ph1, 63). While the first can be characterized as general and separated from the self, the elucidation of the second is actually integral to the constituting of a comprehensive and philosophical concept of selfhood. However, Jaspers contended that these two realities are "linked to each other within a mutual movement" (Ph1, 63). One cannot avoid then the impression that although Jaspers acknowledged the value of an understanding of reality as independent of the subject being, his more dominant commitment to the subjective viewpoint nevertheless tied his understanding of this concept strongly to Existence's self-explication needs.[17] This interpretation of the dialectic, accompanying Jaspers' growing interest in external reality, can find supplementary support in the concern he expressed that "the urge to have an understanding of existence" would turn "destructive". That would lead to a dangerous immersion, if not to wallowing in the world in a way that would detract from the uniqueness and particularity of Existence (Ph2, 3). Although Jaspers previously considered that urge as an inseparable part of one's self-recognition as a worldly being, he introduced Existence as a being that was "required by its own self to be distinguished from the world" (Ph2, 3). Finally, Jaspers' concept of reality, consolidated within his philosophy of Existence, is revealed as functional by its very nature, i.e., it was mainly meant to facilitate a better and more complete understanding of the being by which Existence is surrounded and which is meaningful to it.

The apparent return to former insights that where characteristic of Jaspers' pre-philosophical writing, or at least the maintaining ties of the idea of Existence to them, can explain the fact that many of Jaspers' commentators hardly discerned his progress towards attaining an understanding of external reality. Nevertheless, in my opinion, by the very expression of that concern, Jaspers did not retract his understanding of Existence as a worldly being, but revealed his difficulty in overcoming his early solipsistic inclination that characterized his initial concept of subjective being. My contention is that what shaped Jaspers' attitude towards the reality external to the subjective being was his innermost anxiety that acknowledging the worldly character of Existence in the reality of the world would influence also the understanding of Existence. If that happens, Existence, like other things in the world, would be conceived via the objective tools of consciousness. These are accessible to the objective dimensions of the world, but nonetheless incapable of representing Existence's unique fullness. This analysis of Jaspers' hidden consideration can be strengthened by his later assertion in the text, according to which "possible Existence separates itself from the world in order that it *afterwards* genuinely enters into the world" (Ph2, 4). By this contention, Jaspers managed to secure the uniqueness of Existence as a worldly being, so that it would be considered as existent in the world and yet be tested and characterized according to criteria derived from its authentic self-understanding.

Only at this point can we understand the relevance of the world, or better, the value of the disposition towards the world as external reality to the self-determination Existence: the world acknowledged by Existence as an arena of possibilities through which it can achieve its self-fulfillment. In a way, the world

---

[17]See: Samay, op. cit., 66f; Mader, op. cit., 58; Heinemann, op. cit., 78.

exists for it only as a stockpile of possibilities for self-fulfillment. Nonetheless, Existence itself is not identified by any of these possibilities (Ph2, 32). This specific perspective of the world as perceived by Existence prevents us from regarding the possibility it chooses as derived from a logical or objective understanding of the world's reality. It is only Existence that can see a certain possibility as its own, and hence the whole meaning bestowed upon the reality of the world is necessarily subjective by its very nature. It transpires, then, that Existence shifts between two languages: the existential, which is necessarily subjective and subjected to Existence's needs for self-fulfillment and self-understanding, and the objective, attributed to the external reality of the world. Not only does Existence use these two languages, but it is the instance which marks both the connection point and the dividing point between them.

Against this background we can discover the complexity that characterized Jaspers' attitude to external reality, which can also be regarded as the relation towards the immanent dimension of the being of Existence. On the one hand, he conceived of the being of Existence as the result of an experience of self-constitution, but, at the same time, Existence was understood as a being that finds itself already in the world as external to itself. Existential freedom is located exactly between these two poles; although forced by conditions indifferent to its wishes and needs, Existence has the ability consciously to transcend concrete situations (*Situationsein*) and to avoid identification with anything external to it. Thus Existence incessantly seeks after new possibilities in a world that appears to it as concealing possibilities for a more complete self-fulfilling. True, Existence may abandon a concrete option, in favour of a speculative possibility that at a certain point seems better than the one formerly chosen. While this does not mean that Existence is motivated by caprice or irrational mood, it expresses the dynamic of the way it experiences life and world. Constant movement between actuality and possibility is therefore characteristic of Existence as long as it strives to live as Existence (Ph2, 21).

This dynamic, where Existence knows itself as part of the world external to it, while at the same time separated from it, reflects the dialectic that accompanies Jaspers' concept of reality as developed within his philosophy of Existence. This dialectic is not only clear evidence for the continued presence of residual traces from the early solipsistic understanding of subjective being, but also reveals the struggle for priority or even exclusiveness between two representatives of reality in Jaspers' thinking at this stage: while the *internal* is intended to serve as part of the comprehensive and more complete self-awareness of Existence, the *external* is supposed to be independent of Existence's self-understanding. Though the first bears decisive weight in the context in which Existence is elucidated and the second only comes up without being fully discussed, they nonetheless are in conflict. In my opinion the conflict involved in this duality stems from the irreversibly achieved insight, according to which, despite its uniqueness, Existence is located in the same world towards which objective consciousness (*Bewußtsein Überhaupt*) is directed. Hence, overcoming this dialectic, i.e. loosening the polarity between the idea of the self and that of reality as external to it, only became possible after the subjective dimension ceased to be at the core of Jaspers' philosophical thought. This could occur only with his thought directing itself at a new independent target: namely to establish a philosophical concept of Being (*Sein*).

Reality as Being

Posing the classic philosophical question "what is Being?" at the beginning of his first book of philosophy (Ph1, 1), clearly indicated Jaspers' intention to widen the scope of his discussion.[18] The term Being (*Sein*) which gradually became pivotal in Jaspers' discussion and took the place formerly granted to Existence turned out to be broader and more comprehensive than 'World', which remained to a large extent tied to the elucidation of Existence's subjective point of view.[19] The extension of the range of the reality to which philosophizing was directed was referred to as the 'Encompassing' (*das Umgreifende*), Jaspers' unique term for the idea of Being. The 'Encompassing' includes immanent components as well as transcendent ones. The latter are inaccessible by their very nature, both to the objective viewpoint of consciousness, and, in their completeness, also to Existence. Nonetheless, Jaspers made a considerable effort to maintain the link with his concept of Existence, which reflected at the present stage of its explication not only its understanding as a worldly being, but also as one that constituted a relationship with the surrounding world. Accordingly, Jaspers contended that 'Being' as a subject for philosophical explication is an inseparable part of the subjective being that seeks it, to such an extent that searching for 'Being' is identified with the very existence of Existence, while abstention from the search is analogous to its cessation.[20] These words ended the aforementioned dialectic that characterized the idea of Existence, and so a new context of discussion was established in Jaspers' philosophical writings.

It was especially the distancing from the solipsistic inclination that functioned as a precondition for this far-reaching change in Jaspers' philosophizing. It is clear that only a self-conscious subject is a being who can shift the focus of his or her thinking away from his or her own personality, yet not become detached from it, and who is able to open his or her view towards what

---

[18] On the use of "fundamental questions" characteristic of the German philosophical tradition, see: Bernhard Bollen, *Existential Thinking, A Philosophical Orientation*, Duquesne University Press 1968, 1-35.

[19] This contention concerns all the writings that appeared between *Philosophy* (*Philosophie*, 1932) and *Out of Truth* (*Von der Wahrheit*, München: Piper & Co., 1948, from now on Truth). Mayer suggested a different interpretation of the 'reality' sought in the writings from the above period. According to him, in *Philosophy of Existence* it a question of Existence and Transcendence, while in *Out of Truth* Jaspers did not search for Being's reality but for its truth; Ernst Mayer, "Philosophie und Philosophische Logik bei Karl Jaspers", in: Piper Klaus [ed.], *Offener Horizont: Festschrift für Karl Jaspers, zum 70. Geburtstag*, München 1953, 63f.

[20] Jaspers, "Metaphysik", vol. 3 of *Philosophy*, Heidelberg 1994, 1-3 (from now on referred to as Ph3). Jaspers' link between Existence and Being is well reflected in what he termed 'internal awareness' [*Innewerden*] of Being' [*Von der Wahrheit*, 357]. See his usage of this term in: Truth 307f, 344, 487. See also Hoffman's contention, according to which the 'internal awareness' of Being serves as a bridge between objective thinking and the thinking of something not objective. See: Kurt Hoffman, "The Basic Concept of Jaspers' Philosophy", in: Schilpp, op. cit., 104-106.

exists beyond himself or herself. Though the distancing from the solipsistic inclination started already within the establishment of a philosophical concept of selfhood, i.e. with Existence, it was first in this new context, aiming at an explication of Being, that distancing became a much more conscious process. To be more precise, distancing now occurs concurrently with the consolidation of the awareness of the restrictions imposed upon the philosophical horizons by the very concept of Existence as a particular and individual being. Anyway, this change aided Jaspers in breaking more significantly from the framework of assumptions that had characterized his former concept of Existence.

Jaspers' contention according to which 'Being', as an 'origin' and 'purpose' of one's life,[21] is prior to one's thoughts, rejects them and subordinates them to itself (E, 59f), prominently reflects the rejection of the solipsistic view of the self. Consequently, the required reality is anti-Cartesian by its very nature, i.e. it does not exist only within the boundaries of what can be analyzed by objective thinking, nor of what exists merely subjectively. Furthermore, Jaspers himself tells us that this reality is present within its absence, for those who desire a reality that they do not recognize and which is not their own reality (Philosophy of Existenz, 56). Along the same lines, he depicted Existence as "establishing its own life not just out of self-willing or of mere discipline, but because it faces Being in its completeness", an Existence therefore that is beyond itself (Truth, 221). Therefore, even though the very seeking of Being is necessarily attributed to one's Existence, one can no longer see oneself as located at the center of Being itself. From this point of view, the reality sought by Existence - both as external to it and as independent of it – reflects at the same time the maturity of the mode of its being, i.e., a self-consciousness unoccupied by itself, while open towards a Being beyond itself.

One can point to two results of the shift from philosophizing upon the self to philosophizing upon Being: *from point of view of the content*, this development was reflected in the new image of Existence. From this moment on, Existence was not conceived as isolated, or as a center of attraction that determines the scope of discussion or the meaning bestowed upon other components in the framework of philosophizing. *From the structural point of view*, Jaspers' argument was no longer directed at a sole object, but was anchored in multiple components as reflected in the concept of 'Encompassing', each grasped as a mode (*Weise*) of Being. Jaspers used the following table to expose his concept of the 'Encompassing' (Truth, 50).

---

[21] Jaspers, *Existenzphilosophie*, Frankfurt a. M. 1964, 12; from now on referred to as Philosophy of Existenz.

	The Encompassing that we are ourselves	The Encompassing that is Being itself
Immanent	Existence (*Dasein*) General Consciousness Spirit	World
Transcendent	Existence	Transcendence

This table includes components (*Weisen*) that I cannot discuss in this paper. However, at first glance, we can see that some of them appeared already in Jaspers' earlier writings, which focused on elucidating Existence. These components have taken on a different meaning due to the transformation that has occurred in their use, according to which they have been understood as an expression of a comprehensive Being, as that of Existence.[22] For example, in addition to its usual meaning as the sphere for Existence's experience, 'Existence' (*Dasein*) is now presented as an expression for the direct presence of Being itself (Truth, 53). Consequently, the term 'Existence' serves as a starting point for a discussion about a kind of reality that transcends the borders of the world's phenomena and immanence as a whole.

A similar orientation can be seen in the redefinition of the term 'objective consciousness'. Alongside the familiar understanding of this term as a tool through which consciousness achieves information about objects, in this context Jaspers described it as a means for opening ourselves towards the possibility of an 'Other' which we do not recognize and that it transpires that we cannot know (Truth, 65). Hence the objective point of view, the one whose restrictedness was constantly emphasized during the elucidation of Existence, is revealed from the perspective of the 'Encompassing' as no less than a source uncovering Being itself.[23]

However, the wide perspective of 'Encompassing' did not abolish the particular meaning of each of its components. No less fundamental for Jaspers than Being's comprehensiveness was the fact that precisely its partial manifestation enables us to have contact with Being itself (Truth, 39). As an "unclosed wholeness" that philosophy and human consciousness cannot exhaust, "(Being) incessantly facilitates the New" (i.e., thing, phenomenon etc.) "to face us as a particular Being" (Truth, 38). In this spirit, Jaspers characterized his own concept of Being, i.e. the 'Encompassing', as a representative of just one of the

---

[22] Jaspers explains each of those components, adjusting them to his concept of Being. See: Truth, 53-122, and *Vernuft und Existenz*, München 1987, 38-50. For further details about each of the components, see Gerhard Knaus, "The Concept of the 'Encompassing' in Jaspers' Philosophy", in: Schilpp, op. cit., 152-161.

[23] The same orientation can be seen in Jaspers' redefinition of the rest of the components. A different interpretation has also appeared in the literature, according to which the elimination of the objective viewpoint serves as a prerequisite for establishing a philosophical attitude towards Being. See: Samay, op. cit., 48f; and Mader, op. cit., 55f.

ways to access Being, one that in any case remains as the "unclosed itself" (Truth, 149).[24]

Undoubtedly, the change that occurred in Jaspers thinking and enabled him to focus directly on Being rested on deep modifications of his concept of the self, as a result of which Existence was no longer conceived as motivated solely by seeking after self-understanding of its uniqueness as a particular being. This change was reflected not only in Jaspers' attempt to grant a wider philosophical expression to the reality external to the subject, nor just in the reinterpretation of idioms formerly bound to the concept of Existence. Moreover, within the context of the 'Encompassing', Jaspers explored the important distinction between the immanent and the transcendent dimensions of that reality. This distinction opened new horizons in Jaspers' thought, within which it was possible to explore a more complex concept of reality, encompassing more than just the experiences of Existence, and out of which its identity is established.

At first glance, 'experience', 'world' and 'transcendence' are located in three different cells within the table of the 'Encompassing'. It is clear that transcendence is not identical to the reality external and immediate to subject, i.e. to 'situation being'. Likewise, transcendence is not identical to the world – a term whose meaning embodies a wider reality than what serves for Existence as a ground of experiencing. In other words, the term 'transcendence' does not relate to the reality that surrounds Existence or to the consciousness in which it relates to that reality. Although Jaspers never accounts for the basis from which he derived the reality of a transcendental being ('transcendence'), it seems that his understanding of this point originated in an *a priori* intuition.[25] In any case, it is clear that the concept of 'transcendence' transcends both meanings bestowed upon immanence within the context of the elucidation of Existence: as the external reality of the 'world', and as the self-consciousness that relates to the 'existence' in which a person's living takes place.[26]

From the suggested interpretation, one can intimate Jaspers' shift from philosophy of Existence to a philosophizing directed at the explication of Being in two ways: Firstly, as an attempt to withdraw from the standpoint in which he located his philosophy of Existence to a more primordial reality – a reality where Existence represents just one of the possibilities it contains, or, in Jaspers words: "the One that [exists] in everything, to the final purpose, to the first-base (*Urgrund*), the completeness of world and God" (Truth, 36). Secondly, it is possible to conceive Jaspers' concept of Being as an endeavor to transcend his

---

[24] Truth, 149; nevertheless, Jaspers kept the same framework of the Encompassing's components from its first appearance in his writings until the last one [see: *Der Philosophische Glaube angesichts der Offenbarung*, München 1962, 111-122].

[25] See also a different interpretation, according to which Jaspers' concept of Being was not based on an *a priori* intuition. Heinemann op. cit., 72.

[26] It is important to note that the components included in the 'Encompassing' did not represent Jaspers' ontological understanding of Being, for he rejected the very idea of an ontological attempt to give an account of Being. As an alternative to ontology, Jaspers coined his unique term of 'Periechontology' [Truth, 158], which maintained the non-objective understanding of Being. For the etymology of this term, see Knaus, op. cit., p. 141f. For further discussion, see: Heinemann, op. cit., 70f, and Urs Richli, *Transzendental Reflexion und sittliche Entscheidung. Zum Problem der Selbsterkenntnis der Metaphiysik bei Jaspers und Kant*, Bonn 1967, 119f.

own idea of Existence and to find the words for what he vaguely described as 'thinking bounded-into-one" (*in-eins-bindend*) (Truth, 2). One way or another, the philosophizing that was directed at Being reflected not only a loosening of the ties imposed by his own concept of Existence, i.e., the relevance to its self-understanding, but also the desire to find a comprehensive and lasting perfection that could substitute the ephemeral and wasteful part of subjective human life. In this context, there was no longer any need to divide the external reality into 'situations', which from this point were integrated as whole into the vast framework of the 'Encompassing'.

Reality as a 'Cipher' of Transcendence

The wish to live unlocked possibilities that were opened by the awareness of the reality external to Existence – thanks to which Jaspers' work was characterized as "the adventure of the radical openness"[27] – may explain why Jaspers left the question of the scope of the reality that was covered by the idea of the Encompassing unanswered: whether it includes 'transcendence' as one of its components, whereby the explanation given indicates that this component would in principle be explicable. By this very explication, the scope of the reality to which Jaspers' philosophizing is directed is expanded, whereas the reality within which Existence is illuminated remains mainly immanent; or else the component of transcendence as "the Encompassing of all Encompassings" (Truth, 109) is different from the others which are in principle explicable, due to its very location beyond the philosophical explication of Being, i.e. of the concept of Encompassings. From this perspective, the reality towards which Jaspers' concept of the 'Encompassing' was directed at this stage remains the immanent one, namely the same as that underlying his concept of Existence.

Though this question remained unanswered in the explication of the 'Encompassing', it is possible to clarify the scope of reality towards which Jaspers' philosophizing was directed by his unique term of 'cipher' (*Chiffre*). This term, which appeared in Jaspers' writings parallel to that of the 'Encompassing', was also used for the explication of Being. Central to this concept is the idea that immanence contains a metaphysical depth thanks to its function as a sign or symbol of transcendence.[28] As will become clear later, within the concept of 'cipher', the split between two kinds of 'Encompassing' – 'the Encompassing that we are ourselves' and 'the Encompassing that is Being itself' – was replaced by the unified understanding that recognized transcendence already in immanent reality, without identifying the two.

Jaspers' argument that immanence was granted a metaphysical depth rested upon both meanings bestowed upon immanence within the discussion of 'Encompassing': as the *concrete reality* of the world and as one's *consciousness* of the world of objects (*Bewußtsein überhaupt*) and of one's own self (*Existenz*).

---

[27] Heinemann, op. cit., 61f.
[28] Jaspers usually used the terms of cipher and symbol as synonyms. See: Aloys Klein, *Glaube und Mythos, Eine kritische, religionsphilosophisch-theologische Untersuchung des Mythos-Begriffs bei Karl Jaspers*, München 1973, 88; Johannes Thyssen, "The Concept of 'Foundering' in Jaspers' Philosophy", in: Schilpp, op. cit., 310; and Hoffman, op. cit., 108.

The first meaning consolidated the understanding that the reality of the world is not derivative from the consciousness that relates to it. The second maintained the affinity to the previous infrastructure anchored in his philosophy of Existence. Consciously or unconsciously, Jaspers managed to outline the development of his own thought from its very solipsistic beginning up to the present stage in which his philosophizing was directed towards transcendence:

> To me as Existence, absolute independence is indeed my true unconditionality in temporal existence, but it also drives me to despair. I am aware that as flatly self-based I would have to sink into the void. For my self-realization I depend on a fulfillment that comes to me. ... The test of the possibility of my Existence is the knowledge that it rests upon Transcendence. (Ph3, 4)

With these words, Jaspers pointed to the roots of the crisis encountered by his concept of Existence, but also indicated the direction of its possible solution. That is to say that the comprehension of Existence as distinctive beings independent of external reality, i.e. a comprehension characteristic of Jaspers' writings included in the so-called first period, is revealed as pointless, and therefore "drives Existence to despair". However, when Existence acknowledges itself as based upon what exists beyond itself, it can be free to achieve a genuine and more complete self-consciousness, and as such a person will be free to realize himself or herself as Existence. This insight not only concerns one's close reality, i.e. one's 'situation-being' or even the more general reality of the 'world', but it encompasses the reality of transcendence. Only after achieving such a mature self-understanding will it become possible to view immanence in its genuine depth, namely as a 'cipher' of transcendence.

Furthermore, the essentiality of Existence to the very conception of the 'cipher' is prominent in the definition of immanence itself as a 'cipher script' (*Chiffreschrift*).[29] In the same way as the existence of a language depends upon its understanding by human beings, the 'cipher script' dependent upon Existence, so as to uncover the metaphysical depth concealed in immanence. Jaspers characterizes the 'cipher script' as a mediating language (Ph3, 134), so that thinking transcendence as an expression of the contemplative immersion of Existence striving to contact what lies beyond its very existence, again reaches out for transcendence (Ph3, 135). Now it becomes clear that from the point of view of Existence, there can be no access to transcendence except via immanence, or rather, through the two dimensions in which Existence takes place: in the reality of the world and as a being that has consciousness.[30]

Nevertheless, 'cipher script' is not merely a product of the self-seeking of Existence or just an expression of the creativity of human beings. Actually, this

---

[29] Ph3, 35; Jaspers exposed his concept of 'cipher script' mainly in: Ph3, 128-172. About the three languages of the cipher see: Ph3, 130f. For further discussion, see Olson's interpretation of those languages, in: Alan M. Olson, *Transcendence and Hermeneutics, An Interpretation of the Philosophy of Karl Jaspers*, Boston and London 1979, 139f.

[30] See other commentators who pointed to the role of Existence in the establishing of the understanding of immanence as a cipher of Transcendence: Thyssen, op. cit., 309; Tilliette, op. cit., 390-391.

kind of language reveals the very nature of transcendence as a masked reality, but not as a disappearing one (Ph3, 205f). Jaspers clearly emphasized that, while Existence's point of view uncovers the metaphysical faces of immanence, it cannot exhaust the full meaning of the being of transcendence. In his words: "there is no simple parallelism between the fullness of the sensual and that of the content of Being" (Truth, 1034). That is to say that defining the 'cipher script' as rooted in the existential infrastructure (Ph3, 33) does not abolish the gap between human beings, who establish a metaphysical attitude towards transcendental reality, and the object of this attitude, which is inexhaustible by any kind of philosophizing. Hence Jaspers claimed that a "complete and genuine" meeting with Being is impossible (Ph3, 136).

Yet, it is necessary to point out that the reality of transcendence, as a being that transcends immanence, is not a speculative matter for Jaspers. Unlike the reality-beings (*Wirklichsein*) that exist for empirical knowledge only within contexts and connections (*Beziehungen*), he claimed that "the being of the symbol (*Symbolsein*) as a 'cipher' of 'transcendence' does not take place in a connection" (Ph3, 146). Therefore, the reality of Being and that of transcendence is perceived by Jaspers as independent of the very existence of any consciousness that is able to confirm it, since immanence itself is "full of transcendence" (Truth, 1031f). From this point of view, the concept of the 'cipher' reflects not only an explication of the search of Existence for meaning, but also the attempt to bestow a philosophical expression upon the concealed reality present in immanence itself.

The conception of immanence as a 'cipher' of 'transcendence' consciously undermines the classical positivistic approach to reality that identifies beings with the empirical and the finite (Ph3, 140). Jaspers' contention according to which the fixed logical categories of reality cannot be applied to the elucidation of the being of transcendence (Ph3, 39), at the same time denied the concept of immanence in which they were anchored (Ph3, 137f). Obviously, having said this, by no means is it said that an ascetic worldview considering immanence was latent in the concept of 'cipher'.[31] Just as uncovering the limitations of the objective viewpoint in the elucidation of Existence (Ph3, 11-12) was not accompanied by a negation of the reality of the world, so, in this context, the disagreement with the empirical approach to reality did not serve as a basis for negating immanence as such. The very use of the anchor of the concept of transcendence in immanence, including its immediate dimensions, first made it possible to understand transcendence as the source for meaning concerning human reality. As a matter of a fact, Jaspers contended that the idea of the 'cipher' redefines the whole of human beings' lives as a totality that variously expresses Being itself (Ph3, 142f). In another words, observing phenomena via the perspective of the 'cipher' we become able to reveal the metaphysical depth inherent in the existence of human beings.[32] Therefore, it is clear that the unique contribution of the notion of the

---

[31] Jaspers' criticism was directed at the ascetic approach as well as the pantheistic approach. See: Ph3, 137f.
[32] Jaspers demonstrates the metaphysical depth inherent in the routine [Ph3, 130], physical nature [Ph3, 178], history [Ph3, 182] and art [Ph3, 192]. For further discussion, see: John Hennig, "Karl Jaspers' Attitude towards History", in: Schilpp, op. cit., 565-591 and Johannes Pfeiffer, "On Karl Jaspers' Interpretation of Art", in: Schilpp, op. cit., 703-717.

'cipher' to the understanding of reality is not only that this viewpoint did not detach the concept of Existence from the immanent reality of the world, but that it also gave rise to a far-reaching change in the understanding of objects that appear in immanence itself. These objects symbolize for Existence that which will never become an object, namely Being itself (Truth, 256f). Thus, alongside the notion of immanence, which 'world orientation' identifies with empiricism, the cipher's viewpoint "poses another mythical reality". [33] However, it is clear that ontologically there is no difference between existence (*Dasein*) perceived as empirical from the viewpoint of objective consciousness, and existence that from the cipher's viewpoint is grasped as containing within itself the being of Transcendence. According to Jaspers these are two dimensions of one world accessible to different viewpoints (Ph3, 16). While the empirical reality demands the objective viewpoint, the metaphysical reality requires the cipher's viewpoint.

Herewith it became possible to achieve a more accurate definition of the sort of reality inherent in the idea of 'cipher': this is without doubt the reality of immanence, but it includes a unique remnant (*Rest*) that cannot be completely assimilated in immanence as such (Ph3, 171). This remnant is responsible for the understanding of the reality of immanence as containing wealth that cannot be accessed by the immanent consciousness. According to Jaspers, this wealth is able to "speak" by itself within the immanent reality (Ph3, 197). Yet, it represents "unity without identity with immanence" (Ph3, 138), for a remnant will always last and will refuse any rational explication. As the matter of fact, the very idea of the 'cipher' reflects both the awareness of the fact that we are consciously and existentially and helplessly trapped in immanence, as well as of the attempt to find a door to a reality that transcends the borders of immanence itself. Via the idea of the 'cipher' a wide concept of immanence is consolidated, which can neither be exhausted by Existence's attitude towards it, nor by an account given by objective consciousness. Despite the fact that the meaning of the transcendent Being itself remained obscure in Jaspers' writings, the idea of the 'cipher' enlarged the scope of reality toward which his philosophizing was directed, compared to the scope that underlay the former context of Existence. Additionally, a possible reply to the unanswered question that arose from the idea of 'Encompassing' is suggested by the proposed interpretation of the idea of the 'cipher'. Jaspers' concept of reality, which was consolidated within his reflection upon being, does not overlap with immanence but transcends it. By the same token in both ideas of 'cipher' and 'Encompassing' a new and more mature concept of self was developed. According to this concept, Existence is not solely focused on itself but strives to establish an attitude towards a reality that exists beyond itself and its own existence. Transcendence is the name of that reality.

---

[33] See: "Die Phänomenologische Forschungsrichtung in Psychopathologie", 128. For a more general understanding of the symbol as an expression of the duplicity between the immediate world and the world of meaning, see: Robert Doran, "Aesthetics and the Opposites", *Thought*, 1977, vol. 52, 117-133.

Conclusion

It transpires that the existential infrastructure in Jaspers' thinking *hinders* the development of a concept of reality as well as *facilitating* it. As we have seen, focusing on the elucidation of the particular being of the self, which characterized Jaspers' early writings, led to the consolidation of a solipsistic concept of Existence; this left no place for the exploration of the philosophical concept of reality. Although in the writings of the first period, Jaspers did not reject the very existence of a reality external to self, such reality was not recognized as a significant element in the process in which a person establishes its identity. A change with far-reaching consequences occurred in Jaspers' later philosophical writings, in which the reality external to the subject appeared as a meaningful factor that must be taken in consideration in any explanation of what was now termed Existence. It is true that at this stage traces of the early solipsistic inclination were still visible; traces that are regarded as responsible for the restriction of the discussion to the reality in which Existence finds its being. Nevertheless, the thought directed to Existence created a real basis for a confrontation with what was called above 'the problem of reality', this time at a more explicit level. Furthermore, as has been shown in the above discussion of the concepts of 'cipher' and 'Encompassing', that reality was to become a central theme of Jaspers' writing. Thanks to a further distancing from the assumptions that supported the early solipsistic inclination, the domain of reality broadened, and a transcendent dimension was added to it.

This essay has attempted to explicate the dynamics of Jaspers' engagement with the problem of reality – from the early stage of overlooking the relevance of external reality up to that moment when he comes to terms with the most encompassing reality of transcendence. These dynamics can explain not only the fact that many concepts of reality appeared in Jaspers' writings, but also that they mirror the wider philosophical development occurring in his thinking. In fact, the three meanings bestowed upon reality in the philosophical writings expressed three stages of distancing from the solipsistic inclination contained in the early works. This is exactly why a sufficient explanation of Jaspers' early ideas becomes possible only *vis à vis* the later ones; ideas that mostly realized the latent potential inherent in those that preceded them, and which thus created a real basis for a new understanding of a philosophical sense of reality in Jaspers' thinking. From this we may conclude that concept of reality consolidated in Jaspers' writings remains connected to his concept of self and to its unique problematic nature. Finally, Jaspers' philosophical project can be seen as a door to other philosophical systems that, by being anchored in the being of the subject, turn the nature and meaning of external reality into a problem or at least raise meaningful questions about it.

Was Jaspers Really a Kantian?

Preface

"If I ever write a book on Jaspers," so stated Jaspers' colleague in Basel, "I will call it 'Karl Jaspers: The first and the last Kantian'".[1] So far, such a book does not exist. However, the existing scholarly literature that deals with Jaspers' relationship to Kant is in almost complete agreement about the affinity and even indebtedness of Jaspers to Kant. Olson, for example, contends that the adaptation of "critical epistemological insights of Kant to the language of Existenz" is so obvious that it seems, in his monograph on Kant, Jaspers was "really speaking of his own".[2] Therefore "formally and historically Jaspers' philosophy is virtually unthinkable apart from the influence of Immanuel Kant".[3] Olson's detailed account is preceded by an historical reasoning according to which, "Because the self... is involved so intimately in the process of determining what is known, many after Kant... developed an utterly skeptical attitude towards the possibility of all metaphysics... In Jaspers, however, the opposite is the case... Jaspers recovers what he believes to be the essential intent and purpose of Kantian *kritik*".[4] A comparable understanding emerges also from Gerber's commentary, as he argues that Jaspers accepted Kant's dichotomy between two kinds of thinking: that of Understanding (*Verstand*) that stays within the confines of immanence and objectivity, and that of Reason, which seeks whatever lies beyond the grasp of concepts.[5] This dichotomy between the senses and the transcendent, was realized in Jaspers' understanding of Existenz, so that "the Kantian epistemology becomes an anthropology".[6] Yet Gerber suggests a different setting to support his understanding of Jaspers as Kantian, pointing to the fact that whereas in Jaspers' early works "he adopted the label of Existentialism to characterize this humanist motivation... this existential coloring is abandoned, however, after Sartre appropriates that label for himself in 1946. Having now rejected that label...

---

[1] Quoted from Ehrlich, 211.
[2] Olson, 73-74.
[3] Ibid., 72.
[4] Ibid., 73.
[5] Gerber, 405-406.
[6] Ibid., 414-415.

Jaspers prefers to call his philosophy one of 'reason'".[7] Lastly, Walker, the only commentator who refers both to Jaspers' early career as a psychiatrist and to his philosophical work, contributes the far-reaching statements, according to which, "Jaspers in his *General Psychopathology* has provided a Kantian critique of psychopathological reason",[8] whereas "Jaspers' philosophy is the philosophy of Kant in the twentieth-century context".[9] However, citing the aforementioned quotation of Jaspers' colleague in Basel, Walker alludes to the historical context of post-WWII, when Jaspers left Germany and accepted the invitation of the university of Basel to serve as professor of philosophy.[10]

The recurrence of the use of an historical setting in the above illustrations, especially that referring to the context of German philosophy after 1945, may provide a key to what seems more or less unanimous agreement that Jaspers was a consistent successor of Kant. Olson is right when he distinguishes between Jaspers and both the formal mechanics of the deduction in neo-Kantianism and the prevalent skeptical attitude towards the possibility of all metaphysics.[11] Compared to that culture, Jaspers seems much more Kantian than many other figures. Moreover, the affinity between Jaspers and Kant seems even stronger when one views it from the perspective of a second setting. Undoubtedly Jaspers was one of the outstanding German thinkers who were looking to reestablish what was then called "another Germany" upon universal and cosmopolitical values. In contrast to others, Jaspers insisted that the German heritage of *Bildung* was as relevant then as ever.[12] Thus, he contended:

> Once reason gets lost, everything is lost. From its very beginning its task has been, and still remains, to acquire reason, to restore itself as reason, albeit as reason proper. This reason submits to the logical necessities of the understanding and appropriates its methods and results without succumbing to its limitations. (VuW, 49)[13]

This clear call for rehabilitation of universal reason appears throughout Jaspers' writings after WWII.[14] Undoubtedly, when the recovery of reason stands at the core of Jaspers' effort, it is understandable that readers recall Kant's critical philosophy, especially as one can find other reasons for regarding Jaspers as Kantian. Firstly, there is a prominent repetition of central characteristics in the writings of the two philosophers. Thus, the three topics discussed by Kant in *Critique of Pure Reason* - world, self and God – are parallel to Jaspers' division

---

[7] Ibid., 401-402.
[8] Walker 1993, 210.
[9] Ibid., 238.
[10] In the literature about Jaspers, his relationship to Kant is mentioned on various levels also in: Richli, 117f.; Young-Bruehl, 13-21, 73f., 104f.; Samay, 25f.; Sarin; Kelemen; O'Connor; Walters, Radbruch; Holz; Kornmüller; Lichtigfeld; Milmed; Grünert.
[11] Olson, 73.
[12] For a wide view concerning the cultural forces in Germany after World War II (WWII), see: Plümacher, 20.
[13] This quotation appears also in Gerber's article. See: Gerber, 402. See also Jaspers' opening preface (*Geleitwort*) to the periodical *Die Wandlung*, 1, 1945.
[14] See especially: VuF; BuM.

of his work *Philosophy* into the same three themes: *Philosophical World Orientation, Existential Elucidation, Metaphysics*. Additionally, the basic orientation of both philosophers is based on common distinctions, in particular: the separation of Being and appearance[15], the centrality bestowed upon freedom of consciousness, and the use of the transcendental method. Lastly, Jaspers himself can be considered a trigger for promoting such an understanding of his thinking, for he himself mentioned his debt to Kant.[16]

Although these explanations are not dismissed as being erroneous or banal, in my opinion they are not sufficient to support the understanding of Jaspers' thinking as Kantian. Instead of external reasoning – be it the historical setting of Jaspers' work or the resemblance in specific characteristics between the two philosophers – I will suggest a rather immanent reasoning for Jaspers' conscious drawing away from Kant's positive ideas. In that case, even Jaspers' admission of his debt to Kant cannot make any real difference, especially as such admissions are not rare in his writings.[17] Besides, when one takes into consideration Jaspers' fundamental stance towards the philosophical text, i.e. "To experience contradictions, we must look for the source of contrariety" (Nietzsche, 17), such acknowledgments seems more an a-priori approach than evidence of an identification of himself with a specific way of thinking.[18] In fact, my answer to the question appearing in the title is negative. In my opinion, the divergence between Jaspers' and Kant's thinking had already occurred at the stage of meta-philosophy, and the seemingly external resemblance covers up deep differences; such that could not have permitted the loaning of Kantian contents and concepts to Jaspers' work. Thus the disparities between the two philosophers add up to a different philosophical project. Yet the negative answer is followed by 'but', for Jaspers did not simply reject Kant's ideas, but was aiming to position his own philosophizing vis-à-vis Kantian thinking. In fact, Kant's philosophy functioned for Jaspers as a landmark beyond which he sought to locate his own philosophical vision. Jaspers himself admitted that his view of Kant "brings to something which is not to be found in Kant, and which, where it appears in another philosophy, does not refute Kant but complements him and complements his purifying reason" (GP, 373).[19] In my opinion, the words "another philosophy" refer to Jaspers' thinking, which was not represented in his commentary upon Kant, but rather, alluded indirectly to the criticism and evaluation of Kant's way of philosophizing. In any event, by scrutinizing the relations between the two, this paper will neither aim to add a new interpretation to the existing literature about

---

[15] In order to avoid confusion, hereafter the word 'Being' will signify the German word *Sein* and the word 'being' will indicate the meaning of existence, or what Jaspers frequently referred as *Dasein*.

[16] Ph1, 2; OmP, 137; GP 1, 381; PA, p. 86

[17] For Jaspers' acknowledgment of Nietzsche and Kierkegaard, see: *Vernunft und Existenz*, München (1935) 1987, 7-34 (hereafter: Wisdom and Existence). For his acknowledgment of Weber, see: PA, 55f.

[18] See especially other monographs by Jaspers: *Schelling, Nietzsche* and *Weber*. Besides, he frequently referred to other philosophers and sometimes even integrated a historical excursus within the course of the exposition of his own ideas. See: PW, 109-117.

[19] Hereafter, the numbers in brackets in the body text refer to Jaspers' writings according to the abbreviations in the list.

Kant, nor seek to determine whether Jaspers was a good commentator of Kant or not. Indeed, Jaspers' relation to Kant is seen here as another viewpoint, through which one can view the entirety of Jaspers' mind as a psychiatrist and as a philosopher as well. Thus, my question leading to the topic under discussion is: in what way may Jaspers' own ideas function as a response to the unanswered questions in Kant's philosophy? In order to show that, I shall confront Jaspers' commentary of Kant[20] with his own writings, regarding the two main issues from which both philosophies were consolidated as a whole: Objectivity and Subjectivity. Obviously, the whole interpretation of the present issue is directly influenced by the understanding of each of these philosophies. That is to say, that every determination about the discussed relationship is necessarily dependent on the interpretation of both sides, hence one can fall into an infinite regression. The immanent method employed – which confronts Jaspers' exposition of Kant's ideas with Jaspers' own conceptions, i.e., by confronting Jaspers with himself – is designed to avoid this problem, inherent in every comparative interpretation. Therefore, the analysis of Jaspers' attitude to Kant's Philosophy should be regarded mainly as an implementation of a comprehensive interpretation of Jaspers' thinking.

Jaspers' Elementary Understanding: Kant as Transcendental Idealist

There is nothing new in Jaspers' commentary on Kant's *Critique of Pure Reason*. The reading he suggests can be classified according to the conventions in the existing literature, which can roughly be divided into two ways of reading Kant's idealism. The first regards it as a metaphysical theory that affirms the unknowability of the "real" ('things in themselves') and accordingly reduces the knowledge to pure subjective matter or to mere representation ('appearance'). This view actually includes Kant within the phenomenalistic heritage in philosophy, which provided an account of the experience of the mind that assumed it to be 'affected' by things in themselves, thought nothing is being claimed about these (including the claim concerning their existence). The second reading emphasizes the transcendental meaning of Kant's idea about the limitation of knowledge to appearances, namely regarding it "as an epistemological claim about the dependence of human knowledge on certain a priori conditions which reflect the structure of the human cognitive apparatus".[21] According to this view, these conditions do not determine how objects appear, in the empirical sense; rather they express the universal and necessary conditions for recognizing something as an object at all. It is exactly the understanding of Kant as a philosopher who did not investigate objects but our knowledge of objects that does not allow one to expect him to provide an account of Being. Clearly, both have epistemological and metaphysical implications, yet the first interpretation

---

[20] Jaspers dealt systematically with Kant's philosophy within two contexts: IL, in: Psychology, 465-486; GP, 230-381.

[21] The background of the first course of study and the representative scholars of it are depicted by Allison as 'the standard picture' (see: 3-10), while the second express Allison's own interpretation, among others who regarded Kant as a 'transcendental idealist' (10-13; 25-34).

places more emphasis on the metaphysical ones, whereas the second on the epistemological ones.

Jaspers' focus on the various implications of Kant's theory of knowledge provides real substance that enables us to count his commentary on Kant within the view that regards him as transcendental idealist. So, Jaspers contended that "Kant is referring to the grounding of the objective validity of a priori concepts... he excludes from his discussion [the idea that] representations come into being as reactions of the mind to external things... the transcendental is concerned not with matters of empirical facts but with justification of validity" (GP, 260). Yet, it is important to note that in his discussion Jaspers switches indiscriminately between 'object' and 'objectivity'. Thus, in the same breath he contended that there was "objectivity as such", and in support of it he added that "object" even had "the character of substance" (GP, 247). However, not only are 'object' and 'objectivity' not synonyms for Kant, but the term 'objectivity' does not appear in Kant's *Critique* at all, whereas "object" has two central meanings: it may be taken as signifying content (*Inhalt*)[22], or as affecting the mind.[23] In the first meaning, intuition appears as referring immediately to objects as purely subjective, while in the second, intuition appears as affected by objects, which are accordingly acknowledged as independently real. Clearly, the two meanings of 'object' in Kant's thinking cannot coincide. Nevertheless, in Jaspers' specific perspective on Kant's thinking, not only do the two meanings of 'object' not bring about different implications, but in fact, letting things slide from 'object' to 'objectivity' becomes understandable, for objects appear especially as a source of knowledge. This analysis becomes apparent in Jaspers' following clarification, where he explains that he "entitles transcendental all knowledge which is occupied not so much with objects as with the mode of our knowedge of objects in so far as this mode of knowledge is to be possible a priori... His goal is no longer the metaphysical knowledge of another world but knowledge of the origin of our knowledge... with his transcendental method he strives to transcend while remaining within the world. He thinks about thought" (GP, 262). It transpires, then, that what Jaspers refers to as Kant's idea of 'objectivity' is especially suited to the first meaning of 'object', i.e., content of knowledge. As to the second meaning, it is not ignored and is even alluded to by the reference to Kant's famous phrases: "Thoughts without content are empty, intuitions without concept are blind" (IL, 465; GP, 254).[24] Moreover, as will become clear later on, Jaspers' criticism of Kant was directed precisely to the vanishing of the understanding of the object as independently real.

Objectivity and Subjectivity: Jaspers versus Kant

Jaspers' understanding of Kant's ideas of subjectivity and objectivity indicates the knowing subject and the object of thinking. The subject is defined by his sensibility, which spontaneously receives what is given to it through the senses. Sensibility is the knowing of something through intuition, without which no

---

[22] See: PR1, 51; PR2, 75.

[23] PR1, 119, 226.

[24] PR1, 51; PR2, 75.

reality can be assumed. However, sensibility as such is indeterminate and hence it is "meaningless... mere existence, which does not yet stand before me... It is a reality which being undefined is not yet a reality" (GP, 254). Thus, sensibility cannot suffice to grasp what is given by the senses, but needs the mediation of understanding (*Verstand*), which confers forms by which the endless material turns out to be an object of thinking.[25] On the other hand, Kant's idea of objectivity appeared to Jaspers as referring to the specific shape of sense data under the guidance of exact science patterns (GP, 247), which actually subordinate the empirical reality to the particular formulation of mathematics that can be known a-priori. Thus, with the help of understanding, intuition is replaced with discursiveness. So the categories are inserted into the materials of the given senses, which on the one hand are "something universal" that subsumes all particulars of the same kind (GP, 252), but on the other hand are the subjective form of our thinking (GP, 249). Consequently, the representation of the senses' data can never reach the object for "what we perceive has phenomenal reality but is not reality as such" (GP, 249). The idealness of things in Kant's philosophy is, then, not for their illusive nature, but for the very fact that what appears to us is not 'things in themselves' but only the mathematical shape of reality by the categories that can be known a-priori (GP, 248). However, "to interpret Kant's thoguht as meaning that the world is produced by the subjectivity of man's mental constitution or the condition of his brain is to reduce it to absurdity" (GP, 261). It is only the discursive understanding that knows the object "through concepts which are never the object itself". Having said all this , it is clear, then, that "everything that exists for us is an object of thought" (GP, 252) and without sensibility, as our witness to reality, there can be no reality for us at all. Nevertheless, besides the relatively consistent understanding of Kant, Jaspers integrated within his exposition parts, which do not fall in line with the entire reading suggested by him. This is very prominent when he pointed to the deficiencies in Kant's two core ideas of object and subject. So, concerning the idea of object, which due to the above analysis is revealing also concerning the idea of objectivity, Jaspers stated:"Kant does not... investigate objects; what he inquires into is our knowledge of objects. He provides no doctrine of the metaphysical word, but a critique of the reason that aspires to know it. He gives no doctrine of being as something objectively known, but an elucidation of existence as the situation of our consciousness" (GP, 276). The negative approach is maintained regarding the idea of subject: "It is not the individual, but the 'I think'... the subject of consciousness as such is not the empirical psychological subject, which I can observe and investigate. It is not accessible to self-observation but only of self-certainty... in the cognitive act of my self-consciousness, I do not gain knowledge of myself as a particular object. ... The

---

[25] Jaspers himself did not note the exact place in Kant's writings to which his interpretation referred, or from where his citations were taken. Henceforth, I will point to the main places in which Kant dealt with the subject of discussion. I follow the customary way of referring to Kant's *Critique of Pure Reason*. The pagination of the 1st edition (1781) is given as PR1, the 2end edition (1787) as PR2. In this context, see, for example: PR1, 68, PR2, 93; PR1, 86, PR2, 118. On the ability of understanding to determine the content, which is given to us by sensation, see: PR1, 261, PR2, 317.

more this knowledge identifies itself with thinking, the more it eludes psychological observation" (GP, 257-258).

The feeling of surprise is even increased as one reaches the section of the evaluation where Jaspers accuses Kant of communicating no vision of the world; of creating no symbols (GP, 372); of leaving "many men dissatisfied, as though deprived of food and air. They yearn for a transcendent content" (GP, 373). Obviously, this criticism involves terminology that may suit transcendental realism, or better his criticism uncovers expectations and philosophical wishes that can be addressed to a transcendental realist, someone who treats mere representations as 'things in themselves'.[26] That is to say that Jaspers' criticism of Kant does not agree with his own exposition of his ideas, the same that promised that "In considering them [Kant's ideas], we must keep in mind…the fundamental direction of Kant's thinking" (GP, 246). This situation raises, then, the question: why does Jaspers criticize Kant for not achieving philosophical goals that in regard to his own reading could not even have been expected from it?[27] The answer, as will be clarified below, is inherent in fundamental difference in the understanding of the ideas of subjectivity and objectivity by the two philosophers.

The decisive point that generates the divergence between Jaspers' thinking and that of Kant – as exposed in Jaspers' commentary – is the understanding of the manner in which subjectivity and objectivity are interrelated. According to Jaspers, Kant regarded them as two poles on a single axis, mutually conditional, relative to each other and hence as dependent on mediation. In contrast to that, Jaspers put most of his effort into establishing these two as independent from each other. Additionally, Jaspers and Kant did not share the same content concerning the two ideas. For Jaspers, subjectivity – which is denoted also by the terms of '*psyche*' and 'Existenz' – refers first and foremost to the particular dimensions of the self, which, in general, are not accessible to rational predication. Objectivity, on the other hand, represents generality, the scientific approach accessible to rational reasoning and the reality external to the subject being.[28] The discussion of the ideas of subjectivity and objectivity appears throughout Jaspers' writings. Yet, regarding the present issue, one can divide Jaspers' writings into two main periods: the one covers his early writings that deal with the issues from Psychiatry and Psychology (1909-1919), whereas the second covers his philosophical writings (1932-1947). Thus, Jaspers contended that "in the Psychiatric practice" the interest always turns to "the human being in his singularity and totality" (Psychopathology1, 1). In contrast to the positivistic approach, Jaspers granted priority to the individual personality of the mentally ill person (Psychopathology1, 3)[29] and to understanding the 'psychic' elements that

---

[26] For Kant's distinction between 'transcendental idealism' and 'transcendental realism', see: PR1, 543/ PR2, 571; PR1, 369; PR1, 490-91/ PR2, 518-19. For an analysis of these references, see: Allison, 14-16.

[27] See also: PR1, 536/ PR2, 564; PR1, 740/ PR2, 768. See also: Allison, 14-24.

[28] For a more detailed analysis, see: Miron, 2004, 151-152 (reprinted in this collection as Miron, 2004c).

[29] The individual differences between individuals assumed to be the guiding concept of the psychological approach, therefore, turn out to be no less crucial to the Psychopathology than physiology. The fact that in certain cases psychology cannot be practically implemented by psychiatrists, should serve as to encourage Psychopathology to explore its

accompany the physical illness (Psychopathology1, 12)[30] over the investigation of the symptoms (Psychpathology1, 3). [31] Thus, the abnormal symptoms were considered as unique expressions of one's own singular personality, and not as a mirror of a concrete disease. [32] Moreover, according to Jaspers, as the investigation of the physiological symptoms progresses, the mental elements that are linked to it evade examination; so much so that inquiring into the mental symptoms finally reaches a certain point when one can no longer find any accompanying physical aspect (Psychopathology1, 5). Therefore, the 'singularity' (*Einzelnheit*) with which the human being is imbued (Phen., 408) restricts the very possibility of making comprehensive and scientific claims about pathological psychic phenomena as such. Jaspers' description of the psychic element of mental illness as "foam that floats from the ocean depth" (Psychopathology1, 14) provides an idea of the elusive nature of the subjective being to which he strived to obtain access, and hence the uselessness of representing it with the inflexible patterns of the science of psychopathology.[33]

Parallel with the exploration of the idea of subjectivity, an understanding of objectivity was consolidated in the early writings. This is apparent in referring to the scientific approach, which is depicted as devoted to "identifying and recognizing, characterizing and analyzing not the single person but the General" and to integrate its findings in the conceptual framework of science (Psychopathology1, 1). Hence the physical dimensions of the mental illness, which can be accessed by rational tools of science are especially objective. Jaspers did not ignore the possible relevance of the scientific approach, but opposed the positivistic view that identifies the phenomenon of mental illness with its physiological symptoms, and sometimes even reduces the one to the

---

own psychology that will complete the unique elements that are irrelevant to normal people (Psychopathology1, 3-4). Jaspers himself pointed out initiatives that already took up this challenge (Psychopathology1, 4, note 1).

[30] This idea appears as vaguely as described above in the first edition of *General psychopathology* (1913), but it is largely explored in the enlarged version that appeared as the fourth edition (1942), which contained the philosophical infrastructure that was explored during the intervening years. See: Psychopathology, 624-686.

[31] Jaspers' criticism of positivism was not accompanied by denying the relevance of objective investigation to the understanding of the phenomenon of mental illness. Moreover, Jaspers himself exposed an objective terminology of his own (Psychopathology1, 94-144). Actually, his critique was directed against medical training (*medizinische Bildung*) that did not evaluate a wide understanding of the patient as human being as a first condition for practicing psychiatry (Psychopathology1, 22). As an alternative to this approach, Jaspers proposed exploring the appropriate personal qualifications of the psychiatrist (especially empathy) (Psychopathology4, 254; Phen., 391-397). For more on this issue, see: Spiegelberg 1972, 186; Walker 1995, 247-266; O. P. Wiggins, M.A. Schwarts, M. Spitzer (eds.) 1992, 56ff.

[32] Jaspers critically designated the comprehensive theories of psychiatry "prejudices", and in the same spirit he labeled as 'brain mythologies' the contemporary theories of his time, that identified mental diseases as brain diseases (Psychopathology1, 8). This critique was mainly directed at the psychiatrist Griesinger and other contemporaries. For extensive perspective See: Häfner; Janzarik; Leonard.

[33] On this point, there is a recognizable affinity between Jaspers' and Jung's concepts of hidden subjectivity (see: Jung). Jaspers refers occasionally to Jung's conception. See: AP4, 277f, 300f, 341.

other. Jaspers' goal was, then, to perform a "demarcation" of the scientific approach to what he termed as 'objective Psychopathology'[34] and to attach to it the awareness of the subjective and particular aspects that concern the mentally ill person as a human being. Indeed, the need to supplement the science of psychopathology with such insights – which generally remain obscure in this context – is also a result of the fact that the science of psychopathology did not achieve a uniform concept of illness (Psychopathology1, 3; Psychopathology4, 651f).[35] The idea of objectivity does not appear, then, in the present context as opposed to that of subjectivity, but as representing a narrowed perspective about the subjective being. This should not be renounced, but rather supplemented with a wider one based on the intuition according to which one's subjective being is a particular and unique entity.[36]

The Explicit Departure: Jaspers' Answer to Kant

Against this background, one can easily understand why in the writings from his first period Jaspers could not adopt the ideas of Kant concerning subjectivity and objectivity. In the first place, Jaspers rejected the role, which was given to sensibility, according to which it is our witness to reality or "measurement that provides the criterion to reality" (GP, 246). The reality to which Jaspers devoted his search – firstly that of subjectivity and then that of Being – is hidden from the senses in the most part. Besides, our senses are restricted to the observation of the physical symptoms, which are not revealing for the entire reality of subjectivity out of which the mental illness developed. Moreover, not only do the senses not provide immediate contact with the reality of subjectivity, but they even appeared to Jaspers as obscuring it. Therefore, instead of the direct perspective employed by the scientific approach, Jaspers' approach speaks for the need for non-sensual intuition. This is not essentially a matter of distinction between external features and internal ones, but of an evident persuasion of Jaspers about the nature of subjectivity, whose entirety is not represented by rational tools, but via an immediate contact (Psychopathology4, 464) that cannot be predicted and needs "witty thoughts" (Psychopathology1, 12).[37] The path chosen by Jaspers rejected

---

[34] Jaspers also explored his own 'objective Psychopathology', see: Psychopathology1, 94-144.

[35] See especially the chapter "concepts of health and illness' (Psychopathology4, 651-661). This idea is acknowledged as a landmark in the process of integrating the phenomenological method into the field of psychiatry and psychopathology, see: Spiegelberg, xxxiv- xxxv.

[36] The focus on the particular dimensions of subjectivity found its continuation in *Psychology of Worldviews* (Psychology) where Jaspers entirely liberated himself from the scientific discourse. This attempt will not be discussed here, for it makes no real difference concerning the discussed ideas.

[37] Already in the first edition (Psychopathology1) Jaspers appointed to philosophy an important part in the exploration and in designing the methodological instruments of Psychopathology (Psychopathology1, 6-7). However, in the enlarged version (1942) he granted to philosophy a clear and positive role: it appeared as determining the true borders within which Psychopathology takes place and as facilitating an approach, which is not subordinate to prejudice (Psychopathology 4, 40). Moreover, philosophy was exposed then

not only the meaning of intuition in Kant's thinking, as an immediacy that should be substituted in order to achieve knowledge (GP, 256) and its connection to sensibility. For Jaspers, intuition is merely the primordial contact with a wholeness, which is already given to us. Hence, Jaspers defined his approach as aiming at the "whole of the psychic" (Psychopathology1, 13).[38] The starting point is thus an undivided unity or an evident intuition, and following it does not add anything to it, but elucidates what is already given.

It goes without saying that Jaspers' rejection of Kant's idea of intuition dismissed also its implementation on the idea of the subject. Jaspers not only does not agree with Kant's representation of the subject by his sensibility, namely, as one who spontaneously receives the given through the senses; moreover he refuses the very idea that the subject can be represented at all or be reduced to his abilities. Instead, the subject appears to Jaspers as someone to encounter, to experience in a way that one cannot be put in words.[39] In contrast to Kant, for Jaspers, then, filling the information of the senses with conceptual content does not provide significant understanding, but actually appears as a narrowing perspective that indeed damages the whole, which is already given as a non-sensual intuition. Accordingly, in order to achieve an understanding of the subject one needs to withdraw and even to overcome what one receives from the senses.

Within the second period of Jaspers' writings, a prominent change took place: the shift of the focus of the discussion from the idea of subjectivity to that of Being (*Sein*). The conditions that facilitated this change are important for the understanding of Jaspers' mature thinking. Yet, at present it should be sufficient to note that it stemmed from problems that were inherent in Jaspers' idea of subjectivity, in particular that of solipsism, which is described as "insufficiency in myself alone" (Ph2, 56).[40] However, the initial interest in subjectivity – presently denoted by the term of 'Existenz'– was not relinquished, especially as the very search for Being was acknowledged as existential search (Philosophy of Existenz, 1, 21-22). Moreover, like subjectivity, the intended Being was exposed as a primordial unity and as a self-sufficient entity too. Yet, in the later writings, a consistent effort was made to achieve a philosophical understanding of Being (*Sein*) – an understanding which is independent of one's self-understanding, or 'objective' in Jaspers terms. Accordingly, Being is regarded as prior to one's thoughts, rejects them and subordinates them to itself (Way, 59-60)

At the same time, new concepts were inserted into the discussion: world, reality, 'encompassing' (*Umgreifende*) 'cipher' (*chiffre*) and Transcendence. Indeed, these appeared as various constituents of Jaspers' entire conception of Being.

One can phrase Jaspers' shift from philosophy of Existenz to the philosophizing directed at the explication of Being in two ways: either as an

---

as no less than an instrument through which one can achieve contact with the fullness of human life (Psychopathology4, 644).

[38] Jaspers explored this thesis later on. See: Psychopathology4, 624-686.

[39] Jaspers demands thus close contact with the concrete being of the patient. This point reveals an influence of Dilthey' idea of 'Understanding' upon Jaspers' thinking. See especially: Dilthey 1927; 1977; Walker 1995.

[40] See also: Ph3, 4; Ph1, 12; Ph2, 61. Concerning the implications of solipsistic nature of Jaspers' early idea of subjectivity. See: Miron, 2006 (reprinted in this collection as 2006a).

attempt to withdraw from the starting point in which he located his philosophy of Existenz to a more primordial reality – a reality where Existenz represents just one of the possibilities it contains. In Jaspers' words: "[to] the One that [exists] in everything, to the final purpose, to the first-base, the completeness of world and God" (Truth, 36); or as an endeavor to transcend Existenz and to find the way to what he vaguely described as "thinking bounded to one thing" (Truth, 2). One way or another, the philosophizing that was directed at Being reflected the desire to find a comprehensive and lasting perfection to one's self-understanding that may substitute the ephemeral and wasteful part in subjective human life. Additionally, compared to the previous period in Jaspers' writings, as he was critical of the possibility that the objective aspects could be helpful in the understanding of subjectivity. One can regard this development as an effort to rehabilitate of the idea of objectivity into his discourse. Yet, as will become clear later on, even this modification could not enable Jaspers to adopt the corresponding ideas that he recognized in Kant's thinking. Likewise and not independently, the search for objective understanding of Being did not dismiss the decisive role of intuition in Jaspers' thinking.

The above-depicted modifications are recognizable already at the opening to *Philosophy* where Jaspers stated that "Philosophizing starts with our situation" (Ph1, 1). What was new about that was not the understanding of human beings as existing in concrete reality, but the insight that in addition to the freedom to fulfill one's possibilities one is also indiscriminately imposed upon by necessities.[41] These necessities are actually limitations stemming from reality's factuality, and as such are considered as objectivities that human beings cannot change but are obliged to handle within their lives. What Jaspers calls 'world-orientation', which can be achieved by scrutinizing the conditions of the reality external to Existenz, is the aim of what Jaspers calls 'world-orientation'.[42] Thus, independence of one's own self-understanding's needs, and externality to Existenz, signify the foundation of Jaspers' idea of objectivity in the second period of his writing.

The initial understanding of objectivity as externality transpired as playing an important role Jaspers' conception of Being, which he denoted by unique idiom of 'Encompassing' and demonstrated by the following table (Truth, 50):

	The Encompassing that we are ourselves	The Encompassing that is Being itself
Immanent	[Dasein] Existence General Consciousness Spirit	Word
Transcendent	Existenz	Transcendence

---

[41] Jaspers discussed these possibilities in: Ph2, 9,18, 134f. A first version of the idea of 'situation' appeared in: Spiritual Situation, 23. Jaspers continued to explore this term in the context of his famous concept of 'Ultimate Situation' (*Grenzsituationen*). See especially the later version that appeared in: Ph2, 201f (the earlier appeared in: Psychology, 229f).

[42] See especially: Ph1, 61-148.

The 'Encompassing' consists, then, of immanent components (Weisen) as well as transcendent ones.[43] The latter are inaccessible by their very nature, both to the objective viewpoint of consciousness, and to Existenz.[44] The location of 'existence,' 'world' and 'Transcendence' in three different cells signifies different grades of externality to subjectivity, or else various stages in overcoming the particular starting-point, i.e. advancing towards something objective. Moreover, the very fact that Existenz itself is included in the encompassing, and especially including it under the category of 'Transcendent', in the first place indicates that it represents a kind of being which cannot be exhausted by its self-consciousness. This is merely the idea of subjectivity that is identified with the search for Being as something beyond one's self, i.e., something that has also an objective dimension. As one continues elucidating phrases that are more extensive and hence occupy wider externality, one might obtain a comprehensive grip on the idea of Being and hence objective insights are accumulated within the scope of philosophizing. In fact, all the modes of the encompassing are aiming at becoming more lucid. Yet, with the growing lucidity grows also the wish to transcend towards the transcendental dimensions of the encompassing until achieving some sense of 'Being in itself'. Therefore, the mode of 'transcendence', which is defined as the "encompassing of all encompassings" (Truth, 109), is the supreme aspiration of Jaspers' philosophizing upon Being.

Additionally, within the present context, Jaspers made an effort to integrate the viewpoint of 'objective/formal consciousness' (*Bewußtsein Überhaupt*). The very presence of the idea of formal consciousness represents a modification in Jaspers' thinking, for only in regard to the idea of Being did he consolidate a more positive attitude to the objective viewpoint.[45] In fact, Jaspers had never ignored this function of consciousness. Yet, in this context he described 'objective consciousness' as a means for achieving an experience of the presence of Being-in-itself, or of opening ourselves towards the possibility of an 'Other' that we do not recognize and that seems as something we cannot know (Truth, 65). Hence the objective point of view is revealed from the perspective of the 'Encompassing' as no less than one of the sources for uncovering Being itself.[46] Contradictory as that may sound, 'objective consciousness' (*Bewußtsein Überhaupt*) appears as giving support to what it was employed in order to give.

---

[43] It is important to note that the components included in the 'Encompassing' did not represent Jaspers' ontological understanding of Being, for he rejected the very idea of an ontological attempt to give an account of Being. As an alternative to ontology, Jaspers coined his unique term of 'Periechontology' (Truth, 158), which maintained the non-objective understanding of Being. For the etymology of this term, see Knaus (1957), 141-142. For further discussion, see: Heinemann, 70f, Richli, 119f, Kelemen.

[44] Jaspers explained each of those components, adjusting them to his concept of Being. See: Truth, 53-122, Wisdom and Existence, 38-50. For further details about each of the components, see Knaus (1957), 152-161.

[45] This attitude substituted the restrictive and even negative one evoked both from the early writings, where the idea of subjectivity stood at the core of discussion, and in the later writings (see especially Ph2, 4-5; Ph1, 14-15).

[46] The same orientation can be seen in Jaspers' redefinition of the rest of the components. A different interpretation has also appeared in the literature, according to which the elimination of the objective viewpoint serves as a prerequisite for establishing a philosophical attitude towards Being. See: Samay, 48-49; Mader, 55-56.

Obviously, such a perception avoids subordinating the object of observation to the shape of consciousness itself. One may state the contrary, namely that for Jaspers it is consciousness that is adapting itself to object of Being. This is exactly why the use of 'formal consciousness', together with the continuing presence of the non-sensual intuition, do not exclude but complement one another in the context of the elucidation of Being.

The main factor that makes the objective viewpoint of general consciousness relevant to the elucidation of Being is Jaspers' insight that mere "existence in time" (*Zeitdasein*) or the concrete reality does not constitute an actuality on its own but only when one comes to terms with it (Truth, 30-31) and consolidates an active elucidating attitude towards it (Truth, 1, 308f). Hence, what stands behind the appeal to the objective viewpoint it is precisely the need to arrive at an understanding of Being, beyond the unmediated and evident experience of it. Moreover, the understanding of the objective viewpoint as applicable for a multiplicity of objects may suit the elucidation of Being which is also consists of a few elements (*Weisen*) as reflected in the idea of the Encompassing. Here the multiplicity not only reflected the changing faces of the awareness that refers to Being (Truth, 703) that is nourished by different objects (Truth, 36). It also manifested an essential characteristic of Being itself, which is depicted in terms of "splitting" (*Zerrissenheit*) (Truth, 703) and as a "Being of rupture" (*Aufgebrochensein*) that is unable to "close" itself (Truth, 706).[47]

Thus, the multiplicity calls for a varied method that will access each element as well as the entirety that they create altogether. However, the objective viewpoint of general consciousness can be only one of the methods of approaching Being, and is by no means exhaustive. It is especially incapable for transcendent dimensions, which are central to Jaspers' conception of Being. As in his discussion of Existenz, so too in his conception of Being, Jaspers did not back away from his understanding of general consciousness as relative and limited. Nonetheless, instead of dismissing the objective viewpoint for being incomplete, he assigned it to the illumination of the immanent components of the Encompassing.

Apparently, the initial understanding of objectivity as externality to Existenz plus the understanding of 'transcendence' as the furthest reality from the one where Existenz lives, indicates that 'transcendence' is the most objective among the modes of encompassing. On the other hand, the fact that nowhere in all his writings did Jaspers introduce the basis from which he derived the reality of Transcendence, indicates its origination in an a-priori intuition.[48] Yet, this situation does not point to a contradiction within Jaspers' approach to Being, but only to one of its bottomless insights, according to which, within the philosophizing upon Being, mediated objectivity and primordial intuition to join one another. Accordingly, objectivity – to be precise, to search for it – is a means to elevate the particular self-consciousness of oneself and to become open to what exists beyond the subjective being as such (Ph3, 2). Yet at a certain point –

---

[47] See also: Truth, 261, 873, 956. Jaspers used the term "*Zerrissenheit*" also in his discussion on the concepts of "*Welt*" (Ph1, 64f, 78f, 104f, 218f) and "*Dasein*" (Ph2, 249f).

[48] See also a different interpretation, according to which Jaspers' concept of Being was not based on an a-priori intuition. Heinemann (1954), 72.

specifically, after the illumination of the immanent aspect of Being – objectivity is shifted aside in favor of intuition which itself does not need any reasoning.[49]

Concerning the present discussion of Jaspers' Kantianism, the interesting aspect in the above-depicted development is the fact that though Jaspers' thinking was seeking an objective infrastructure to the idea of Being, and was even granted general consciousness by the role of its achieving, Kant's idea of objectivity was not acknowledged as relevant to it. Jaspers' own conception of objectivity, which is elaborated within his discussion of Being, clearly demonstrates that the barrier to the adoption of the Kantian ideas was not Jaspers' rejection of the possibility of achieving some knowledge of it, but the specific conditioning of such knowledge to subjective faculties which might mistakenly lead to the reduction of Being into discursive knowledge. To put it positively, Jaspers was looking for an unconditioned idea of objectivity, something that he was expecting to find in Kant's *'noumena'* or 'thing-in-itself', but was critical of its elimination from Kant's theory of knowledge. Though Jaspers acknowledged the value of the kind of representation of Formal Consciousness, unlike Kant he was reluctant to grant it the total status which he realized in Kant's thinking, but supplemented it with a symbolic approach.[50] This is also an inevitable result of the fact that Being, towards which Jaspers' philosophizing was aimed, is not an object, in both Kant's meanings , as one clearly realizes in the reading suggested by him to Kant. The end is not an object to be known as in the older metaphysics but an awareness of the limits of our knowledge.

The fundamental difficulty is that Kant, in striving to disclose the conditions of all objectivity, is compelled to operate within objective thinking itself, hence in a realm of objects, which must not be treated as objects.

> With his transcendental method he strives to transcend while remaining within the world. He thinks about thoughts (GP, 262).

The case is not that Jaspers did not notice that like him also for Kant "Being remains the central interest" (GP, 256). Moreover, Jaspers even describes the start of the Kantian thinkingin terms that can be in accord to his own. Thus, he wrote, "Kant wishes to think beyond the dichotomy to the ground from which it springs". Yet, "he [Kant] does so only by means of categories and objectivizations which themselves belong to the dichotomy" (GP, 259). This, and not Kant's original wish with which Jaspers could easily have identified himself, is the explanation for the dualistic ending that led to the result in which "the question of Being becomes the question of being-thought" (GP, 251). Indeed, Jaspers' determination that with Kant "everything that exists for us is an object of thought" (251) can be misleading, and hence needs an explanation. Elsewhere Jaspers himself determined that "to interpret Kant's thought as meaning that the world is

---

[49] The joining of the intuitive aspect with that of 'formal consciousness' is most explicit within the discussion of the 'cipher', which signifies the understanding that both the immanent reality and objectivity are a symbol or cipher of transcendence. See: Ph3, pp. 128-173; Truth, 1022-1054. Usually Jaspers used the terms 'Symbol' and *'Chiffre'* as synonyms. See: Hoffman, 108; Thyssen, 310; Klein, 88.

[50] Jaspers explored his symbolic view within his conception of the "reading of the Ciphers" (*Chiffreschrift*). See: Ph3, 128-168.

produced by the subjectivity of man's mental constitution... is to reduce it to absurdity" (GP, 261). In addition to that, he rejects as a mistake the judging of Kant as a dualist due to the two stems of the human thinking: sensibility and understanding. Yet, all that cannot change what seemed to Jaspers as a fact, that:

> In the elucidation of the medium in which we live and think, Kant is dualistic. But the two sources of knowledge are not to his mind two principles of Being; rather Being is invoked as the one root, which remains unknown to us. Being is conceived dualistically only in respect to the form through which we gain awareness of it. Kant's metaphysics is not dualistic in the sense of conceiving two primal powers... But he [Kant] is impelled to think dualistically for the purpose of exploring a field in which paths to unity are subsequently sought and found. (GP, 255).

Jaspers, then, clearly distinguished between Kant's primordial origin and the actual performance of his thinking. Whereas the latter refers to the consequence about which he is critical, with the former Jaspers could easily have identified. The criticism refers to the inability to preserve and give representation to what Jaspers regarded as Kant's 'desirable' beginnings that consequently did not last within that thinking itself. However, when one takes into consideration Jaspers' own thinking, one cannot be sure whether describing the start of the Kantian thinking in terms of 'unity', 'mystery' and 'secrets' is not actually a self-depiction. In that respect, Jaspers is decent for addressing his judgment to the actual carrying out of the Kantian thinking. If Jaspers is correct, then one can tell that Kant is more faithful to his method, i.e. to the analytical tools that he explored, than to his original wishes as a philosopher. Therefore, when Jaspers states that Kant "does not abandon himself" (GP, 259), he refers especially to the actual performance of his thinking and not to its initial interest, i.e. the interest he realized as motivating the Kantian thinking. Against this background one can understand the conclusion according to which Kant's philosophy was "not self-sufficient" (GP, 372), i.e., it was not so only if one confronts it with the beginning that Jaspers attributed to it. Finally, for Jaspers, the decisive factor in the evaluation of Kant's thinking was especially the bottom line, or what he acknowledged as the end results of it.

However, whereas Jaspers' assumption concerning the beginning of Kantian thinking remains vague and is not supported with a discernable reasoning, the connection of such a beginning to his own philosophical project is very prominent. Jaspers' aiming towards a mysterious entity, which was present already in the early writings, where it functioned especially as a critical argument against the positivistic approach of the sciences, finds its more explored continuation within the discussion of Being. There he regards the feeling of enchantment (Truth, 1031), the experience of wonder as one finds himself standing before a reality which is imbued with a secret (Truth, 1048), as indispensable to standing before Being. Moreover, Jaspers determines that "only the loosening of possible Existenz lets intrinsic Being be grasped, so that all relativity, all sublimation of the modes of Being, serves this one suspension that makes me aware of Being" (Ph3, 162).

However, the state of mind required for getting a grip on the idea of Being, by no means conflicts with the consistent effort to rehabilitate the above-discussed idea of objectivity. The following clarification by Jaspers is designated precisely to prevent any mystification of the philosophical conception of Being:

> Immersion in symbols is not the mystical immersion, the entrance into non-objectiveness of transcendence by way of an objectless and thus incommunicable union. Rather, as I hear the symbolic language, the phenomenon of transcendence is articulated for my Existenz in the medium of lucid consciousness, with the subject-object dichotomy maintained... Like the elucidation of consciousness in world orientation, elucidation in the symbol proceeds here by way of objectivity... (Ph3, 16-17).

Undoubtedly, both the maintenance of the dialogue with the subject-object dichotomy, and the accompanying emotional experience are connecting points between Jaspers and Kant. Nonetheless, sharing the same sensation of standing in front of a mystery – be it true or not – was not sufficient to treat Kantian thinking a source of contents to adopt. These are only beginnings, intentions, that according to Jaspers do not survive in Kant's thinking as a whole, or at least lose their genuine meaning. Thus, when intuition and the sense of mystery are dissolved, the subject-object dichotomy is taken to the extreme, until it ends in dualism. At the present point, Jaspers' accusation of Kant for "creating no symbols" (GP, 372) becomes transparent by its comprehensive implications. By these words Jaspers is not only referring to what he regarded as Kant's inability release himself from the oppression of the discursive thinking which remains attached to its formulations, and thus erodes the primordial intuition; the same intuition which Jaspers realized as existing in Kant's critical philosophy. Moreover, it is especially evident to the specific stance of Jaspers when facing Kant's thinking: as a completion to the unfinished voyage towards Being in itself.

To be sure, Jaspers did not ignore the value of Kantian thinking. As a matter of a fact, exactly what Jaspers appreciated in Kant, i.e., "the depth of his fundamental philosophical idea lies precisely in the involvement of his method... in the fact that all the aspects we thus clarify belong to an idea which itself cannot be elucidated as a determinate, particular idea" (GP, 270), itself provided the reason for criticizing it: firstly it refers to the supreme principle according to which, "everything we know as reality must enter into some mathematical forms that can be known a priori" (GP, 249).

Concerning this, Jaspers claims that "Kant forgoes richness of content, because he wishes to convey pure consciousness of 'forms'. Forms are superior to philosophical embodiment" (GP, 372-373). Additionally he explains, "When we unravel these methods, we are left with a number of philosophically ineffectual parts. The fundamental idea cannot be defined by any method... it is only in their interplay that the truth of the philosophical insight is disclosed" (GP, 270). This criticism stands not only for Kant's concept of Being, which includes by the same token his idea of objectivity, but also for the previously discussed idea of subjectivity.

Jaspers, then, was longing for positive contents about the subjective being and Being, namely exactly what appeared to him as absent the actual performance of Kant's philosophy. For Jaspers, the substance of one's thinking is not necessarily the form or the method one creates, but the embodiment of real objects, of ontological entities which one acknowledges as already given to him in an undivided unity. So are the ideas of subjectivity and of Being, i.e. they do not represent a conscious representation of what Kant would have called Being-in-itself, but are first-given through an intuition. It is exactly the absence of any definition of these in Jaspers' writings that express their primordial given nature. A conscious synthesis appeared to him more as subsequent to what is already given then as a constitutive process. Thus, differently from Kant's mediated way of approaching the ideas of objectivity and subjectivity which led to the perception of them as a discursive synthesis which is never the object itself (GP, 252) – a way of which he is critical – Jaspers himself remains faithful to the primordial intuition which is not damaged by the philosophical explication. Thus, Jaspers' thinking assigns itself especially to the illumination of the way intuition functions within the experience of thinking and to the uncovering of a suitable way that represents its most comprehensive objects: I and Being-in-Itself. Thus, instead of the vision that regards the ideas of objectivity and subjectivity as analytical concepts that function in a theory of knowledge, Jaspers treats them as independent targets of philosophizing. Finally, Jaspers' distance from what he recognized as Kantian ideas cannot be exhausted by the differences in the "formulation" or historical context as suggested in the literature. Also, there are substantial differences in the "content" that fills the ideas themselves and which could not have met the meaning of objectivity and subjectivity, which appeared to Jaspers as Kantian. In that respect, Jaspers is quite minor in the way he proclaims his criticism of Kant.

Postscript and Summary

My understanding of Jaspers' work as reacting to that of Kant is the main reason for employing a comparative method. This is intended to demonstrate how Jaspers' acquaintance with Kantian thinking was influential on the consolidation of his meta-philosophy. In this context, the standard picture concerning Jaspers' Kantianism played an important role. Indeed, the challenge of reconsidering the existing agreement among scholars was taken up only after an effort had been made to uncover the logic behind such an understanding of Jaspers' thinking. Paying attention to the significance of the historical setting, which was demonstrated at the beginning of the discussion, was helpful in revealing the specific method employed by the representatives of the reading of Jaspers as Kantian, i.e., reading his writings backwards, or from the relatively later ones to the earlier. Indeed, reading Jaspers' work as Kantian appears sympathetic compared to the familiar evaluation of it, that has often accused him of suggesting no consistent philosophical instruments[51]; of being 'a hovering philosopher' who cannot determine anything positive given his extreme faithfulness to the

---

[51] Hoffman, 95.

adventure of a radical openness[52]; of being immersed in the movement towards the whole and hence unable to express his own ideas.[53] All these appear as outcomes of Jaspers' expressive writing. However, regarding Jaspers as Kantian grants him the advantages of Kant's thinking, in particular an epistemological reasoning to his ideas.

Notwithstanding, reading Jaspers backwards seemed to me not only as granting his thinking an epistemological reasoning, which he actually does not need due to the great weight of intuition in it; but also failing to notice the ontological implications that emerge from the specific reaction to Kant, and so misses Jaspers' specific stancewhen facing Kant's thinking. Additionally, my feeling of difficulty in accepting the standard picture was even intensified as I realized the gap between Jaspers' empathic reading of Kant's philosophy, which by no means manipulated it, and his criticism of it where that reading seemed to vanish. In order to give reason to these arguments, I suggested reading Jaspers' work forwards, i.e. from the early writings to the later ones, and so follow concurrently Jaspers' understanding of Kant's ideas of subjectivity and objectivity and his own exploration of the same themes. Obviously, this compelled referring to the writings where Jaspers consolidated his conception of these ideas, namely those which cover the two distinguished periods, while those writings written after WWII were excluded from the discussion.[54] Admittedly, thismethod also has its own historical setting, i.e., the criticism of the positivistic approach in sciences that generated Jaspers' early ideas of subjectivity and objectivity, out of which his whole philosophical project developed. However, this choice seemed to me as naturally derived from the actual carrying out of Jaspers' philosophizing, whereas the inverted perspective seemed problematic for imposing something alienated from it. One wonders why at all base the understanding of Jaspers as Kantian on presumable benefits that he could have derived from it, and not on what Jaspers actually found in Kant's thinking? In other words, what is needed is to demonstrate in what way Kant may contribute to the understanding of Jaspers' entire project. The fact that the understanding of Jaspers as Kantian did not provide an answer to this decisive question, is thus the reason for substituting it with the immanent method; a method that phenomenologically follows the echoing of Jaspers' stance towards Kant, both within the actual performance in his writings, and in his commentary on Kant's critical philosophy.

Consequently, unlike the common understanding of Jaspers as Kantian, the suggested interpretation clearly shows that though he had Kant's thinking in the back of his mind, it did not appear as a resource for contents to adopt, but as a basis to transcend from. To be precise, I contend that Jaspers' criticism of Kant – especially of the ideas of subjectivity and objectivity to which the exposition above referred – can be seen as a crucial infrastructure to his own philosophy. Indeed, the early split between the two philosophers, gives reason to the different outcomes of their work. Instead of the Kantian dualism which consolidates a

---

[52] Heinemann, 65, 71. See also: Mader, 58.
[53] Richli, 119, 142-143.
[54] The accurate referring to the time of writing and not to that of appearance takes into consideration the fact that in at 1938 the Nazi regime enacted a prohibition against the publishing of Jaspers' books, and they only appeared after the war .

theory of knowledge in which objectivity and subjectivity are mutually conditioned, Jaspers' thinking was led by a non-sensual intuition; the ideas of objectivity and subjectivity that appear in it not only do not function in a theory of knowledge, but also there is no theory that could pave the way to them since they are already given. The philosophical explication cannot constitute these ideas, but uncovers their independent given nature. Lastly, Kant appeared to Jaspers as remaining in a dichotomy in which objectivity and subjectivity do not touch each other but subordinate one another. Conversely, in regard to the content granted to both ideas in Jaspers' thinking they appear in a consecutive order where subjectivity precedes objectivity but is also preserved in it in a more ripe shape as a subject being who searches for Being.

My analysis intended to show that the same thing that did not enable Jaspers to rely on what he regarded as Kant's idea of subjectivity was the reason preventing him from making use of the idea of objectivity, i.e., the consistent commitment to a non-sensual intuition. Yet the contribution of Kantian thinking was not totally dismissed, for the disagreements about contents do not exclude the possibility of being inspired by structure. This can find both positive and negative support. On the one hand, for Jaspers, the "greatness in Kant's thinking" lies in the thinking of forms and limits that dominate it but "not in any academic knowledge of Kantian concepts" (GP, 373). This acknowledgment is clearly reflected in Jaspers' idea of seeking the borders of philosophizing and of the human experience and in his scrutinizing of the possibility of transcending them. Moreover, also Kant's distinction between limits (*Schranken*), which are "mere negations which affect a quantity so far as it is not absolutely complete, and 'bounds' (*Grenzen*) which always presuppose a space existing outside a certain definite place and inclosing it",[55] is evidently echoed in Jaspers' division between 'contextual borders' (*jeweilige Grenzen*) and 'principle borders' (*prinzipielle Grenzen*) (Ph1, 45). Whereas the former are temporal and disappear once the philosopher has reached an understanding of his objects, the latter undermine the understanding of the human world as a phenomenon, since in the face of them the rational tools cease to be functional and hence they bring the philosopher to an unsurpassable barrier, which signifies his finitude. Yet, they still open the question of having an idea about what lies beyond the human world, i.e., the Transcendence (Ph1, 45). Therefore, exactly as Kant, so also Jaspers aimed to mark the space in which his philosophizing would take place, namely achieving a concrete content. On the other hand, Jaspers' different implementation of the thinking of limits provides the support from negative side. Actually, the common structure of marking the limits resulted in different goals of philosophizing: Kant withdrew into the realm of Reason related especially to its product, i.e., knowledge. So he stated: "Our reason… sees in its surroundings a space for knowledge of things in themselves, though we can never have definite concepts of them, and are limited to appearances only".[56] Conversely, Jaspers could not be satisfied only within the realm of reason or in what can be crystallized as knowledge, and was longing for what transcends the marked limits of reason

---

[55] Kant, *Prologomena*, 101.
[56] Ibid.

from both directions – to the particular that cannot be generalized and to the transcendent that is beyond generalization as such. In Jaspers' words:

> In philosophizing on the ground of possible Existenz we take up everything conceivable and knowable we meet in our search; we want Existenz to come out of this, but Existenz is not the final goal. The philosophizing urge goes beyond it. It wants Existenz to dissolve again, in transcendence. Philosophical thought is a beacon (*Scheinwerfer*); it means not only the lighted object but the light itself... (Ph1, 27).

Jaspers, then, exposed two ways of radicalizing of Kant's ethos: either to begin earlier than him or to continue to philosophize after the point where Kant's philosophy culminated. Thus, the two specific objects at which Jaspers' thinking was aiming, subjectivity or Existenz and Being, are not elaborated in Kant's thinking. One can put it also in the following way: Jaspers idea of subjectivity could not have met that of Kant because of the objective shape which eliminated from it any concrete aspect due to the method of transcendental deduction. Additionally, the idea of objectivity, as it arose from Jaspers' explication of Being, is also far from that of Kant, which nonetheless appears as conditioned upon the subjective facilities of the human consciousness. In other words, according to his understanding of Kant, Jaspers rejected Kant's idea of subjectivity for being too objective and that of objectivity for being too subjective. Thus a complicated mode of an influence between Jaspers and Kant was revealed, namely adopting the frame or better the ethos of seeking borders, but not the content with which it is filled. Accordingly, Jaspers' hunger for positive content about his objects of Philosophizing could not find then a relief in what was suggested in Kant's philosophy, for it did not dare to break through the limits imposed by itself, and hence was not radical enough for him. In the end, Jaspers not only rejected the specific contents which were achieved in Kant's philosophy, but especially the very possibility that a theory of knowledge could become accessible to the two targets of his philosophizing: subjectivity and Being. Instead of the definable way traced by Kant, Jaspers suggested something that he regarded as secured against any need of reasoning: an ontological persuasion that Existenz and Being are present to the one who looks for them. Nonetheless, one may still hesitate whether the above-explicated disparities between the two philosophers might allow viewing Jaspers as complementing Kant or actually put their work on separate scales.

Jaspers' books and their abbreviations in this article

1912. "Die phänomenologische Forschungsrichtung in Psychopathologie," *Zeitschrift für die gesamte Neurologie und Psychiatrie*, 9, (1912), 391–408 (Phen.).

1913. *Allgemeine Psychopathologie, Ein Leitfaden für Studierende, Ärtze un Psychologen*, Berlin. (Psychopathology1).

1937. *Existenzphilosophie*. 3rd edition. Berlin: Walter de Gruyter, [1937] 1964 (Philosophy of Existenz).

1942. *Allgemeine Psychopathologie*, Berlin-Heidelberg, 8. Aufl. 1965 (Psychopathology4).
1931. *Die geistige Situation der Zeit*, Berlin-Leipzig (Spiritual Situation).
1946. *Die Idee der Universität*, Schriften der Universität Heidelberg, Heft 1, Berlin (IdU).
1919. "Kants Ideenlehre" in: *Psychologie der Weltanschauungen*, Heidelberg (IL).
1958. *Max Weber, Politiker-Forscher-Philosoph*, München (Weber).
1950. *Nietzsche, Einführung in das Verständnis seines Philosophierens*, Berlin (Nietzsche).
1941. "On my Philosophy", trans. F. Kaufmann, in: *Existentialism from Dostoevsky to Sartre*, ed. W. Kaufmann. Cleveland, 1956 (translation of "Über meine Philosophie") (OmP).
1932. *Philosophie* (1-3), Heidelberg (1994) (Ph1, Ph2, Ph3).
1957. "Philosophical Autobiography", in Schilpp (ed.), 3-94 (PA).
1955. *Schelling, Größe und Verhängnis*, München (Schelling).
1962. *The Great Philosophers*, Ralf Manheim (trans.), Hannah Arendt (ed.), London (GP).
1951. *Über Bedingungen und Möglichkeiten eines neuen Humanismus*. München (BuM).
1950. *Vernunft und Widervenunft in unserer Zeit, Drei Gastvorlesungen*, München 1950 (VuW).
1959. *Vernunft und Freiheit*, Ausgewählte Schriften, Stuttgart-Zürich-Salzburg (VuF).

Secondary literature

Allison, E, Henry (1983), *Kant's Transcendental Idealism: An Intepretation and Defense*, Yale University Press, New Haven and London.
Cesana, Andreas (1993), "Philosophie als dritter Weg. Zum Philosophieverständnis von Jaspers und Kant", in: Ehrlich, H. Leonard & Wisser, Richard (eds.), *Karl Jaspers: Philosoph under Philosophen*, Würzburg, 22-27.
Dilthey, Wilhelm (1927), *Der Aufbau der geschichtlichen Welt in den Geisteswissenschaften*, Leipzig, 79-188.
----- (1927), "The Understanding of the Other Person and Their Expressions of Life", in: *Descriptive Psychology and Historical Understanding*, (R.M. Zaner and K.L. Heiger, trans.) 1977, The Hague, 127-147.
Ehrlich, Leonard (1975), *Karl Jaspers: Philosophy as Faith*, Amhurst.
Gerber, J. Rudolf (1969), "Karl Jaspers and Kantian Reason", *New Scholasticism*, Vol. 43, 400-423.
Grünert, Erich (1956), "Der Einfluss Kants auf Karl Jaspers: Zugang zur Transzendenz bei Kant und Karl Jaspers", *Freiburger Zeitschrift für Philosophie und Theologie*, Bd. III, 21-28.
Häfner, Heinz (1986), "Einleitung in den Psychiatrischen Teil", in: Hersch 1986, 83-87.

Heidegger, Martin (1921), "Anmerkungen zu Karl Jaspers' Psychologie der Weltanschauungen (1919)", in: Saner, Hans (ed.) (1973), *Karl Jaspers in der Diskussion*, München, 1973, 70-100.

Heinemann, Fritz (1954), *Existenzphilosophie—lebendig oder tot?*, Stuttgart.

Hersch, Jeanne & Lochman Jan Milic & Wiehl Reiner (eds.) (1986), *Karl Jaspers—Philosoph, Artzt, politischer Denker*, München & Zürich (Hersch, 1986).

Hoffman, Kurt (1957), "The Basic Concepts of Jaspers' Philosophy", in Schilpp (ed.), 95-113.

Holz, H. (1977), "Philosophischer Glaube und Intersubjektivität: zum Glaubsensproblem bei Immanuel Kant und Karl Jaspers", *Kant-Studien, Philosophische Zeitschrift der Kant Gesellschaft*, 68, 404-419.

Janzarik, Werner (1986), "Jaspers, Kurt Schneider und die Heidelberger Psychopathologie", in: Hersch (1986), 112-126.

Jung, Carl G. (1966), *Persönlichkeit und Übertragung, Grundwerke*, 2, Zürich und Düsseldorf.

Kant, Immanuel (1933), *Critique of Pure Reason*, N. Kemp Smith (trans.), Basingstoke and London.

Kant, Immanuel (1950), *Prologomena to Any Future Metaphysics*, New York.

Kelemen, Janos (1993), "The 'Thing-in-itself' and the 'Encompassing'" in: Ehrlich, H. Leonard & Wisser, Richard (eds.), *Karl Jaspers: Philosoph under Philosophen*, Würzburg, 18-21.

Klein, Aloys (1973), *Glaube und Mythos, Eine kritische, religionphilosophische thelolgische Undersuchung des Mythos-Begriffs bei Karl Jaspers*, München.

Knauss, Gerhard (1957), "The Concept of the 'Encompassing' in Jaspers' Philosophy", in: Schilpp (ed.), 141-176.

Kornmüller, Hellmuth (1965), "Karl Jaspers' Philosophy of History", *Modern Schoolman: A Quarterly Journal of Philosophy*, 42, 129-152.

Leonard, Joachim-Felix (ed.) (1983), *Karl Jaspers in seiner Heidelberger Zeit*, Heidelberg.

Lichtigfeld, Adolf (1962), "Jaspers' Philosophical Basis (Kant or Hegel)", *Kant Studien, Philosophische Zeitschrift der Kant Gesellschaft*, 53, 29-38.

Mader, Johann (1975), "Das Seindenken bei Karl Jaspers", *Wissenschaft und Weltbild*, 10, 50-58.

Milmed, Bella K. (1954), "Theories of Religious Knowledge from Kant to Jaspers", *Philosophy, the Journal of the Royal Institute of Philosophy*, 29, 195-215.

Miron, Ronny (2004), "From Opposition to Reciprocity—Karl Jaspers on Science, Philosophy and What Lies Between Them", *International Philosophical Quarterly*, New York, 44/2 (2004), 147-163. (Reprinted in this collection as 2004c).

Miron, Ronny (2006), "Towards Reality: The Development of the Philosophical Attitude to Reality in Karl Jaspers' Thought", *Journal of the British Society for Phenomenology*, 37/2, 2006, 152-172. (Reprinted in this collection as 2006a).

O'Connor, B.F. (1988), *A Dialogue between Philosophy and Religion: The Perspective of Karl Jaspers*, MD: University Press of America.

Olson, Alan M. (1979), *Transcendence and Hermeneutics, An Interpretation of the Philosophy of Karl Jaspers*, Boston-London.
Plümacher, Martina (1996), *Philosophie nach 1945 in der Bundesrepublik Deutschland*, Hamburg.
Radbruch, Knut (1993), "Ein mathematischer Blick auf die Philosophie von Kant und Jaspers" in: Ehrlich, H. Leonard & Wisser, Richard (eds.), *Karl Jaspers: Philosoph under Philosophen*, Würzburg, 11-17.
Richli, Urs (1967), *Transzendental Reflexion und sittliche Entscheidung, Zum Problem der Selbsterkenntnis der Metaphysik bei Jaspers und Kant*, Bonn.
Samay, Sebastian (1971), *Reason Revisited: The Philosophy of Karl Jaspers*, Dublin.
Sarin, Indu (1993), "Freedom and Reason. Jaspers and Kant", in: Ehrlich, H. Leonard & Wisser, Richard (eds.), *Karl Jaspers: Philosoph under Philosophen*, Würzburg, 29-40.
Schilpp, Paul Arthur (ed.) (1957), *The Philosophy of Karl Jaspers*, New York.
Spiegelberg, Herbert (1972), *Phenomenology in Pscyhology and Psychiatry*, Evanstone.
Thyssen, Johannes (1957), "The Concept of 'Foundering' in Jaspers' Philosophy", in: Schilpp (ed.), 297-335.
Walker, Chris (1993), "Karl Jaspers as a Kantian Psychopathologist, I: The Philosophical Origins of the Concept of Form and Content", *History of Psychiatry*, Vol. 4, 209-266.
Walker, Chris (1995), "Karl Jaspers and Edmund Husserl – IV: Phenomenology as Empathic Understanding", *Philosophy, Psychiatry and Psychology*, Vol. 2, No. 3, 247-266.
Walters, G. J. (1988), *Karl Jaspers and the Role of 'Conversion' in the Nuclear Age*, Langham, MD: University Press of America.
Wiggins, O.P., Schwarts, M.A., Spitzer, M. (1992), "Phenomenological/Descriptive Psychiatry: The Methods of Edmund Husserl and Karl Jaspers", in: Spitzer, Manfred & Uehlein, Freidrich & Schwarts, Michael A. (eds.), *Phenomenology, Language & Schizophrenia*, New York-Berlin, 46-69.
Young-Bruehl, Elisabeth (1981), *Freedom and Karl Jaspers' Philosophy*, New Haven.

Between Freedom and Necessity: The Conception of Guilt in Jaspers' Thought

> We should absolutely not say that we have already lost everything. As long as we have not wasted in desperate rage what could have been for us unlosable: the elements of history—for us [this element is] first and foremost the thousand years of German history, then the history of the west, and finally the history of the entire human race ... We will gain contact with what human beings have experienced all over the world in the most extreme manner. A German ostracized in his fatherland will find his support in the spaces of this humanity.[1]

These words, appearing in the opening of the periodical *Die Wandlung* (*The Change*), which started publication in 1945, express to a large extent the central issue that occupied Jaspers in his writings published after the war, including the essay *Die Schuldfrage* (*The Question of Guilt*)[2], whose analysis forms the core of the discussion in this article. The immediate reality to which this essay responds is post-war Germany, a reality characterized by far-reaching changes to the social and political being of the Germans. Jaspers accepted the offer of Basel University in Switzerland to serve as Professor of Philosophy, and left Germany in 1947. However, he participated in the effort of German intellectuals in this period—Gadamer, Habermas, and others—to propose a new substrate upon which would be formed a new German identity with universal values, without being detached from the German past and heritage.[3] Jaspers feared that along with the efforts to constitute what was termed a "different Germany" the cultural tradition developed in German would be forgotten, as would dealing with the guilt related

---

[1] Karl Jaspers, *Die Wandlung* 1 (1945): 5, cited in Plümacher 1996, 20. Jaspers founded this periodical along with the journalist Rudolf Sternberger.
[2] Karl Jaspers, *Die Schuldfrage*. Heidelberg: L. Schneider, 1946; Karl Jaspers, *The Question of German Guilt*. Trans. E.B. Ashton. New York: Fordham University Press, 2000 (hereafter: The Question of Guilt). All citations of this work in this article refer to the English version, and any page numbers in parantheses in the article body and notes refer to this English version.
[3] On the various trends in the writings of German intellectuals during this period, see Plümacher 1996, 23-29.

to the crimes committed during the Nazi period. Like the other writings Jaspers published after the war, characterized by a more fluent style compared with his philosophical writings, and aimed at a wide readership, the essay *The Question of Guilt* presented human freedom and its determinations regarding the truth and necessity of universal humanistic values as the corner stone upon which the new Germany would be constituted.

Contemporary events play an important role in understanding Jaspers' turning to deal with the issue of German guilt, and his understanding and interpretation of the essay *The Question of Guilt*. However, I argue that we can expose the full meaning of Jaspers' position in this essay only by turning to the perspective of his philosophical writings. Jaspers systematically and uniquely developed the concept of guilt already in his early essay *Psychology of Worldviews*, published in 1919, and discussed it in depth in his important work *Philosophy* from 1932. The discussion of the concept of guilt in his philosophical writings is very abstract and different in nature to that appearing in *The Question of Guilt*, which is accompanied by examples taken from post-war German reality. However, Jaspers' appeal, at the beginning of *The Question of Guilt*, "Philosophy and theology are called on to illumine the depths of the question of guilt" (22), hints at the wide horizon from which he started clarifying the question of German guilt.[4] The article aims to present from the wide perspective of the whole of his oeuvre Jaspers' perception of guilt, from which his position to the worthy character of post-war German society and culture was derived. I will show the covert presence of some of Jaspers' most central philosophical ideas in this essay, which seems to have granted him a special opportunity to examine the possibility of their implementation in a real-life context. The discussion will focus on three ideas: selfhood (*Selbstsein*), historicity (*Geschichtlichkeit*), and boundary situations (*Grenzsituationen*). A different view of guilt was formulated around each of them, but the three viewpoints join together in a process with one purpose: to recognize the guilt and turn it into a permanent element in the identity of Germans and human beings in general—as individuals and as part of a culture and a nation.

The Question of Guilt from the Viewpoint of Selfhood

This essay is unique compared with other writings of Jaspers' in this period thanks to Jaspers' personal tone, sometimes verging upon confessional, as can be seen in the following:

---

[4] The requirement for philosophical support will be answered in this article through revealing and elucidating the hidden presence of Jaspers' philosophical ideas. In contrast, the statement that a theological perspective is also required is strange, since Jaspers anchors his discussion in *The Question of Guilt* in a process of personal clarification (as transpires below), and in light of his explicit words: "The question of original sin must not become a way to dodge German guilt. Knowledge of original sin is not yet insight into German guilt. But neither must the religious confession of original sin serve as a guide for a false German confession of collective guilt, with the one in dishonest haziness taking the place of the other" (94). Jaspers' theological position was clarified in several contexts. See for example EM, Philosophical Faith in the Face of Revelation.

> We Germans differ greatly in the kind and degree of our participation in, or resistance to, National-Socialism. Everyone must reflect on his own internal and external conduct, and seek his own peculiar rebirth in this German crisis. Another difference between individuals concerns the starting time of this inner metamorphosis... In these matters we Germans cannot be reduced to a common denominator. We must keep an open mind in approaching each other from essentially different starting points (98).

Against the background of recognizing the variety of attitudes toward the Nazi regime that characterized German society, Jaspers concluded that "In this kind of talking none is the other's judge; everyone is both defendant and judge at the same time" (8). The central role granted to the personal dealing of individuals with Nazism greatly reduces the role of the objective or external observation directed to the German by those who are not German, but does not completely negate it. Indeed, Jaspers himself states that "The guilt question is more than a question put to us by others, it is one we put to ourselves" (22). The explanation given for the focus on the individual stems from the philosophical perspective directed at clarifying the issue of guilt: "philosophically, the first thing required of anyone dealing with guilt questions is that he deal with himself" (101). So guilt expresses the person's relationship with himself, and thus recognizing it requires the range of emotional and mental skills involved in forming self-consciousness. Indeed, a demand from an external source—other people, the state, or general moral norms—influences the individual and the formation of his personality. However, the arena in which handling the guilt occurs is the internal boundaries of the individual's selfhood. In any case, and to remove doubt, Jaspers clarified that the philosophical perspective he offered as a tool to deal with the guilt does not express any comfort or a distant attitude to the factors that cause the guilt, quite the opposite: "For the first thing each of us needs in disaster is clarity about himself. The foundation of our new life must come from the origin of our being and can only be achieved in unreserved self-analysis" (84).[5] The basic starting point in Jaspers' approach to the question of German guilt is anchored, it transpired, in appealing to the Germans as individuals to observe themselves inwardly and examine their attitude to the Nazi regime.

However, beyond stating that the philosophical examination of selfhood is essential for clarifying the issue of guilt, *The Question of Guilt* contains no clarification of the nature of the selfhood behind Jaspers' determinations regarding the personal stance of German individuals vis-à-vis Nazism. In contrast, in his pre-war writings, starting with his early works on psychiatry and up to his mature philosophical works, he dedicated extensive space to clarifying the issue of selfhood and the foundations upon which it is constructed. This is not the place to offer a philosophical discussion of Jaspers' perception of selfhood, which I have discussed elsewhere[6]. For our discussion of the issue of guilt it

---

[5] Throughout the essay, the discussion of guilt is anchored in the idea of the "self": e.g., 6-17, 32-37, 78 ff.

[6] See Ronny Miron, "Transcendence and Dissatisfaction in Jaspers' Idea of the Self", in: *Phaenomenologische Forschungen*, NS. 10, 2005, 221-241 [Reprinted in this collection as Miron, 2005].

suffices to mention the main milestones in Jaspers' attempt to exhaust the particular viewpoint of the individual's subjective being. So, for example, in his early days as a psychiatrists and researcher into mental illness, Jaspers sought to form an understanding regarding the patient's complete personality and world as a basis for determining the relevance of scientific definitions to his needs and concrete situation (Psychopathology1, 1). His main argument was that the person's individuality places a boundary (*Grenze*)[7] that cannot be crossed or overcome through the objective criteria derived from the conceptual system of the science of psychopathology (ibid., 1-2). Jaspers did not suggest ignoring scientific considerations in treating mentally ill patients, but to add to them considerations related to the patient's subjective personality in order to enable a meeting with what he termed "the mental in its real reality" (ibid., 12).[8]

Jaspers' interest in the particular aspects of the individual continued and even deepened after he decided to leave the field of psychiatry and turn to philosophy. In *Psychology of Worldviews*, Jaspers placed the subjective being at the focus of a systematic and structured discussion describing and elucidating the individual experiences that determined its self-perception—a perception whose encompassing expression is the "worldview" (*Weltanschauung*) the individual forms by himself.[9] Unlike knowledge (*Wissen*), acquired in a defined context that determines its boundaries and sets "objective" criteria for testing it, the worldview according to Jaspers expresses the entirety of a person's world. It embodies simultaneously both the person's concrete experiences and his ability to objectivize these experiences in order to obtain wider understanding of himself in reality (Psychology, 1-2). Jaspers argued that the infinite variance, reflected in the ways people experience reality and the ways they perceive themselves, does not enable the achievement of an exhaustive and complete understanding of a person's private being: "We do not seek the frequent or the average... we seek

---

[7] Jaspers' usage of the concept of boundary to demonstrate the particular nature a mental illness may wear with individuals who suffer from it is generally equivalent to Kant's distinction between limits (*Schranke*) and bounds (*Grenze*) (see Immanuel Kant, "Prologmena to any future metaphysics that will be able to come forward as a science". Trans. Gary Hatfield. In : *Immanuel Kant: Theoretical Philosophy after 1781*. Henry Allison and Peter Heath (eds.) New York: Cambridge University Press, 2002, 142. In his philosophical writings, Jaspers made this distinction into one of the central parameters in his method of philosophizing that brought him to its clearest crystallization in the concept of "boundary situations" to be discussed later in this article. See in this context Jaspers' basic distinction between *jeweilige Grenzen* and *prinzipielle Grenzen*. See note 27 below.

[8] In the background of this was Jaspers' criticism of the positivistic viewpoint that was prevalent in the science of psychopathology during his period. Jaspers called this approach "prejudices" of psychiatry, and defined as "mythologies of the brain" the perceptions based on the contemporary premise viewing mental illness as a disease of the brain (Psychopathology1, 8).

[9] The concept of worldview is one of the most central in German culture, and has various philosophical and psychological meanings. The tension between "world-knowing" (*Welterkennen*) and "self-knowing" (*Selbsterkennen*) characterizes the various thinkers who clarified the issue of worldview. For further discussion, see Heidegger's interpretation of *Psychology* and the interpretations of Dilthey and Max Scheler to the issue of worldview, which have many connections to Jaspers' interpretation. See Saner 1973, 70-100; Dilthey 1962; Scheler 1954.

the specific patterns even if these are quite rare. Our field... [is] what we notice in the historical, internal, living experience, and [the experience] present in the peculiar thing, even if it is unique" (ibid., 14). So, in this context too the handling of the general and structural aspects characteristic of worldviews is pushed to the margins of the discussion in favor of focusing on subjectivity as a being whose efforts to obtain better self-understanding are expressed in its worldview.

Jaspers' interest in the particular dimensions of subjectivity reached its peak crystallization in the philosophy of Existenz. While in his early writings subjectivity was discussed through the mediation of other topics ("mental illness", worldviews), in *Philosophy*—Jaspers' mature and best-known philosophical work—subjectivity is discussed directly and was termed henceforth Existenz.[10] At the center of the philosophical elucidation of Existenz is the requirement *"to be from within the source of my selfhood"* (Ph2:6).[11] The possibility of forming an objective understanding of a person was also examined in this context, this time through testing the possible contribution of the formal and objective viewpoint of consciousness. Jaspers admits that it is possible to indicate what is the person's "objective existence" in the world as reflected in his activity and the contexts in which it takes place. However, the constant gap Jaspers identified between the person's being and the contexts in which he participates,[12] due to the freedom characterizing his activity within them, provided Jaspers with a basis and justification for perceiving the individual as a being in which the particular elements dominate.[13]

This brief review of the perception of selfhood in Jaspers' philosophy clearly shows the dominance of his interest in the particular aspects of selfhood compared with its objective dimensions. The meaning of the argument that selfhood constitutes an essential substrate for clarifying the issue of guilt is that the private aspects in the individual's being have a decisive weight in determining Jaspers' concept of guilt, since these aspects are accessible to the individual himself, and he can evaluate them through self-examination. In contrast, the objective or formal viewpoint, whose boundaries and criteria are determined mainly by the collective, is marginalized due to its lack of access to the individual's subjective being.

What implications could the implementation of Jaspers' perception of selfhood, as developed in his pre-war writings, have for his handling of the issue of German guilt? The danger that such a move would undermine the discussion of German guilt, and perhaps even make redundant the various distinctions Jaspers himself offered in *The Question of Guilt*, seems very tangible considering the abstractions and sometimes even vagueness typical of Jaspers' approach to it.

---

[10] For interpretations of Jaspers' concept of Existenz in the research literature, see Miron, Monograph, 2012, 81-100.
[11] On the perception of Existenz as a "source" (*Ursprung*), see also Ph2, 336-337.
[12] In his words: "If I want to know what I am then my objective existence presents itself, in the trains of thought I experience, in the scheme of my being. I perceive myself inside it, but I experience that I am not completely identical to it: *what has thus become an object does not reach absolute identity with me myself*, since in my expansion I must lose myself in this scheme" (Ph2, 32).
[13] On Jaspers' perception of existential freedom, see Ph2, 175f, and also Tennen 1977, 47-57.

However, I believe that such a result is not unavoidable. While Jaspers did state that the starting point for handling the issue of German guilt should be anchored in the personal reflection of individuals, he did not sweepingly reject the objective and general viewpoint of guilt, and even examined the relevance of this viewpoint in his discussion of the four concepts of guilt he developed in this essay: criminal, political, moral, and metaphysical.[14] The first stage shows this viewpoint as relevant precisely for the criminal and political guilt: the former applies to those who committed crimes that are "acts capable of objective proof and violate unequivocal laws" (25). The second, "involving the deeds of statement and of the citizenry of a state, results in my having to bear the consequences of the deeds of the state whose power governs me and under whose order I live. Everybody is co-responsible for the way he is governed" (25). These two guilts are mainly the matter of the individual, and are determined according to his actions, but the individual's viewpoint is not usually decisive regarding the determination of criminal or political guilt; these are determined in accordance with objective criteria. In other words, these types of guilt apply to the individual as the person who owns the guilt and who must bear its consequences, but he cannot influence them himself, but they are determined according to general and wide considerations exceeding his private domain.

On the face of it, the subjective viewpoint, in which the person observes himself, seems relevant primarily to the "moral guilt" and perhaps also to the "metaphysical guilt". In Jaspers' opinion there are no objective or formal criteria by which these two concepts of guilt are determined. "Moral guilt" relies on recognizing the individual's responsibility for actions he takes as an individual or those he avoids taking, an avoidance whose results are undesirable for him. Here the decisive jurisdiction is the personal conscience and the person's response to the demands it sets him (25-26). No authority, including legal authority, can release a person from guilt the individual recognizes in his personal conscience (55). The "metaphysical guilt" is founded upon "a solidarity among men as human beings that makes each co-responsible for every wrong and every injustice in the world" (26). Jaspers sought to grant tangible expression to this argument by claiming that "This solidarity is violated by my presence at a wrong or a crime. It is not enough that I cautiously risk my life to prevent it; if it happens, and if I was there, and if I survive where the other is killed, I know from a voice within myself: I am guilty of being still alive" (65). However, this does not blur the fact that Jaspers' discussion of the concepts of moral and metaphysical guilt is characterized by a generality that explicitly rejects any horizon of concretization. This fact is undoubtedly related to his general perception of the concepts of morality and metaphysics, which constitute key concepts in his thought as a whole. Jaspers did not assume a theory of morality in the sense of setting norms for appropriate human behavior nor an ethics clarifying the human qualities one should nurture in the spirit of the Aristotelian tradition.[15] Also, his concept of metaphysics is not based on a defined ontological system. However, it is precisely

---

[14] Jaspers first defined the concepts of guilt concisely (25-26) and later expanded upon them (45-67).

[15] For an extensive historical and philosophical discussion of Jaspers' ethics and morality, see Tennen 1977, 9-24. The ethical orientation is also characteristic of the approaches of Salamun 1985 and Young-Breuhl 1981.

the generality typical of these concepts, which rejects a real possibility of concretization and objective observation, which grants the individual's particular being a decisive status in determining the very existence of moral and metaphysical guilt and the weight they are granted in his world. In this respect the concepts of moral and metaphysical guilt denote only types of the person's reference to himself, based on self-judgment and self-criticism. However, the determination of the existence of guilt does not in itself indicate a certain action performed or a breach of a specific law, but is mainly related to the individual's presence in a setting where evil or injustice occurred, and to the meaning he grants to this presence that links him to them.

At this stage we can state that Jaspers' various concepts of guilt assumed two different modes of the individual's dominance: regarding the criminal and political guilt, the individual's behavior in practice is decisive. In contrast, moral and metaphysical guilt are based on consideration, judgments, and perceptions originating in his personality. The objective or formal viewpoint can be relevant only regarding actions that can be measured or evaluated by an external body. However, in the case of moral and metaphysical guilt, there can be no room for any objective consideration, since they grant clear precedence to the individual's perceptions and personality. Against the background of the discussion of his early perception of selfhood, we can state that Jaspers assumed a mismatch in principle between the individual's particular being and an objective observation of the individual and his actions.

But the discussion of the disputed status of the objective viewpoint, which served as a tool for developing the concepts of moral and metaphysical guilt, also projects onto the other two concepts. Jaspers' argument in principle was that the "guilt of human existence" (28), related to the most fundamental factuality of ourselves as human creatures, cannot accept what exists as a guideline. Indeed, "Power and force are indeed decisive realities in the human world, but they are not the only ones" (51). Precisely because "Truth and probity fail to come by themselves" (110), "For in human affairs reality is not yet truth. That reality, rather, is to be confronted with another. And the existence of this other reality depends upon the human will" (51). Therefore, the "difference between *activity* and *passivity*" (63), relevant primarily in determining the punishment (30, see also 110), is not decisive regarding the determination of the existence of guilt. Indeed, Jaspers develops this argument in direct relation to the moral guilt. As he puts it: "passivity knows itself morally guilty of every failure, every neglect to act whenever possible, to shield the imperiled, to relieve wrong, to countervail"; thus "each one of us is guilty insofar as he remained inactive [...] The moral guilt of compliance, of *running with the pack*, is shared to some extent by a great many of us" (63-64). However, this can easily be connected to the political guilt too, which he phrases more concretely than the other concepts of guilt. In his words: "The destruction of any decent, truthful German polity must have its roots also in modes of conduct of the majority of the German population. A people answers for its polity. Every German is made to share the blame for the crimes committed in the name of the Reich" (55). Jaspers did not attribute the guilt to the absence of opposition to the regime, precisely because he recognized the limited power of citizens versus a terror state: "To ask a people to rise even against a terrorist state is to ask the impossible" (77). At the same time, Jaspers rejected the argument that there are non-political people, as a basis for avoiding sharing the guilt. In his opinion, in a modern state, in which the lives of citizens are granted to them through the order prevailing in the state, there is no real possibility of non-political existence, and in any case it cannot remove the sharing of political liability (56), "from which no individual can altogether escape and which have political significance as well" (73). These two poles, opposition to the regime on the one hand and refraining from political activity on the other hand, which greatly reduce the concept of guilt to a concrete level, are in stark contrast to Jaspers' general position aiming to expand the guilt through connecting it to the substrate of our humanity. Obviously a position whereby the actual behavior of individuals is not the decisive thing in determining guilt also reflects on the perception of criminal guilt. From this viewpoint, whoever lives in a society where criminal acts are prevalent should ask himself what in his behavior or the actions he avoids has contributed to this reality. The argument that against what exists and is reprehensible we should place what is worthy and good applies to both political and criminal guilt. In other words, one should not determine the existence or non-existence of guilt based on the individual's actual personal involvement in it. Jaspers thus shows that even individuals who are not tainted with criminal or political guilt still bear these two guilts and they bear them exactly as individuals.

These determinations regarding criminal and political guilt reaffirm my argument that selfhood serves as a very fundamental substrate in Jaspers' discussion of the issue of guilt. Moreover, as for the moral and metaphysical guilt, for the criminal and political guilt too the connection to selfhood reinforces the argument regarding the weakness of the objective viewpoint as a decisive criterion for guilt. Indeed, at an earlier stage of the discussion, this viewpoint played a role in distinguishing between the concepts of guilt and determining the individual's decisive weight in establishing it. But now, after it transpired that the actual behavior is not the full story regarding guilt, the difference between the four concepts of guilt is blurred to some extent. This means that a person's self-knowledge as a human being makes him guilty, even if he has done nothing. Through the linkage of guilt to the person's selfhood, Jaspers posits an opposite position to the one that has become established in western culture, seeking to see a person as innocent until proven guilty. In contrast to this, Jaspers claims that a person, by being human, inevitably carries guilt. However, this guilt has nothing in common with the idea of original sin (94), but embodies a very basic human element that simultaneously grants it meaning and an infinite horizon.

One of the inevitable questions arising at this stage of the discussion is: Can the fact that the withdrawal of the objective viewpoint from the discussion of guilt takes place in a controlled manner still enable a public discussion of German guilt, or perhaps despite his complex position regarding the status of selfhood, Jaspers' approach endangers the possibility of conducting such a discussion? This question, raised at an early stage of the discussion, arises once again at this point, even more forcefully. But Jaspers was well aware that emphasizing the personal element could serve as a means of evading the concepts of guilt and eventually the entire question of guilt:

> Political liability—all right, but it curtails only my material possibilities; I myself, my inner self is not affected by that at all. Criminal guilt—that affects just a few, not me... Moral guilt—I hear that my conscience alone has jurisdiction, others have no right to accuse me... Metaphysical guilt... none can charge it to another... That's a crazy idea of some philosopher. There is no such thing. And if there were, I wouldn't notice it. That I needn't bother with it. (68)

Against the background of these words and the discussion of the individual's viewpoint as the substrate for clarifying the question of guilt, we can state that selfhood, no less than it can serve as a basis for the very recognition of guilt, may also serve as a tool for avoiding it. But just as Jaspers' rejection of the objective viewpoint regarding selfhood was not sweeping, so also his handling of the harmful implications of the status he granted to selfhood within the process of clarifying the German guilt did not lead him to completely reject his position but rather to locate the problematic element it contained that might enable evasion of guilt. The difficulty in particularism for dealing with guilt stems from the fact that in its extreme form it leaves no room for any of the four concepts of guilt.

As will transpire later, the strategy Jaspers employed to handle the evasion possibilities entailed in the subjective viewpoint of guilt was aimed to restore the status of the objective viewpoint within the discussion of guilt rather than to negate its relevance. However, beyond indicating the possibility of guilt evasion embodied in his position, in *The Question of Guilt* he does not discuss the problematic in the understanding of selfhood as a basis for guilt. In contrast, in his earlier philosophical writings Jaspers dealt directly with the restrictive implications of the particular understanding of selfhood. Through several original philosophical terms, including the central concept of "historicity", Jaspers constantly moderated his earlier emphasis on the particular and isolating understanding of selfhood in favor of opening it to an objective viewpoint and to other people in general.

Guilt from the Collective's Viewpoint

In parallel with the personal tone through which Jaspers sought to connect individuals and himself to the German guilt, his discussion is also threaded with many expressions indicating that the guilt under discussion is the guilt of those belonging to the German nation as a collective. Thus, he described himself as "a German among Germans"[16]; "the German—that is, the German-speaking individual—feels concerned by everything growing from German roots" (73); "all of us speak the German language, and we were all born in this country and are at home in it" (13). Jaspers also gave tangible expression to his being part of the German collective when he dealt with arguments common among the German public regarding the question of guilt. In his discussion of what he termed

---

[16] This citation appears in the introduction to the German edition, *Die Schuldfarge, Von der politischen Haftung Deutschlands*, Munich: Piper, 1996, 7, but not in the English translation.

"possible excuses" (76 ff.) he demonstrated positions expressing avoidance of blaming the Germans for the crimes of the Nazi regime, such as Germany's geographical situation that enforced the militarism and its results (80-82), the world-historical situation that expressed a comprehensive spiritual and religious crisis (82-84), the guilt of other nations involved in the war (84-91). His participating and accepting tone indicates that his words are not an expression of a moralizing or preaching position, but contain a large degree of proximity and empathy toward German society.

Jaspers clarified that speaking about Germanness as a characteristic that turns the Germans into a collective is "altogether different from making the nation absolute" (74); after all, this was the Nazi perception of the German nation, attributing to it an apriori essence unconditional upon the individuals composing it. Against this, Jaspers argued that "There is no such thing as a people as a whole" (35). The collective is a continuation, expansion, and development of the individual's selfhood. In his words: "The self-analysis of a people in historical reflection and the personal self-analysis of the individual are two different things. But the first can happen only by way of the second. What individuals accomplish jointly in communication may, if true, become the spreading consciousness of many and then is called national consciousness" (96). Jaspers gave sharp expression to the merging of the two perspectives I have presented regarding guilt—that appealing to the individual and that anchored in the relation to the collective—through stating that "Every one [of the Germans], in his real being, is the German people" (74).

The argument that there is continuity between the two perspectives about guilt has two important implications for the discussion of the issue of guilt. First, like the individual's selfhood (84), the concept of German collectivity also requires clarification and reflection and does not refer to a permanent and agreed object. This point returns several times in *The Question of Guilt*, for example: "in Germany... We have no common ground yet" (5); "Common is the non-community" (12); "Now... we seem to each other as if we had come from different worlds" (13); "All these differences lead to constant disruption among us Germans... the more so as our existence lacks the common ethical-political base" (16). Since there is continuity between the individual and the collective, we can state that Jaspers' argument that Nazism had dismantled the collective (14) also enfolds the understanding that this regime damaged the selfhood of each and every German individual.

However, in my eyes the most important significance of the continuity between the two perspectives stems from its contribution to establishing Jaspers' principle of not anchoring the guilt in the concrete level of the action. Just as anchoring the guilt of individuals in actions can serve for many Germans as a justification for evading it, it was clear to Jaspers that relying on the concrete element could help disprove the collective perspective regarding the guilt: "One cannot make an individual out of a people. A people cannot perish heroically, cannot be a criminal, cannot act morally or immorally; only its individuals can do so. A people as a whole can be neither guilty nor innocent" (35). Jaspers went further, stating that from the practical point of view alone there is no point in referring to the Germans' sole guilt for the crimes of the Nazis: "Shall we admit that we alone are guilty? No—if we as a whole, as a people, as a permanent species, are turned into *the* evil people, the guilty people as such. Against this world opinion we can point to facts" (90).

Jaspers did not dismiss the importance of the viewpoint of others, meaning of those who are not Germans, for clarifying the issue of German guilt. First and foremost, Jaspers states, "we know we are part of mankind—are human before we are German" (22). Moreover, "That the victors condemn us... has the greatest consequences for our life" (22). However, in his opinion more important than the viewpoint of others is the observation or individuals and of the German collective regarding itself: "But even more important to us is how we analyze, judge and cleanse ourselves. Those charges from without no longer are our concern. On the other hand, there are the charges from within... They... are the source of whatever self-respect is still possible for us. We must clarify the question of German guilt. This is our own business" (43). The marginalization of the others' accusatory viewpoint thus joins previous clarifications that rejected a metaphysical and comprehensive perception of the concepts of people and nation; all these together detract from the concept of collective that served Jaspers in his discussion of guilt as generalizing and deterministic elements that were alien to his general metaphysical perception, centered around the individual's particular being.

However, can we find in Jaspers' discussion a positive clarification of this concept, which would enable a real understanding of the individual's relation to the German collective? It appears that in *The Question of Guilt* Jaspers based the concept of the German collective largely on general features, especially the language and the shared political and social fate that befell the citizens of Germany upon the end of the war. But his statement that "We further feel that we not only share in what is done at present—thus being co-responsible for the deeds of our contemporaries—but in the links of tradition. We have to bear the guilt of our fathers... our national tradition contains something, mighty and threatening, which is our moral ruin" (73-74), shows that the concept of the collective that he assumes exceeds the boundaries of the present and its implications relate not only to the way the German public faced the crimes of the Nazi regime. However, it is not clear what he bases this upon. The question why the German must accept the guilt of the previous generations, and see himself as responsible for the outcome of their perceptions, remains unanswered in *The Question of Guilt*. It seems that the discussion of the collective viewpoint regarding guilt, like the discussion linking guilt with the individual's selfhood, requires the wider philosophical substrate developed in Jaspers' pre-war writings.

In order to understand the nature of the collective viewpoint of guilt, the general philosophical conceptions that led Jaspers to move the focus of discussion from the individual to the collective are particularly important. As we recall, the perception of selfhood, which occupied Jaspers' work from its inception, stressed the particular aspects of the individual's subjective being. These continued to interest Jaspers even later in his work, but his writings from the early 1930s onward gradually formed an awareness of the restrictive implications of this approach for the perception of the human being as an individual.[17] One of the clearest expressions of this awareness is reflected in the following words:

> Standing itself absolutely on itself alone is indeed for Existenz *the truth of its independence on the reality of time, but this becomes despair for it*. It (Existenz) is itself aware that being completely self-standing, it must sink into vacuum (Ph3, 4).

Dealing with the collective's viewpoint was henceforth places against the closeness enforced by the individual's viewpoint regarding guilt. For our discussion of the issue of guilt, particularly important are the conceptions achieved within the idea of historicity, through which Jaspers sought to explain the individual's connection to his past as an individual and as part of the collective.

The idea of historicity[18] is based on the classical Hegelian distinction between the two meanings of the German word *Geschichte*: history and story.[19] The former denotes the objective clarification of the details of a historical occurrence whose guiding principles serve as a foundation of the scientific approach to history. The second, following the formation of the consciousness of the past by people and its use as a basis for their understanding of themselves in the present, expresses the subjective meaning of history. Against the background of this distinction, with which Jaspers was undoubtedly familiar, he sought to distinguish between "historical consciousness" and "historistic consciousness". A person's role regarding *historical consciousness* is exhausted by his ability to observe past occurrences and learn from them about various historical periods. These occurrences do not necessarily touch upon his personal life. Also, in the mental activities related to historical consciousness the person is not present as an individual making subjective discoveries typical of his selfhood, which is sometimes perceived in this context as a disruptive element, but as having rational and abstract theoretical abilities. In contrast, in the *historistic consciousness* a person perceives himself as existing in a concrete time and context and as part of a continuity whose boundaries exceed the boundaries of his personal existence, meaning that he is a continuation of previous modes of existence, and serves as a basis for a future reality that will continue after him (Ph2, 118-119). The person's understanding of himself as a historistic being

---

[17] On Jaspers' handling of the difficulties entailed in a solipsistic understanding of a person, see Miron, Monograph, 2012, 65-80.

[18] Jaspers' term *Geschichtlichkeit* preserves the two main components: First it denotes the physical aspect of time as a sequence, upon which the objective examination of time in science relies. This means that each present point in time was preceded by another point in time, and it will be succeeded by a new point in time. This facet is relevant to the discussion of Existenz as a real being in concrete time. Additionally, the term "historicity" contains a representation of the experience of reality through consciousness, in a process of constructing the personal identity that continues throughout a person's lifetime. This facet relates to Existenz as a being aiming to achieve consciousness of the facts of its existence and of its patterns of dealing with them.

[19] Hegel, *Vorlesungen über die Philosophie der Geschichte*, ed. G. Lasson, Leipzig, 1974, 142 ff. On the relation between these two components and their role in forming historical consciousness, see also Rotenstreich 1955, 9-24.

inseparably combines reflection aimed at clarifying the data and circumstances of the past on the objective level and at the same time the subjective meaning that he gives them, through which he connects himself to them. Jaspers expressed the connection between the objective and subjective dimensions by saying: "Here [in historistic consciousness] are inseparably connected at source *being* and *knowledge*... Without knowledge, meaning a clear perception and being within it, there is no historistic being, and without a historistic reality there is no knowledge" (Ph2, 119).

However, the distinction between the objective level, dealing with historical knowledge, and the subjective one, through which the individual links himself to the image of the past emerging through this knowledge, does not mean these two are detached. Quite the opposite, through the concept of historicity Jaspers sought to harness the mental skills involved in forming historical consciousness, aimed primarily at establishing the scientific nature of history as a discipline, to the service of the historistic consciousness, and to turn it into an integral part of the individual's self-consciousness:

> *From this historistic source, the historical too becomes for the first time really historistic.* Without it, it would only have had the meaning of a certain occurrence referring to the existence of the present evaluated positively or negatively. However, *my theoretical knowledge of history turns through the entire science of history into a function of possible Existenz*, to the extent that its contents and images direct themselves at me, turn to me, demand from me, or push me away from them, not only as distant patterns existing as closed within themselves, or in other words: to the extent that it [historical knowledge] is appropriated to the function of the eternal present of things that exist within philosophical-historistic consciousness (Ph2, 119-120).

The idea of historicity, it transpires, enfolded the understanding that historical knowledge itself does not reflect a mere objective generality. The individual's reflexive turning to historical knowledge creates a fundamental change within him, as a result of which the general and impersonal element is expropriated from this knowledge and it serves as a framework within whose boundaries a person organizes his life story and his consciousness as an individual.[20] From Jaspers' point of view, the change that takes place in historical knowledge as a result of the individual's turning to it is not perceived as a distortion, but reveals its original meaning: "[through Existenz historical knowledge] *proves its power* in the ability of its results [meaning its capacity] to be replaced by real historistic consciousness of the self in existence" (Ph2, 120). In fact, the meeting between a person and historical knowledge creates a mutual change: on the one hand, the

---

[20] Jaspers' relation in principle to general and objective knowledge, directed in this context to historical knowledge, is a continuation of his early position as a psychiatrist and active researcher of mental illness. Like his criticism of the science of psychopathology or general psychology as the formal settings of knowledge that cannot enable access to the fullness and uniqueness of human being, the assumption was apparently also made here that general and formal historical knowledge cannot serve as a source of self-understanding.

existential view reveals new and unfamiliar facets of historical knowledge, enriches it, and mainly exposes its dynamic nature that enables it to address the world of present-day people. On the other hand, the individual's turning to historical knowledge expands the boundaries of his existence and introduces into them belonging, context, and depth. Thus the concept of historicity links the individual to the past and to the knowledge of the past. Knowledge of the past does not expropriate from the individual his individuality, but grants it a fuller meaning that is not exhausted within the boundaries of personal existence.

These ideas arising from the discussion of historicity are essential for understanding Jaspers' approach to the issue of guilt, which deliberately avoided anchoring it in committing crimes at a given time. First, it is impossible to separate between Germans as such and the Nazi period of German history. As we have seen, a person's past is an inseparable part of his present-day existence. Present-day people—whether they continued living after the war or were born after it—should therefore be considered as a continuation of the Nazi past, or as the future of this past. Second, dealing with historical knowledge, in which the past events are presented in general patterns appealing to objective thought, also has implications regarding the future discussion of guilt, when the criminals who obeyed the Nazi regime have passed from the world. In this situation, there would be a predictable increase in the protests of individuals who have not committed crimes themselves, or who committed them against their will, and they would want to avoid the German guilt, as has indeed happened. But connecting Jaspers' discussion of the guilt issue to the philosophical theme of historicity can make historical knowledge about the Nazi crimes into an inseparable part of the selfhood of all who belong to the German collective. This knowledge does not revolve about what was and is no longer, or about the crimes of others, but all Germans are required to see it as referring to them personally. The historistic viewpoint regarding guilt enables the joining together of the existential observation of guilt, from the viewpoint of present-day Germans, and the objective observation of it that examines its connection to the cumulative knowledge about the Nazi period. The determination that served as the basis for the discussion of the collective viewpoint regarding guilt, whereby "We have to bear the guilt of our fathers" (73), receives its full meaning through its linking to the philosophical idea of historicity: "German guilt connects to it every German due to the Germanness anchored in the shared past and future. Through this, Jaspers' central argument in *The Question of Guilt*, whereby recognition of guilt does not depend on committing the crimes themselves, receives further support. Now it transpires that like the viewpoint anchored in the individual, the one regarding the German collective too requires reflection turning to a general and not necessarily concrete element in the German being. The two viewpoints regarding guilt join together on a mainly subjective and abstract basis.

One of the central problems raised by the discussion of the two viewpoints regarding guilt relates to the place of freedom in the face of guilt: what space for choice is left by the perception of guilt appealing to such a deep human element in the being of the German—his selfhood, his being part of a collective with a past and heritage, and a future continuing from them? It seems that Jaspers was well-aware of this danger, and so he clarified:

> The effects of natural causes depend also on how man takes them, how he handles them, what he makes out of them. Cognition of history, therefore, is never such as to apprehend its course as flatly necessary. This cognition can never make certain predictions..., nor can it retrospectively perceive an inevitability of general events and individual actions. In either case it sees the *scope of possibilities*, only more richly and concretely in the case of the past (79-80, my emphasis).

In this spirit he added, after listing and criticizing the considerations that could serve Germans to evade guilt, that:

> ... however true this basis trait of our reflections may be, it is important for us not to interpret it as absolute necessity...

> In fact, we always describe national character in terms of arbitrarily selected historical phenomena. Yet these in turn have always been causes by events, and by conditions marked by events. At every time they are one group of phenomena, appearing only as one of many types. Other situations might bring entirely different, otherwise hidden character traits to the fore. A distinct natural character complete with talents may very well exist, but we simply do not know it.

> We must not shift our responsibility to anything like that. As men we must *know ourselves free for all possibilities* (81-82, my emphasis).

These words clearly show that Jaspers assumes the existence of freedom as a permanent element in human being, and thus it should not be seen as depending upon the existence of possibilities to realize it, nor is it damaged by the existence of facts or circumstances that cannot be changed by human beings. Therefore, just as Jaspers requires the individual to create through his will "[an]other reality" (51) against the undesirable existing reality, so he also requires the collective not to see the circumstances of its concrete life as finished factuality.

To be precise, Jaspers does not reject factuality as irrelevant to the discussion of the guilt issue, but only the objective viewpoint that identifies it with actions that can be measured and judged. In the section "Differentiation of German Guilt" (45 ff.), Jaspers addresses the concrete facts around which the uniqueness of German guilt, compared with that of other nations, is crystallized. So, for example, he states: "there can be no doubt that Germany planned and prepared this war and started it without provocation from any other side" (47); "Germany... has committed numerous acts resulting in the extermination of populations and in other inhumanities... This war did not break out between opponents alike in kind... It was conceived and executed by criminal cunning and the reckless totality of a destructive will" (47-48). Additionally, Jaspers does not avoid the concrete implications of the actions of the Germans during the war: "We must experience mortification if required by our political liability. Thereby, symbolically, we experience our utter political impotence and our elimination as a political factor" (46-47). The actions and the consequences stemming from them represent the element of necessity involved in guilt. Although this element was not at the focus of Jaspers' discussion in *The Question of Guilt*, he did not ignore it. Moreover, in this context the objectifization of guilt is also important—not only an action aimed at Germans as individuals from the outside, but it also expresses an essential ability for the individuals' facing themselves:

> Our darkest feelings do not mind being trusted out of hand. Though immediacy is the true reality, the presence of our soul and our feelings are not simply there like given facts of life. Rather, they are communicated by our inner activities, our thoughts, our knowledge. They are deepened and clarified in the measure that we think. Feeling as such is unreliable. To plead feelings means to evade naively the objectivity of what we can know and think (23).

However, Jaspers believed that dealing with the guilt cannot rely only on an honest stance in the face of the necessity it entails, but also requires reference to the element of "possibility" (*Möglichkeit*) or freedom that constitutes guilt but is also present in it as an open and undecided horizon.[21] This element has great importance for the clarification of the guilt issue. First, exposing the element of possibility in the context of the discussion of the collective viewpoint regarding guilt contributes to establishing Jaspers' argument that the German nation does not express an apriori essence, and its character is not determined by necessity: "being German is... not a condition but a task" (74). Second, this idea adds a layer to Jaspers' continuing effort to avoid reducing guilt to the concrete level of the actions, circumstance, or reasons. Such a reduction could lead to avoidance of the clarification of guilt.[22] In his words: "We distinguish between cause and guilt. An exposition showing why things happened as they did, and why indeed they could not but so happen, is automatically considered an excuse. A cause is blind and involuntary. Guilt is seeing and free" (78-79).

But Jaspers' discussion progressed beyond indicating the necessity and the freedom as two distinct elements within guilt. His statement that "It is not the liability of a national but the concern of one who shares the life of the German spirit and soul—who is of one tongue, one stock, one fate with all the others—which here comes to cause, not as tangible guilt, but somehow analogous to co-responsibility" (73), also indicates his attempt to rank these elements in the issue under discussion. Like the hierarchy existing between source and its analogies, the two levels present in guilt—the concrete embodied in actions or facts, and the abstract that transpires during the reflexive process—are not located on one level and are not granted an equal degree of importance. While Jaspers' choice to deal with the guilt issue as "an inner process which is never ended but in which we continually become ourselves" (114), which constantly exposed his discussion to its infinite and undefined horizons, expressed the importance he granted to the abstract element in his perception of guilt. However, he believed that the clarification of the defined and distinct aspects typical of the concrete actions conducted during the Nazi period should be given precedence. The element of

---

[21] For more on the concept of freedom in Jaspers' thought, see Tennen 1979, 47-57; Young-Bruehl 1981, 64-65, 105-106.

[22] Indeed, after Jaspers addressed the world's demand for a punishment for the German people, he states "The temptation to evade this question is obvious" (21).

necessity in guilt, representing a finite layer responding to distinct criteria, is therefore revealed first, even though it is perceived as having an analogous, and thus merely secondary, meaning in comparison with the element of freedom active within guilt. Although the element of freedom is considered as prior to and more important than the element of necessity, it can only be clarified after the clarification of the concrete acts for whose evaluation distinct criteria exist. This movement from the concrete and vague to the abstract source is reflected in his statement that "these distinct concepts [the various concepts of guilt] are to lead us back to the one source" (27). From this point of view, even the concepts of guilt discussed in *The Question of Guilt* are partial and relative, and clearly indicate the unconcrete target to which the discussion is aimed.

But the importance of the hierarchy between the two elements is not exhausted by illuminating the relative and fluid status of the four types of guilt presented in *The Question of Guilt*, which makes them dependent on the observer's viewpoint. As he put it: "The distinctions are, of course, not absolutely valid. In the end, what we call guilt has one all-embracing source. But this can be clarified only by what is gained by means of the distinctions" (22-23). Furthermore, he directs to the transcendent horizon embodied in guilt. Thus, while the boundaries of the analogy are finite and dependent on the source, it itself is characterized by openness enabling an infinite variety of meanings. Jaspers goes further, defining guilt itself as a possibility: "In tracing our own guilt back to its source we come upon the human essence—which in its German form has fallen into a peculiar, terrible incurring of guilt but exists as a possibility in man as such" (94). This is the decisive point where the discussion exceeds the boundaries of German guilt and turns to a deeper element in human being, an element that Jaspers states "cannot be flatly referred to as our guilt" (27), meaning it does not relate only to Germans as individuals or as a collective.

The exhausting of the analogous layer in guilt reveals horizons vastly exceeding the boundaries of necessity and placing the discussion of the guilt issue in a new space that Jaspers terms "the inevitable guilt of all, the guilt of human existence" (28). In *The Question of Guilt* Jaspers did not expand upon his meaning in the term "inevitable guilt", which on the face of it seems paradoxical, or upon his meaning when he hinted to "What man, by himself, can experience before the transcendent" (99). Like the concepts of selfhood and the collective, the clarification of the concepts of transcendence and inevitable guilt requires us to turn to the sources of his thought appearing in his philosophical writings. The concepts of inevitable guilt and transcendence, among the most complex in Jaspers' philosophy, enfold the depth of his metaphysical perception whose boundaries vastly exceed the concrete context in which *The Question of Guilt* was written. The main thing we learn about Jaspers' concept of metaphysical guilt is its connection to the idea of possibility, which in itself expresses the openness and presence of an infinite element. However, this general meaning appears unrelated to the German guilt, which raises quite defined and concrete associations. Perhaps the fact that *The Question of Guilt* was written during a period where the presence of the element of necessity in the lives of Germans was felt more than ever contributed to the decision not to delve too deeply into the overall metaphysical meanings of guilt, which undoubtedly exceed the boundaries of the German guilt. However, Jaspers' choice to note the presence of an infinite facet or component in guilt, even in the specific context of this essay, necessitates an examination of his philosophical writings. Once again, as with the need for the collective viewpoint that arose already in the discussion of the individual's viewpoint that was discussed previously, at this point the necessity of the metaphysical viewpoint of guilt arises.

Guilt from a Metaphysical Viewpoint

The presence of the element of possibility in the perception of the collective laid the foundation for the discussion of guilt to exceed the boundaries of the German context. However, the emphasis Jaspers placed on the distinctiveness and uniqueness of the German guilt, as part of the explanation and justification for the difficulties experienced by the German nation after the end of the war, required him to grant the element of possibility a relatively marginal status in his perception of the collective. It appears that the main role of this element was to serve as a barrier to an apriori and absolute perception of the nation and people, as adopted by the Nazi regime. Furthermore, stressing the presence of the element of possibility in the perception of the collective, beyond its role in restraining invalid perceptions of the collective, might have endangered the commitment to deal with the guilt, a commitment to which Jaspers sought to harness every German, no matter what his personal behavior during the Nazi period. "Possibility" denotes the undecided element in collectivism, but this facet can be interpreted in various ways whose implications for the recognition of guilt could be contradictory. On the one hand, it enables avoiding the identification of the German nation with its Nazi past and allows new horizons around which the post-war German collectivism could be crystallized. On the other hand, the possibility element could indicate, precisely due to its openness, a path for evading German guilt for individuals who shake off their relationship to the German collective. These two interpretations show the possibility element as in some respects a liberating element. However, while in the latter the liberation leads eventually to an overall evasion of guilt, in the former it can help precisely in handling it, by leaving the individual room in which he can face it without detaching his basic link to the collective.

At this point, the nature of the continuity between the two first viewpoints regarding guilt—the one anchored in the individual's selfhood and the one addressing the German collective—is clarified. The continuity in this context expresses a process of expansion and development, in which the dynamic of one viewpoint leads to the constituting of another viewpoint, more encompassing than its predecessor. Thus the collective viewpoint regarding guilt expands the one anchored in selfhood and grants it a more inclusive context and identity. However, the first viewpoint is not abandoned, but serves as an instrument for restraining the later viewpoint and limiting the dimensions of its expansion: while the collective viewpoint of guilt constitutes an expansion of the individual's viewpoint of it, it cannot expand to boundaries exceeding the self-understanding of the German as an individual. In other words, the collective viewpoint is positioned as a more effective means of achieving the individual's self-understanding regarding his guilt. But the full meaning of the element of possibility and the relations between it and the element of necessity remains largely undeciphered, since the requirements imposed by the restrictions of the collective viewpoint did not enable this deciphering. This disadvantage can be addressed by the metaphysical viewpoint regarding guilt.

The metaphysical viewpoint regarding guilt starts in the identification of two separate elements in reality: possibility and necessity. The fact that neither of these elements can be removed from reality, or that the contradiction created by their shared and constant presence cannot be solved, grants reality its contradictory nature, or as Jaspers called it following Kant, its antonymous nature (Ph2, 249).[23] Jaspers described this reality from the viewpoint of the person experiencing it:

> [The person] can never remain [only] in the finite and concrete, because everything concrete simultaneously contains both a finite and an infinite nature. In order to deal with what is essential for him, he always encounters ways to the infinite or the whole. He can find in his escape from the infinite to the mystical experience a limited satisfaction and quiet. However, to the degree that he remains alert... then any infinity leads him to the chasms of contradictions known as antimonies (Psychology, 231, my emphases).

The antonymous nature of reality is an expression of the undecided dualism—the simultaneous presence of good and evil, positive and negative, infinite and finite, whole and partial—that people encounter in their existence in the world.[24] This is not the place to go into the perception of reality as antonymous, although it has many implications for Jaspers' thought. For our discussion, it is important to clarify the meaning the two contradictory elements have in the metaphysical perspective of guilt, anchored in this perception of reality. Jaspers linked the element of possibility to guilt as follows: "Since I know myself [as] free, I know myself as guilty... Since I know what I do, I take this upon myself" (Ph2, 196), and also: "My guilt *inside* my freedom is each time something defined, and so something that I experience and not something that I allow to come to me" (Ph2, 197). So Jaspers connects freedom, self-knowledge, and guilt. In his opinion, it is not possible to affirm or reject one element without affirming or rejecting the others as well. Another meaning of the element of possibility in guilt is the absence of an origin that characterizes it:

> If I knew the origin of my guilt, it would be limited and avoidable; my freedom would have been the possibility of preventing it. I would not have to take anything upon myself, not me myself in the sense of self-

---

[23] Jaspers used the Kantian concept of antimony, relating to a logical contradiction between two premises, each of which can be proved by disproving the other. On the ethical implications of this perception of reality, see Tennen 1977, 34-36. Regarding Jaspers' Kantianism, opinions are divided in research; for a review and interpretation of the various directions, see Ronny Miron, "Was Jaspers really Kantian?", *Yearbook of the Austrian Karl Jaspers' Society*, 19, 2006, 73-106 [Reprinted in this collection as Miron, 2006b].

[24] Jaspers refers to these contradictions in several contexts in his thought. See for example Ph2, 248-249; Ph3, 102f.

choice and not the existence [*Dasein*] into which I enter and for which I become responsible by acting (Ph2, 197).[25]

Denying the existence of a starting point for guilt, which does not enable it to be defined and its dimensions to be estimated, indicates the inclusive and encompassing nature of the guilt revealed through the metaphysical viewpoint. In this context, guilt is perceived as an expression of a person's freedom to formulate an independent perception, to act according to it, and to bear the consequences of his actions while seeing himself as responsible for them. Thus the element of possibility, which from the collective viewpoint of guilt appeared quite vaguely, receives real content. However, the unreserved freedom in this context has an additional meaning, linking it to the converse element of human existence: necessity. In the absence of a point of origin, the person is denied the possibility of controlling his own freedom, and in this respect he cannot be defined as its constitutor.[26] We can present Jaspers' arguments in this context as follows: since we cannot place reservations on freedom, we cannot prevent the guilt. The guilt's unavoidable nature is a direct result of the inclusiveness of the freedom in which the guilt is anchored. What is denied a point of origin thus transpires as simultaneously unavoidable. Finally, the guilt based on the freedom leads to a restriction of the freedom to the extent that the guilt becomes a basic given of human existence, meaning inevitable:

> Despite the transparency of my free decision, and through it, *I experience the restriction of my freedom*, which I recognize to the same extent as my own handiwork and simultaneously with *the restriction as guilt*...
>
> I take upon myself... in reality what I must do, without being able to act differently in the situation. It is as though I was able to choose myself in advance, as I am, and this choice, which in practice was not made in terms of my actions, I accept upon myself as belonging to me and as if the realities in which I find myself were even so felt in my consciousness of guilt as if I had created them myself (Ph2, 196-197, my emphases).

These words clearly demonstrate the dynamic leading from the discussion of the element of possibility in guilt to standing before the inevitable necessity it contains. This establishes the thesis of continuity between the two opposing elements in human reality—freedom and necessity—in which Jaspers'

---

[25] The problem of the origin bothered many phenomenologists. Husserl noted the difficulty in determining the point at which the method of philosophical investigation starts being applied (Husserl 1913, § 63) and the nature of the datum this investigation grasps (see Husserl, "Philosophy as a Rigorous Science", in Phenonmenology and the Crisis of Philosophy, trans. Quentin Lauer, New York, 1965, 110-111; Husserl 1913, § 40). One of the conclusions that Husserl reached was that the definition does not help us understand because it contains an arbitrary determination of a point of origin. For more on this issue, see Fulda 1966; Fuchs 1976.

[26] Heidegger defined this situation of the absence of an origin, restricting freedom, as "thrownness" (*Geworfenheit*); see Heidegger 1927, § 29, §38.

metaphysical perception of guilt is anchored. In other words, the simultaneous existence and proximity to each other of two contradictory elements in human reality expresses its antonymous nature. In this respect, we can state that no less than inevitable guilt is anchored in human reality, antonym serves as a reliable mirror image of it.

This perception of reality in which people live and act and of their status within it reaches its peak formulation in the perception of guilt as one of the "boundary situations".[27] This term is composed of two basic concepts appearing in Jaspers' philosophical writings in various contexts: "situation" or "situation being" (*Situationsein*) and "boundary".[28] The former denotes the freedom and necessity revealed in the person's conscious existence (Ph1, 1) and discussed above.[29] Through this concept, greatly reduced compared to the concept of "world" (*Welt*), Jaspers sought to demonstrate a basic fact about human existence, whereby a person never experiences reality as a whole but always in its limited contexts, in which he enjoys freedom but is simultaneously subject to restrictions independent of him that reduce it. Duality also characterizes the concept of "boundary", portraying the range of possibilities of human experience and understanding, but also the human desire to exceed the boundaries of existence and consciousness: "Every boundary immediately raises the question what is beyond it" (Ph1, 45). The two components of the concept "boundary situations" thus reaffirm the fundamental pattern of simultaneous presence of the elements of possibility and necessity. Jaspers described boundary situations as follows:

> Situations like those I always exist within, that I cannot live without struggle and without grief, that I take upon myself inevitable guilt, that I must die, I call boundary situations. They do not change except in their appearances; *in their reference to our existence they are absolutely valid.* We cannot gaze beyond them; in our existence, we cannot see [anything] else behind them. They are like a wall that we push and encounter. *They are not changeable through us*, but we can only bring them to clarity without a possibility of deducing them or explaining them from something else. They exist with existence itself (Ph2, 203, my emphases).[30]

The inevitable guilt, like the constant struggle with existence and the death that awaits all human beings, is a particular example of the general human phenomenon of boundary situations. Jaspers especially stressed the lack of freedom in boundary situations and described the personal sensation of a person

---

[27] Boundary situations is an original concept of Jaspers'. Heidegger believed that this concept alone could grant him his status as a philosopher; see Heidegger 1998, 10. For more on Jaspers' boundary situations, see Bollnow 1964; Latzel 1957.

[28] The concept of the world is discussed extensively in the first volume of the trilogy *Philosophy*, entitled "Philosophical World Orientation"; see in particular Ph1, 63.

[29] An early version of the idea of "situation" appears already in "The Spiritual Situation", 23 ff.

[30] The term "boundary situations" is handled in two contexts in Jaspers' writings: Ph2, 201-254; Psychology, 229-280. On the differences between the two contexts, see Miron, Monograph, 2012, 141-156.

within them as being "a gaming ball" (Ph2, 216), thus expressing the arbitrariness accompanying the experience of these situations. The prominent emphasis on human helplessness in these situations, along with the immediate meaning of the term "inevitable guilt", seems to grant greater weight to the element of necessity compared with the element of possibility. This apparently breaks the balance between the two elements that characterized the discussion of the metaphysical viewpoint regarding guilt up to this point. However, this conclusion, which could have been valid in the perception that links guilt with human actions, was denied throughout the discussion and is once again explicitly denied in relation to inevitable guilt. Let us clarify this.

On the face of it, if guilt is the result of an action, it can be prevented by refraining from the action. But Jaspers rejects this solution to the problem of guilt. He determines that "Inaction [*Nichthandeln*] is itself an action, meaning refraining [*Unterlassen*]. Inaction would have necessarily become a rapid sinking; this could have been a form of suicide. Not entering into the world is a self-denial of the demands of reality that addresses me… to dare and experience what has been formed of it" (Ph2, 247). Avoiding an action bears within it, it transpires, a necessity of its own, since it necessarily leads to sinking. From the viewpoint of guilt there is no difference between the results of inaction and those of action, and thus the guilt cannot be attributed to the difference between them. In other words, a person is guilty whether he acts or refrains from acting. This is undoubtedly one of the reasons why Jaspers did not link guilt to actual behavior, in this context collaboration with the Nazis, but anchored it in the more fundamental fact that the crimes where enabled in the lives of the Germans—as individuals and as a collective. However, avoiding action is a flawed choice, not only because it adds a necessity of its own, but also because in this choice the person reduces, without this being necessary, the share of the element of possibility in his being. As he put it: "Guilt is the prevention of reality and then the deeper guilt comes in abandoning each time other possibilities" (Ph3, 111). Moreover, the antonymy typical of human reality, originating in the mutual influence of the element of necessity and the element of possibility, indicates the pointlessness of avoidance as a means of evading a situation of guilt. Guilt is thus inevitable both from the viewpoint of possibility and from the viewpoint of necessity.

With the perception of guilt as a boundary situation, and hence as inevitable, its realm expands to maximal dimensions. Like the other boundary situations, guilt too is given along with the human existence. This insight can be phrased as follows: I exist, therefore I am guilty. This closes the gap between existence and guilt, and also undermines the various evasion attempts contained in the viewpoint anchored in the self and the one based on the collective. Boundary situations, marking the boundaries of human existence, leave no other room for the existence of guilt, since beyond them human existence ceases. All at once: the boundaries of existence are simultaneously the boundaries of guilt.

One of the disturbing questions arising from the perception of guilt as inevitable is: what is the difference between the guilt of the Germans and that of those who are not German? Between that of the Nazis and that of their opponents? Another question arises regarding the methods of coping proposed, if at all, in Jaspers' thought with its all-embracing reality of guilt. These questions are interconnected, since the perception of guilt as a boundary situation relates to a fundamental human condition, which does not stem from a particular behavior or avoiding it, and in this respect there is no difference between Germans and non-Germans, between supporters and opponents of the Nazi regime. Furthermore, guilt, like the other boundary situations, does not and cannot have a solution, since helplessness is involved in it by its very nature. Indeed, in Jaspers' writings, including *The Question of Guilt*, there is no solution to the problem of guilt, but it is possible to extricate a certain response inherent in the discussion. Thus, for example, in *The Question of Guilt* several expressions indicate the diversion from the channel of action to that of reflection: "The way we answer it [the question of guilt] will be decisive for our present approach to the world and ourselves" (22); "acceptance of the guilt... comes to be a fundamental trait of our German self-consciousness" (111); "purification out of the depth of consciousness of guilt" (112); "where the real guilt consciousness is an indelible prick and has forced a new form on self-consciousness" (115). Expressions such as "guilt consciousness" or "acceptance of guilt" do not refer to the factual level of guilt that cannot be changes, but to the way the person relates to it, to his self-consciousness and honesty with himself; they entail the demand to face the guilt and withstand the temptation of evading it, which Jaspers himself recognized, and to take personal responsibility for the guilt: "Responsibility is the willingness to take the guilt upon himself" (Ph2, 248).[31] Guilt consciousness, it transpires, represents the persons' transparent consciousness regarding the boundaries of freedom and necessity that characterize his existence in the world, and the ability to bear by choice the personal responsibility for the guilt inevitably entailed in human existence.[32]

But the reflection raised by the consciousness of guilt is not exhausted only in distinguishing the antonymous nature of existence and an honest stance facing it while taking responsibility for it. The unique contribution of the reflection raised by boundary situations is expressed in revealing a new datum of human existence that gives them meaning: "Every boundary immediately raises the question what is beyond it" (Ph1, 45). This datum is transcendence;[33] more precisely, becoming acquainted with the existence of a transcendent being, which Jaspers described as an experience in which the person discovers that he is "directed at another freedom", he finds himself "referring to a being that is not himself but is his transcendence" (Ph3, 2). It should be clarified that the actions a person discovered in everyday existence, particularly the self-consciousness achieved outside of the boundary situations, is not perceived as false consciousness that should be rejected. Quite the opposite, Jaspers states that "We live in activity... I *must* want; because wanting must be my last [thing] if I finally want *to be*. But the way that I want freely can open to transcendence" (Ph2, 197).

---

[31] Jaspers demonstrates a possible discourse of avoiding guilt (97). Jaspers believed that the ways of referring to boundary situations and to the antonymous nature of reality in general shows the person's personality and he suggested classifying people according to their various coping patterns; see PW, 240f.

[32] For further discussion of Jaspers' idea of responsibility (*Verantwortung*), see Harries 1994; Tennen 1977, 96-104.

[33] The concept of transcendence is one of the most complex in Jaspers' thought. It was not defined anywhere, but only indirectly. See for example Ph3, 1-35. On the problematic nature of this concept and its philosophical implications, see Collins 1952, 88-127.

If so, transcendence grants meaning to the nature of human freedom as existing in the face of an object that exists beyond it, meaning in the face of a reality that exceeds the boundaries of human existence and consciousness. The boundary that ends the realm of the freedom and necessity in human existence thus denotes also the start of the realm of transcendence that spreads from there onward.

Moreover, the meaning of transcendence for human existence is not exhausted by its sharing a common boundary with it, but primarily in its serving—precisely by existing beyond it—as a source of meaning for human existence: "Were there no transcendence, the question would have arisen why should I want. I can in practice only want when there is transcendence" (Ph2, 198). Wanting, one of the prominent appearances of human freedom, now transpires as lacking direction and meaning without transcendence. In his words:

> Transcendence is not my freedom, but it is present in it. Only in the freedom of my selfhood, with which I think to surround the necessities of... necessity, am I aware that I did not create myself. It transpires to me that where I am completely myself, I am myself alone. Where I was really me myself in desire, I was also at the same time subject to myself in my freedom (Ph2, 199).

So, recognition of transcendence does not deny human freedom, nor does it change the system of limitations to which it is subject. But through its function as an *object* of possibility and necessity, transcendence reveals the real dimensions of the two elements that constitute human existence. These are determined in face of, and perhaps by force of, another entity that exists above and beyond human existence, but that shares a common boundary with it. In this respect, becoming acquainted with transcendence complements the understanding accumulated so far regarding the elements of possibility and necessity, and thus helps position the status of the person in existence more precisely. As he put it: "It transpires to him that what fills him comes toward him... He verifies his possibility only if he knows himself as based on transcendence" (Ph3, 4). Transcendence, as the entity the person faces, simultaneously determines both his possibilities and his restrictions. The two elements, freedom and necessity, thus transpire as what they are only against the background of recognizing the existence of transcendence, which is a more encompassing and whole entity than them.

Against the background of the more complete understanding of the elements of freedom and necessity, a deeper meaning is granted to the concept of inevitable guilt and of boundary situations in general. The main importance of the awareness of the existence of an entity additional to that of human existence stems from its giving the inevitable guilt an object, without which it would have been arbitrary (Ph2, 198). Guilt, just like other human activities, requires an object of reference, without which it would lack meaning and significance. Just as we think about something, want something, and so on, but do not just think or just want, so also guilt refers to an object, meaning we are guilty of something or about something. But transcendence as an object has a more encompassing meaning than that of the other objects of human activity. The perception of transcendence as an entity existing independently of human beings, even if this entity is revealed in human existence and bears a special meaning for people

(Ph2, 22-23; see also Ph3, 164-165), grants it a special status regarding guilt. Guilt is not just guilt of something, it is also guilt in the face of or in relation to something. Jaspers' argument, whereby "the boundaries appear in their real function, to still be immanent and [at the same time] already indicate transcendence" (Ph2, 204), hints at the implications transcendence has for the understanding of human existence. Indeed, the actions of people take place in the world and are apparent there. However, human activity is not exhausted by this, but points to a new ontology existing above and beyond its boundaries.

Transcendence, like any otherness facing which, or in relation to which, human activity takes place, is now positioned "against the tendency for self-sufficiency, against the will's satisfaction with knowledge... against the individual's will, against the drive for self-closure in a life closed in upon itself, against wandering in the existing tradition as a habitual way of life" (Ph2, 61). The metaphysical viewpoint formed in light of recognizing transcendence may serve as a barrier before the ways of evading guilt revealed in the discussion of the two previous viewpoints, centered around closing oneself to the other and to the external world. Thus it transpires that the metaphysical viewpoint provides an explicit response to the problem inherent in viewing guilt from the perspectives of selfhood and of the collective. The distinctiveness of transcendence from the boundaries of human existence is what enables the metaphysical viewpoint formed in relation to it to act as a restraining power against the temptation of evading guilt. Since the boundaries of existence are simultaneously also the boundaries of guilt, the guilt transpires as inevitable.

Conclusion

The analysis of the essay *The Question of Guilt* revolved around three points of view: the viewpoint of selfhood, the viewpoint of the collective, and the metaphysical viewpoint. The path of evading guilt, which arose from the viewpoint anchored in selfhood, led to the discussion of guilt as a collective characteristic of the German nation. The perception of collectivity as an expansion and development of the element of selfhood enabled the rejection of an apriori and absolute perception of the collective, and the prevention of its contrasting to human freedom. However, the presence of freedom within the perception of collectivity expanded the realm of German guilt and showed it as "a possibility in man as such" (94). This opened a real space for the constituting of the metaphysical viewpoint addressing the most fundamental factuality typical of human existence, and revealing that guilt is a boundary situation. From this point of view guilt was discussed as "the guilt of human existence" (28), and at the same time granted real content to the component of freedom that appeared in the collective viewpoint, but was unable to be interpreted within its boundaries. In addition, the basic connection existing between the metaphysical viewpoint of guilt and that anchored in the individual's selfhood was revealed. Like facing himself, in the face of transcendence the person is also alone. However, while anchoring the guilt in the individual's selfhood enabled it in principle to be understood through a particular understanding, its perception as a boundary experience showed that is inevitable, and in this respect it is a permanent and undisputable datum of human existence. In any case, at the same point where the possibilities of the discussion of guilt ended, new possibilities opened before it based in the individual's personal handling of consciousness of the existence of an infinite transcendent entity that shares a common boundary with finite human existence.

In the end, the three viewpoints regarding guilt transpired to denote one reflexive and dynamic motion, constantly expanding the boundaries of the discussion and at the same time illuminating the meaning of the previous stages of the discussion. Jaspers' discussion moves between the personal, the collective, and the metaphysical elements. These do not reflect different degrees of guilt, but appearances of the fundamental patterns of human existence, which as such are raised above the whole concrete context that caused the guilt. This raising of the discussion of guilt above and beyond the historical situation in which *The Question of Guilt* was written also shows its independent importance and value. Focusing the discussion of guilt on the reality of German post-war society could have at most been valid for those Germans who were personally involved in the Nazi crimes. Moreover, they could have argued that their difficult situation in the present was sufficient to punish them for their actions or for standing aside. In contrast, revealing the philosophical depth embodied in Jaspers' later discussion of the issue of guilt through illuminating the inherent presence of three central themes in his philosophical thought—selfhood, historicity, and boundary situations—harnesses the Germans of all generations and human beings in general to handle guilt.

The metaphysical interpretation I have proposed to Jaspers' perception of guilt, presenting the essay *The Question of Guilt* as a sort of reflection of his existentialist thought, can be considered as a problematic perspective for discussing the guilt of the Germans. On the immediate level, the argument arises that an abstract philosophical stance is insufficient to enable the handling of the role of the Germans, as individuals and as a collective, in a war whose victims were real people, and whose results have direct and concrete implications for the lives of nations and millions of people. Secondly, the metaphysical perspective of guilt locates the Germans and their victims on one level, or more precisely, the differences between them do not alter the most basic factuality that they share the same guilt together. The danger in this approach is that turning to the inevitable guilt will itself serve as an evasion route from the inevitable guilt, and there is no doubt that the guilt of the Germans during the Second World War was this type of guilt.

Perhaps we can find in *The Question of Guilt* a sort of brakes that reflect a way of handling the danger of evading the inevitable guilt. Thus, for example, Jaspers notes now and then in this essay certain facts, dates, places, and so on (e.g., 45 ff.). But in my opinion, the appearance of these mentions was not primarily intended to prevent this danger. It is entirely clear that as a philosopher Jaspers could not base his perception of guilt on concrete ground, as defined as distinguished as it might be. It was clear to him that against any concrete fact an opposing fact could be placed, and that there would never be a safe way to decide between them. Thus, instead of working to identify and develop a factual substrate for discussing German guilt, Jaspers chose to anchor his perception precisely in *the question of guilt*, and hence the name of the essay he dedicated to it. Unlike an accusation that invites answers or responses from the addressee, and directs him outside of himself, the question directs the person to himself and encourages him to reflect upon it and pave his own way to understand it. Indeed, there is no guarantee that the reflection would not skip over the avoidable guilt and find its destination within the boundaries of inevitable guilt. In any case, it seems that Jaspers thought that only if the question of guilt continues to be asked would it become a permanent feature in the being of Germans and of human beings in general, and in each generation would people continue to deal with the meaning of their past.

Bar-Ilan University

References

Jaspers' Writings:

The Question of German Guilt. 2000. Trans. E.B. Ashton, New York: Fordham University Press. (*The Question of Guilt*).
Allgemeine Psychopathologie. Ein Leitfaden für Studierende, Ärzte und Psychologen. 1913. First ed. Berlin. (Psychopathology1).
Der philosophische Glaube angesichts der Offenbarung. 1962. München. (Philosophical Faith in the Face of Revelation).
Die geistige Situation der Zeit. 1931. Berlin-Leipzig. (Spiritual Situation).
Die Frage der Entmythologisierung. 1954. München. (EM).
Philosophie. 1932. 3 vols. *Philosophische Weltorientirung* (Ph1); *Existenzerellung* (Ph2); *Metaphysik* (Ph3). Heidelberg, 1994.
Psychologie der Weltanschauungen. 1919. Heidelberg, 1985 (Psychology).

Other Writings:

Bankir, David. 2006. "The Historical Background: Germany in 1945-1947", in Karl Jaspers, *The Question of Guilt*, 9-29, Jerusalem [Hebrew].
Bollnow, Otto Friedrich. 1964. *Existenzphilosophie*. Stuttgart.
Collins, James. 1952. *The Existentialists: A Critical Study*. Chicago.
Dilthey, Wilhelm. 1962. *Weltanschauungslehre, Abhandlung zur Philosophie der Philosophie*, in *Gesmmelte Schriften* 8. Stuttgart & Göttingen.
Fuchs, Wolfgang Walter. 1976. *Phenomenology and the Metaphysics of Presence: An Essay in the Philosophy of Edmund Husserl*. The Hague.
Fulda, Hans Friedrich. 1966. "Über den spekulativen Anfang", in Dieter Henrich and Hans Wagner (eds.), *Subjektivität und Metaphysik*, Festschrift für Wolfgang Cramer. Frankfurt a.M.
Harries, Karsten. 1994. "Shame, Guilt, Responsibility", in A.M. Olsen (ed.), *Heidegger & Jaspers*, 49-64. Philadelphia.
Hegel, G.W.F. 1974. *Vorlesungen über die Philosophie der Geschichte*, ed. G. Lasson. Leipzig.
Heidegger, Martin. 1998. *Pathmarks*. Cambridge.
Heidegger, Martin. 1927. *Sein und Zeit*. Tübingen, 1993.
Husserl, Edmund. 1993. "Philosophy as a Rigorous Science", in Husserl, *Phenomenology and the Crisis of Philosophy*, Quentin Lauer (trans.), New York, 1965, 71-147.

Knauss, Gerhard. 1957. "The Concept of the 'Encompassing' in Jaspers' Philosophy", in P.A. Schilpp (ed.), *The Philosophy of Karl Jaspers*, 141-175. New York.

Latzel, Edwin. 1957. "The Concept of 'Ultimate Situation' in Jaspers' Philosophy", in P.A. Schilpp (ed.), *The Philosophy of Karl Jaspers*, 177-208. New York.

Miron, Ronny. 2004. "From Psychiatry to Philosophy: The Concept of Self in Karl Jaspers". *Iyyun* 53: 123-150 [Hebrew] (Translated and reprinted in this collection as Miron, 2004b).

Miron, Ronny. 2005. "Transcendence and Dissatisfaction in Jaspers' Idea of the Self", *Phänomenologische Forschungen*, NS. 10:221-241 (Reprinted in this collection as Miron, 2005).

Miron, Ronny. 2006a. "Was Jaspers Really Kantian?", *Yearbook of the Austrian Karl Jaspers Society*, 19:73-106.

Miron, Ronny. 2006b. "Towards Reality: The Development of the Philosophical Attitude to Reality in Karl Jaspers' Thought", *Journal of the British Society for Phenomenology*, 37/2,152-172.

Miron, Ronny. 2012. *Karl Jaspers: From Selfhood to Being*. Rodopi, Value Inquiry Series (Miron, Monograph, 2012).

Plümacher, Martina. 1996. *Philosophie nach 1945 in der Bundesrepublik Deutschland*. Hamburg.

Rotenstreich, Nathan. 1955. *Between Past and Present: Ways of Historical Consciousness*. Jerusalem [Hebrew].

Salamun, Kurt. 1985. *Karl Jaspers*. München.

Saner, Hans (ed.). 1973. *Karl Jaspers in der Diskussion*. München.

Scheler, Max. 1954. *Philosophische Weltanschauung*. Bern.

Tennen, Hanoch. 1977. *The Perception of Existentialist Ethics in the Thought of Karl Jaspers*. Ramat Gan [Hebrew].

Young-Bruehl, Elisabeth. 1981. *Freedom and Karl Jaspers' Philosophy*. New Haven.

The Guilt Which We Are: An Ontological Approach to Jaspers' Idea of Guilt

Abstract

This paper suggests a phenomenological reading of Karl Jaspers' writings regarding the issue of guilt. This reading aims to extricate from them an ontological understanding of guilt, at the centre of which stand the various appearances of guilt and not the subjective awareness of its experience. The discussed ontology of guilt does not exist in Jaspers' thinking in its entirety, but rather is only implicitly interwoven in his ideas – some of them referring to the issue of guilt, but spread over his writings in an elementary and not systematic manner, while others, no less central to the phenomenology of guilt, are not exposed by him as referring to the idea of guilt, but according to the suggested interpretation are relevant to the ontology of guilt (for example, the idea of historicity). Although the suggested phenomenological-ontological reading contains a certain reconstruction of Jaspers' ideas, the reconstruction itself serves only as a means for a thematic crystallization of a possible ontology of guilt based upon his thinking but not realized by him as he rejected the very idea of ontology from the outset.

Introduction

This article offers a phenomenological reading of Jaspers' writings with a view to extricating his ontological approach to guilt. First, it is necessary to explain the methodology and the way Jaspers' writings will be read and interpreted here. This will provide background for the specific phenomenological reading of Jaspers' approach. The article will then expose and explicate three different manifestations of guilt that appear in Jaspers' thought.

The ontology of guilt discussed below is not treated explicitly in Jaspers' writings, but is implicit in his philosophy. Some of his ideas refer directly to the issue of guilt, but they are undeveloped and scattered among his writings. There are also other ideas which the proposed interpretation shows are relevant to guilt and will refer to them as its manifestations. I contend that Jaspers' thought expresses notions of guilt, but he identifies only some of them with guilt, and he does not explain the transitions between the various manifestations of guilt. The proposed phenomenological-ontological reading partially reconstructs Jaspers' ideas, but the reconstruction is not the purpose of this article. It is only a means of formulating thematically the phenomenology of guilt derivable from his thought, which was not realized by Jaspers himself.

Readers familiar with Jaspers' writings deserve an explanation regarding the nature of the proposed project, since Jaspers is known in the history of philosophy as one of the existentialist thinkers who explicitly confronted the issue of guilt. Jaspers does indeed discuss it in various contexts, as I shall now demonstrate.

In *Psychology of World Views*, guilt is discussed in the context of the perception of subjectivity. It appears there as an *organon* for the formation of a world view which itself was not constituted in relation to the reality external to the individual. In Jaspers' mature existentialist philosophy, guilt is presented as a human experience which, when dealt with, helps formulate self-understanding.

Guilt is also presented elsewhere as a "boundary situation" (*Grenzsituation*), along with other extreme forms of human experience, such as death, chance and suffering. In this context, Jaspers proposes a distinction between "avoidable guilt" and "inevitable guilt". The former can be avoided by adopting a normative moral code of behavior. Inevitable guilt, the main subject of his discussion, relates to the foundations of human existence, and as such cannot be avoided.[1] The issue of guilt as one of the boundary situations goes beyond the limits of Jaspers' philosophy of Existenz. It is related to his conception of Being. This is not restricted to immanent human existence, but recognizes the independent existence of a transcendent Being towards which the inevitable guilt is directed.[2] In any case, even in his philosophy of Existenz, Jaspers does not grant real and concrete reality any weight or significance with regard to guilt.

The issue of guilt, then, although continuously discussed in Jaspers' writings, does not touch upon the connection between its various aspects. Moreover, from a phenomenological viewpoint, Jaspers' references to guilt raise a problem, since they do not confront the basic fact that guilt is the individual's way of relating to the other, to the norms and moral approaches acceptable in society and to events in concrete reality.

An answer to these problems appears to be provided in *The Question of Guilt*, where Jaspers presents the range of manifestations of guilt in the context of historical reality with a reference, albeit minimal, to the criminal and moral aspect of guilt. Furthermore, in addition to his reference to the real German context, Jaspers refers in this work to the subjective and metaphysical aspects that had appeared in his earlier works. Thus, one cannot conclude from the perception of guilt arising from *The Question of Guilt* that Jaspers changed his approach or that he thought that dealing with concrete reality was incompatible with discussing

---

[1] Jaspers made it clear that his approach had nothing in common with the idea of original sin. Karl Jaspers, *Die Schuldfarge, Von der politischen Haftung Deutschlands* [1946], 1996, München. The discussion will refer to the English translation, which appeared as: *The Question of the German Guilt*, New York, 1947, 100 (hereafter: Question of Guilt). Other references to Jaspers' writings will follow the abbreviations appearing in the list at the end.

[2] Jaspers' perception of Being is discussed directly in the following writings: Ph3; Wisdom and Existenz; Truth.

these aspects. In *The Question of Guilt*, he refers to the guilt of the Germans as individuals and as members of the German nation, but also presents guilt as "the guilt of our humanity", an indisputable datum of human culture. However, it seems that the difficulty in formulating a thematic concept of guilt containing the spectrum of components of guilt scattered in Jaspers' writings is most tangible in this work. The lack of coherent integration between them is particularly prominent at the point where he collects all of them together. The relation between the guilt experienced by an individual and the guilt experienced by the member of a collective is unclear, as is the connection between these two experiences and the metaphysical dimensions of guilt.

In this article I would like to present the three main dimensions where human beings experience guilt – the individual, the collective and the metaphysical. Each of these dimensions in Jaspers' perception of guilt acquires its full significance only within a complete phenomenological explication drawn from Jaspers' entire *oeuvre*.

Guilt as the individual's experience may be understood in terms of the explication of the perception of subjective particularity that Jaspers dealt with in all his writings, while guilt as an experience of the collective is elucidated using aspects of a comprehensive view of Jaspers' philosophy of Existenz. This is a framework in which his perception of subjectivity matured and where various expressions of the individual's transcendence of his individuality are revealed. The deeper significance of the metaphysical manifestation of experiencing guilt, where it appears as a boundary situation, will become clear in the context of Jaspers' perception of Being, with the notion of a transcendent Being as a horizon of Existenz.

This explication anchors the three manifestations of guilt in Jaspers' entire work. Furthermore, the proposed interpretation will seek to examine the relation between the three manifestations of guilt from a genetic phenomenological viewpoint, and thus the discussion will go beyond the framework of Jaspers' thinking.

To begin with the first manifestation, the individual's experience of guilt has an evident and immediate nature grounded in the world of real life. The guilt is first and foremost that of the individual but it does not constitute an experience closed within its own boundaries. Elucidating the individual's experience of guilt, which leads one beyond one's own boundaries, will reveal the second manifestation, the collective horizon contained in it. This complements the discussion of the individual dimensions of guilt.

So far as the ontology of guilt is concerned, the first circle, encompassing the individual's experience, exists within the collective social being that surrounds it. This determines what guilt is, and accordingly marks the boundaries between guilty and not guilty. It also determines the field within which the addressees of the guilt – other humans – are located. The social framework shows that guilt is not just a category through which individuals refer to themselves, and which reveals them as beings yearning for self-understanding in existence. It is also a category that mediates between the individual and others. However, even the collective experience cannot contain itself, and its elucidation leads to the third, most encompassing, circle of the experience of guilt, the metaphysical manifestation.

As in any phenomenological explication, completing the movement gives new significance to the previous manifestations of guilt. The different dimensions of guilt can indeed appear in human experience independently of each other, but the ontology of guilt deriving from them all reveals that they are different stages in dealing with guilt as a basic datum of human existence. Thus, the three stages of the phenomenology of guilt should all be seen as existing in the ontological space of inevitable guilt. This means that it is found in the manifestations of existence that are not the result of the individual's mental constitution but rather the datum into which the individual is thrown. At the same time, the unavoidable nature of this guilt is not revealed all at once – neither in existence nor in the philosophical explication – in each of its manifestations. Instead, the inevitability of guilt is gradually revealed as the experience of guilt deepens. At the more mature metaphysical stage of experience, when guilt appears as a boundary situation, the inevitability of guilt reaches the peak of its clarity.

That each of the three stages can appear independently shows that the experience of guilt is, by its very nature, inexhaustibile. The ontology of guilt connects and elucidates the various stages, thereby making the human experience of guilt significant. The process of phenomenological explication is reflexive in nature. On the one hand it serves as a mirror for the experience of guilt, gradually revealing both the various stages and the dynamic leading from one stage to the next. On the other hand it extricates guilt's inevitability already present implicitly in the first manifestation.

Following this explanation of the nature of the phenomenological reading of Jaspers' thought, let us now examine in detail each of the three manifestations of guilt derivable from his writings.

The Experience of Individual Guilt

Guilt anchored in the individual's subjective experience is presented as the first manifestation in *The Question of Guilt*. The individual nature of guilt is clearly expressed in the following words, bearing the signs of a personal confession:

> We Germans differ greatly in the kind and degree of our participation in, or resistance to, National-Socialism. Everyone must reflect on his own internal conduct, and seek his own peculiar rebirth in this German crisis.
>
> Another great difference between individuals concerns the starting time of this inner metamorphosis... we Germans cannot be reduced to a common denominator. We must keep an open mind in approaching each other from essentially different starting points (Question of Guilt, 104).

The basic premise regarding the distinctiveness of individuals leads inevitably to the recognition in principle of the range of attitudes towards the Nazi regime that typified German society. Jaspers states that: "In this kind of talking none is the other's judge; everyone is both defendant and judge at the same time" (Question of Guilt, 14). Moreover, the individual is not only the addressee of the guilt, he is also its deliverer: "the guilt question is more than a question put to us by others, it is one we put to ourselves" (Question of Guilt, 28). So, guilt has a framework of self-reference with the range of emotional and mental skills involved in the formulation of self-consciousness. Indeed, a demand from an external source – other people, the state laws or general moral norms – affects the individual and the formation of his personality.

However, the arena in which people deal with guilt is limited by the boundaries of the individual's self-reference. Thus, reference to the external dimensions relating to guilt is delayed at the individual stage in favor of the experience (*Erlebnis*) of guilt with its particular aspects. Some of these cannot be communicated and objectivized, since the faults that awaken guilt appear to the individual as aimed at him specifically. At the individual stage, guilt does not appear as a general human experience or as connected to a concrete historical reality but only as tangential to it, and independent of general criteria or standards.

Further study shows that the perception of individuality guiding Jaspers' approach to the individual experience of guilt is drawn from the concept of the subject developed in the early stages of his thought. The recognition that the individual's world is particular and mostly inaccessible to formal knowledge and objective thought as such began to develop already in his early writings dealing with psychopathology. In this spirit, he argued that the human being's individuality places a boundary (*Grenze*) that cannot be crossed or overcome using the objective criteria taken from the conceptual system of science (Psychopathology1, 1-2). Therefore, the possible contribution of psychopathology to the understanding of people suffering from mental diseases was essentially limited.

This approach continued to develop in *The Psychology of World Views* (1919), dealing with the description and elucidation of individual experiences through which people formulate their self-perception. In this context, Jaspers argued that the infinite variety, reflected in the experiences of people in reality and in the ways they perceive themselves, does not allow the philosopher to achieve by mere observation an exhaustive and complete understanding of the person's individual Being. In this spirit, he declared:

> We are not searching for the frequent or the average... We are searching for the specific patterns even if they are rather rare. Our area is... the material that comes into being when we see what we notice in the historical experience, in the living internal [experience] and in the [one] present in the peculiar (*Eigentümliche*), in itself unique, even if this only seems and is built as typical. (Psychology, 14).

Jaspers' interest in the particular aspects of subjectivity reached its full development in the philosophy of Existenz, at whose heart was the requirement "to be from the source of my selfhood" (Ph2, 6).[3] He argued that the constant gap between people's Being and the contexts in which they participate (Ph2, 32) greatly restricts the ability to discuss it using objective tools and justifies the perception of an individual as a Being whose particular elements dominate it. As he phrased it:

---

[3] On the perception of Existenz as a "source" (*Ursprung*), see also Ph2, 336-337.

> If I want to know what I am, then my objective existence presents itself, in the thinking moves I experience, as a scheme of my Being. **I perceive myself inside it, but I experience that I am not completely identical with it:** *what thus becomes an object cannot attain absolute identity with me myself,* since in my expansion I must lose myself in this scheme. (Ph2, 32).[4]

This brief review of the perception of selfhood in Jaspers' writings clearly shows the dominance of his interest in the particular aspects of selfhood compared with its objective dimensions. The perception of subjectivity as a particular Being is essential to the understanding of the stage of the individual experience of guilt in Jaspers' thought, where the extent of its detachment from the surrounding reaches its maximum. Here this perception explains the lack of communication typical of the appearance of guilt at this stage and of its view of guilt as a type of self-reference. In other words, the individual notes in this context not only the field where the guilt appears, but also the context where it has meaning and significance. The objective or formal viewpoint, whose boundaries are determined mainly by the collective, is marginalized due to its inaccessibility to the individual's subjective Being.

However, it is impossible to refer to the individual while suspending the external contexts in which he acts, since the individual's own experience takes place within a concrete field. The individual is always this particular individual, located in a particular environment and place, connected to a specific history and to people with whom he shares a common existence. As one penetrates inwards to subjectivity, the spaces from which its surrounding subjectivity appears are projected.

Jaspers does not present the insufficiency of the experience of guilt at the individual stage explicitly. In practice, this insufficiency arises from his discussion of the four concepts of guilt in *The Question of Guilt*: criminal, political, moral and metaphysical.[5] The first three are attributed mainly to individuals, but the individual's viewpoint is not what determines the fact of guilt. Instead it is objective criteria independent of the individual that do this. Thus, criminal guilt applies to those who perform "acts capable of objective proof and violate unequivocal laws" (Question of Guilt, 31). Political guilt "involve[s] the deeds of statesmen and of the citizenry of a state, result[s] in my having to bear the consequences of the deeds of the state whose power governs me... Everybody is co-responsible for the way he is governed" (Question of Guilt, 31). Moral guilt relies on recognition of the individual's responsibility for what he does as an individual, or for what he avoids doing, an avoidance whose results are undesirable from his point of view (Question of Guilt, 31-32).[6]

Apparently, the situation is different regarding metaphysical guilt, which is not determined by objective or formal criteria. Metaphysical guilt originates in the conscience the individual possesses as part of his Being. Moreover, the

---

[4] For an extensive discussion of selfhood in Jaspers' writings, see: Miron, 2005.
[5] For a more detailed definition of these concepts of guilt, see: Question of Guilt, 31-33, 61-73.
[6] For further discussion of Jaspers' idea of responsibility (*Verantwortung*), see: Harries, 1994.

individual does not bear this guilt as an autarchic subject but as a human being. Metaphysical guilt originates in "a solidarity among men as human beings that makes each co-responsible for every wrong and every injustice in the world" (Question of Guilt, 32); "responsibility [that] is the willingness [of each individual] to take the guilt upon himself" (Ph2, 248). Jaspers tried to make this argument concrete when he stated that this solidarity is breached "if I was present at the murder of others without risking my life to prevent it". If these things happened and I witnessed them, if I survived when someone else was murdered, then I hear a voice that tells me: "that if I live after such a thing has happened, it weighs upon me as indelible guilt" (Question of Guilt, 32).

It seems that even if metaphysical guilt is an experience of individuals, and like the three other types it is self-referential, its meaning breaks through the boundaries of the individual's existence, and does not depend on any particular behavior, or its avoidance. Either way, in all forms of the individual's experience of guilt, he is revealed as insufficient in himself and thus forced to transcend the boundaries of his self-reference. This can be achieved through external objective judgement or through the individual's attempt to transcend the boundaries of self-reference. Since this transcending becomes inevitable for him, it is revealed as a full expression of the individual experience of guilt.[7]

The perception of the individual as a particular Being, implemented in his approach towards guilt, continued to bother Jaspers throughout his works. It was only in his writings from the early nineteen-thirties onwards that he gradually became aware of its restrictive implications. The perception of the individual is restrictive not only as a starting point for clarifying other philosophical issues his thought was destined to address, but also for the individual's self-understanding. This awareness is clearly reflected in the following passage:

> Placing itself absolutely on itself alone is for Existenz **the truth of its independence of the reality of time, but this turns into despair for it**. It [Existenz] knows itself that by standing completely by itself it must sink into a vacuum. (Ph3, 4).

Jaspers sought to solve the closedness that the individual's viewpoint forced on his perception of selfhood by expanding the perspective regarding selfhood. However, his handling of the possible harmful implications of the viewpoint anchored on the individual did not lead Jaspers to completely rejecting the centrality he had granted the individual in his approach. Rather, when discussing selfhood in the philosophy of Existenz and when turning to the issue of guilt, he located the problematic element, the particularity of the individual, whose over-

---

[7] The revolution Jaspers instigated in the individual perspective of guilt, familiar mainly from its psychological discourse (mainly Freudian), is clear against the background of the proposed analysis. While the latter leads to liberating the individual from guilt, or more precisely from guilt feelings, the former aims to anchor the experience of guilt and the process of the formation of self-Being on common ground. For a basic ontological distinction between guilt and guilt feelings, see: Buber. For Jaspers' criticism of psychoanalysis, see: Spiritual Situation, 137-139. See also his essay "Zur Kritik de Psychoanalyse", written in 1950 and published in Report, 260-271. For further reading see: Kolle.

emphasis had contributed to the formulation of the individual in his writings as a solipsistic Being.[8] The meaning of this insight in the current context is that the extreme particular perception of the individual imposes upon the experience of guilt a detachment that conceals its inevitability, or more precisely, creates a false appearance of guilt.

Jaspers' discussion of the individual's attempts to avoid guilt (Question of Guilt, 74) he is indirectly aware of the ontological distortion entailed in the manifestation of guilt at the individual stage.[9] The discourse of escaping guilt raises ethical questions which are not the concern of the current ontological analysis of guilt. Jaspers describes the problem with the experience of guilt by referring to the individuals' consciousness of the different types of guilt. In this way, he contributes indirectly to the discourse of escaping it, since consciousness can be changed, while guilt cannot. Nevertheless, the problematic of escaping guilt touches upon a significant point for its ontology, since it indicates that the individual manifestation of guilt can be distorted.

Beyond the potential for distortion entailed in individual guilt, its ontological representation encounters another basic difficulty. This stems from the fact that it is the very focusing on the individual's particular characteristics that contributes to its concretization. This, in turn, inevitably locates it in the time and place common to the individual and to other people. This is a difficulty typical of the phenomenological discourse based on real human experiences, which requires a constant expansion of the perspective of reference to the human experience in order to achieve an appropriate understanding of it. Thus, the phenomenological explication shows that one cannot reject the external contexts in which the individual operates.

The appropriate weight of the individual's subjective Being in the experience of guilt will be clarified below in the discussion of the next stages, where the individual aims beyond the boundaries of his personal view. Jaspers himself did not suggest an explanation for the transition from the individual stage of experiencing guilt to the next stage, collective guilt. However, his discussion of the possibilities for escaping guilt indirectly laid the infrastructure for this transition, since it was contained in dimensions objective and external to the individual existence, which turned out to be involved in the human experience of guilt. In this context, it is especially important that even when he was aiming to establish the centrality of the individual's personal Being, in the clarification of guilt and in his philosophy in general, Jaspers did not explicitly reject the relevance of objectivity for understanding the individual's Being. He only marginalized or suspended it, and thus did not prevent the possibility of breaking out of the solipsistic individuality that was formulated in his discussions of the issue of guilt and elsewhere in his writings.

---

[8] On Jaspers' handling of the difficulties involved in the solipsistic understanding of man and the turning point in his thought towards another approach of subjectivity, see Miron, 2005

[9] Jaspers demonstrates a possible discourse of escaping guilt (Question of Guilt, 74). He believed that the ways of referring to the boundary situations and to the antonymous nature of reality in general expose the person's character, and he suggested classifying people by their various coping patterns. See Psychology, 240 ff.

The Collective Stage—The Group's Guilt

Two aspects arising from the explication of the individual manifestation of guilt serve as the basic infrastructure, albeit mainly negative, for the second manifestation of guilt, the collective stage. These aspects are the suspension, rather than explicit rejection, of the objective aspects it entailed, and the potential for distortion entailed in the solipsistic manifestation of the individual that conceals the guilt's inevitability. The collective stage in Jaspers' ontology of guilt is basically an expanded observation of the individual experience of guilt and not a diminution or devaluation of this experience. More precisely, the collective stage is merely an explication of the context in which individual guilt manifests itself. It is clear that the character of an experience appearing in a context is different from its isolated representation as expressed in the individual stage of the experience of guilt.

It is not surprising that only in *The Question of Guilt*, a work written in connection with concrete reality, did Jaspers discuss the collective aspects entailed in the experience of guilt. In the other contexts of his thought, which lack this connection, direct references to this dimension are not to be found. This is not to imply that the experience of individuals is not a real experience of guilt, or that the metaphysical aspects related to guilt are not part of this experience. However, it seems that the collective dimension of the experience of guilt appears especially in relation to a concrete historical situation.

Thus, when discussing the guilt of Germans for crimes committed during the Nazi period, he included expressions that indicated that the guilt under discussion was the guilt of those belonging to the German nation as a collective. In this spirit, he described himself as a German among Germans (Question of Guilt, 11), "who feels concerned by everything growing from German roots" (Question of Guilt, 79). Jaspers clarified that speaking about Germanness as a characteristic that turns Germans into a collective "is altogether different from making the nation absolute" (Question of Guilt, 80), and added that "there is no such thing as a people as a whole… One cannot make an individual out of a people. A people cannot perish heroically, cannot be criminal, cannot act morally or immorally; only its individuals can do so. A people as a whole can be neither guilty nor innocent" (Question of Guilt, 41).

In this work, the collective appears as a continuation, expansion and development of the individual's selfhood, clarified as a Being existing in relation to the human reality surrounding it. As he puts it:

> The self-analysis of a people in historical reflection and the personal self-analysis of the individual are two different things. But the first can happen only by the way of the second. What individuals accomplish jointly in communication may, if true, become the spreading consciousness of many and then is called national consciousness. (Question of Guilt, 102).

Not only do the individuals join together to form the collective, the individual also bears the collective within, thus "everyone, in his real being, is the German people" (Question of Guilt, 80). Moreover, understanding the collectivity as a continuation and expansion of the individual's experience enables us to observe the collective experience of guilt as a modification of an individual experience, and thus as also limited within its own boundaries:

> But even more important to us is how we analyze, judge and cleanse ourselves. Those charges from without no longer are our concern. On the other hand, they are the charges from within... are the source of whatever self-respect is still possible for us. We must clarify the question of German guilt. This is our own business. (Question of Guilt, 49).

Thus it transpires that just like the individual, the collective appears in the experience of guilt as a Being to be clarified and examined: "[in Germany] we have no common ground yet" (Question of Guilt, 11), to the extent that "being German is to me... not a condition but a task" (Question of Guilt, 80); "Common is the non-community" (Question of Guilt, 18); "now that we can talk freely again, we seem to each other as if we had come from different worlds" (Question of Guilt, 19).

Jaspers' range of references to collectivity in *The Question of Guilt* indicates the cautious and gradual way in which the immediate experience of guilt anchored in the individual's Being is directed to the surrounding collective horizons. Jaspers wishes to preserve the individual's status within the boundaries of the collective. He also wants to ensure that the presence of individuality in the experience of collective guilt will not entail the failings threatening the standing of individuals in the face of guilt. In particular, individuals closing themselves off from other people and the world, thereby potentially distorting the authentic appearance of guilt as inevitable.

However, even in *The Question of Guilt*, the only context referring to the collective stage, Jaspers did not elucidate the transition between the individual stage and the collective stage of guilt. The basic question what makes a group of individuals into a collective is not answered in *The Question of Guilt*, nor in the other contexts where Jaspers refers to the issue of guilt.

Apart from collectivity providing the context for the manifestation of the individual's experience of guilt, it is not clear what unique quality of experiencing guilt is discovered at the collective stage, nor what is has that the individual's guilt does not. In my opinion, the answer to both these questions, essential for understanding the collective experience of guilt, is contained in Jaspers' original idea of historicity (*Geschichtlichkeit*). Jaspers himself did not link this idea to his perception of guilt, but it throws light on the notion of objectivity as an expansion of individuality. In this idea Jaspers rehabilitates the dimension of objectivity external to the individual and links it to his experience of existence. This concept completes Jaspers' effort, prior to the appearance of the idea of historicity, to re-examine the possible contribution of recognition of the world's reality and of formal knowledge to the development of the philosophical perception of selfhood. This had encountered difficulties due to the over-emphasis of its particular elements, which had led to the view of the individual as a solipsistic Being.[10] Historicity provides Jaspers' notion of collectivity with

---

[10] For further discussion of this issue, see: Miron, 2004c.

content, beyond the formal features of the common language mentioned in *The Question of Guilt* (79), and joins the subjective and objective dimensions, enriching the individual's manifestation in existence.

The idea of historicity was based on the classic Hegelian distinction between the two meanings of the word "history" (*Geschichte*) in German: history and story.[11] The former denotes the objective clarification of the details of an historical event, whose guiding principles serve as a basis for understanding history as a science. The latter, following the formation of the consciousness of the past by people and its use as a basis for self-understanding in the present, expresses the subjective meaning of history. A person's understanding of himself as a historistic Being combines reflection aimed at clarifying the data and objective circumstances of the past with the subjective meaning he grants them. Through these, the person perceives himself as existing in a concrete time and context, and as part of a continuity whose boundaries transcend the boundaries of his individual existence. So, in this context, the individual is manifested as a continuation of earlier forms of existence, and at the same time as a foundation for a future reality that will continue after him (Ph2, 118-119). Jaspers expressed the connection between the objective and subjective dimensions when he wrote:

> Here are originally connected in an inseparable way **Being and knowledge**... Without knowledge, meaning a clear perception and being inside it, there is no historistic Being, and without a reality of historicity there is no knowledge. (Ph2, 119).

However, the distinction between the objective and subjective dimensions of history was not intended to detach and separate them. Quite the opposite: through the concept of historicity, Jaspers sought to harness the mental skills involved in the formation of historical consciousness, mainly aimed at establishing the scientific nature of history as an area of knowledge, to the service of historistic consciousness, to turn it into an integral part of self-consciousness. As he put it:

> **From this historistic (*geschichtlichen*) source, the *historical* also becomes for the first time really historistic**. Without it, it would only mean a particular event attributed to the existence of the present evaluated positively or negatively. However, **my theoretical knowledge from history becomes through the whole science of history a function of the possible Existenz**, if its contents and images aim themselves at me, face me, demand from me or push me away from them, not only as distant patterns existing as closed within themselves or in other words: if it is *acquired* to the function of the eternal present of the things that exist within the philosophical-historistic consciousness. (Ph2, 119-120).

The idea of historicity, it transpires, contained the understanding that historical knowledge itself did not reflect a mere objective generality. The individual's reflexive turning to historical knowledge causes a fundamental change in himself,

---

[11] Hegel, 142 ff.

as a result of which the general and impersonal element is removed from this knowledge. It now serves as a framework within whose boundaries the person organizes his life story and his self-consciousness as an individual.[12]

From Jaspers' viewpoint, the change occurring in historical knowledge as a result of the individual's turning to it is not perceived as its distortion but as revealing its real significance: "[historical knowledge] **proves its power** in the ability of its results, to be replaced by real historistic consciousness of the self-existing in the present" (Ph2, 120). In fact, the meeting between the person and historical knowledge creates a mutual change. On the one hand, the existential view reveals new and unfamiliar facets of historical knowledge, enriches it and especially reveals its dynamic nature that enables it to turn to the world of present people. On the other hand, the individual's turning to historical science expands the boundaries of his existence and introduces to it belonging, context and depth. The concept of historicity thus connects the individual to the past and to the knowledge of the past. The knowledge of the past does not take away the individual's privacy, but bestows upon it a fuller meaning that is not restricted to the boundaries of personal existence.

Through the idea of historicity we can now mark out the boundaries of the collectivity in which the experience of guilt appears. This collectivity has two basic features: it indicates the link between the individual and his contemporaries, and it connects him, along with them, to ancestors and future descendants. The objective aspect of history, portrayed in the accumulated knowledge of the past common to members of the collective, and the subjective dimension comprising the range of references of individuals belonging to the collective towards this past, now turn out to be present in any experience of guilt. The absence of the objective dimension at the stage of the individual experience of guilt has now received a real solution from the perspective of the idea of historicity.

Questions regarding the injustices done to other humans during my lifetime and the crimes committed by previous generations of the collective with which I identify myself may now be seen to be an integral part of the individual manifestation of guilt. Jaspers' aim to establish independence between the experience of guilt and individuals' concrete behavior – an aim apparent already at the stage of individual experience of guilt – now receives additional validity, since the idea of historicity indicates that the person never manifests alone in existence.[13] More precisely, the reference point for human existence is anchored

---

[12] Jaspers' attitude in principle towards general and objective knowledge, in this context towards historical knowledge, is an extension of his early attitude as a psychiatrist and active researcher of mental disease. As in his criticism of the science of psychopathology or of general psychology as formal frameworks of knowledge that cannot enable access to the fullness and uniqueness of human Being, here too it is assumed that general and formal historical knowledge cannot serve as a source for self-understanding.

[13] It is important to clarify that although Jaspers sought to avoid reducing guilt to the concrete level of acts, circumstances or reasons, a level that on its own could lead to avoiding the clarification of guilt (see Question of Guilt, 27: "The temptation to evade this question is obvious"), he did not reject factuality as irrelevant to the discussion of the issue of guilt. Moreover, in *The Question of Guilt* he refers to the concrete facts around which the uniqueness of German guilt was formulated in comparison to that of other nations and did not try to avoid the concrete implications necessitated by the actions of the Germans (see for example, Question of Guilt, 70-71).

in multiplicity, i.e., in society. Indeed, "the effects of natural causes depend also on how man takes them, how he handles them, what he makes out of them" (Question of Guilt, 85). Moreover, the idea of historicity does not remove the uniqueness of the individual and accordingly claim that in the collective manifestation of guilt the objective dimension is granted priority or greater weight than that of the individual manifestation.

In his discussion of the idea of historicity Jaspers referred to the aspects relating to the individual's consciousness in existence. However with regard to the ontology of guilt it is more important that this idea appears in the description of the way that individuals who have this consciousness are present in existence. In other words, they are manifested as part of a collective and there is objective knowledge referring to them as a collective. Thus, the individual is present in the collective and in certain cases may even be an object of knowledge that will be handled with objective tools. However, both the collectivity and the knowledge represent a deviation beyond the manifestation of the individual as such.

From a phenomenological viewpoint, the explication of the collective dimensions, including that of the objective aspects entailed in the experience of guilt, reveals no new dimension that did not exist in the individual stage. It elucidates what was contained but not revealed in the individual manifestation of guilt due to the restricted perception at that early stage. More precisely, the two stages of the experience of guilt supplement each other. The personal link to the reality to which the guilt in its individual manifestation refers is joined by another form of linking to reality anchored in objective knowledge, which indicates a Being going beyond the boundaries of private existence.

Against the background of the discussion of the idea of historicity, we can now understand Jaspers' statement in *The Question of Guilt*: "we have to bear the guilt of our fathers" (Question of Guilt, 79) as summarizing the concrete stage in his perception of guilt. All the individuals in a certain collective inevitably become guilty, merely by their belonging to the collective. The collective thus indicates the horizon of possibility (*Möglichkeit*) at the disposal of the individual in existence at a given time. Even if this individual did not express in practice a behavior harmful to others, his own manifestation was saturated in the collective to which he belonged. Thus, being part of the collective, he inevitably bears the guilt. The component of "possibility" in guilt adds a layer to the general trend seeking to detach the experience of guilt from linkage to concrete actions, thus giving another indication of the continuity between the stage of the individual experience of guilt and the collective stage that expands it.[14] Jaspers went further and defined guilt itself as a possibility. As he put it:

> In tracing our own guilt back to its source we come upon the human essence – which in its German form has fallen into a peculiar, terrible incurring of guilt but exists as a possibility in man as such. (Question of Guilt, 100).

---

[14] The idea of possibility is discussed in relation to the idea of freedom in Jaspers' philosophy. See: Young-Bruehl 1981, 64-65, 105-106.

At this point, the dimensions of the particular collectivity to which individuals belong have been expanded, and the experience of the guilt has been directed to a deep element in human Being, an element "which cannot be flatly referred to as our guilt" (Question of Guilt, 33). This is an element that does not relate to individuals *per se* or as belonging to a particular collective but to the widest collective imaginable, the one to which all humans belong. This wide space, to which "the inevitable guilt of all, the guilt of human existence" (Question of Guilt, 34) refers, leads to the metaphysical stage of the experience of guilt.

The Metaphysical Stage—Guilt as a "Boundary Situation"

The metaphysical stage is the third and final manifestation of guilt. The element of possibility in the collective approach established the status of the second stage as intermediate in the experience of guilt. There is a negative facet entailed in this understanding of the collective that separates it from the perception of people and nation in a-priori and absolute terms. Apart from this it has a positive role in relation to the other two stages. First, the perception of collectivity as a possibility of the individual creates continuity with the stage of the individual experience and enables a more complete manifestation of the individual experiencing guilt. Second, the perception of collectivity as a possibility lays the foundation for the experience of guilt going beyond the boundaries of the individual and the group to which he belongs and turning to the widest context in which he participates. Now the experience of guilt appears as the "guilt of human existence" (Question of Guilt, 34). The realm of the experience of guilt at this stage encompasses human existence as a whole, and thus one cannot mark its starting point or its boundary. As Jaspers wrote:

> If I knew the beginning of my guilt, it would be limited and preventable; my freedom would be the possibility of preventing it. I would not need to take upon myself anything, not myself in the sense of a self-choice and not existence [*Dasein*] into which I enter and for which I become responsible in my actions. (Ph2, 197).[15]

The absence of clear boundaries of guilt prevents us from noting the lack of the beginning of guilt and from determining the boundary beyond which people no longer experience guilt, since human existence ceases where people do not experience guilt. Now it appears that experiencing guilt as an undefined human possibility – positive or negative – has maximal dimensions, and is therefore inevitable. In other words, the area where guilt manifests itself is coextensive with that of human existence and for this reason a person cannot avoid experiencing guilt. The exhaustion and radicalization of the approach that

---

[15] The problem of the beginning has bothered many phenomenological researchers. Husserl noted the difficulty in determining the point at which the method of the philosophical enquiry starts being applied (Husserl 1913, § 63) and also in terms of determining the nature of the datum this enquiry grasps (see Husserl 1913, § 40). One of the conclusions Husserl reached was that the definition does not help us understand since it is an arbitrary setting of a starting point. For further discussion, see: Fuchs, 1976; Fulda, 1966.

translates possibility into necessity exists in Jaspers' conception of boundary situations (*Grenzsituation*).[16]

The term "boundary situation" embraces two basic concepts that appear in Jaspers' philosophical writings in different contexts: "situation" or "situation Being" (*Situationsein*), and "boundary". A "situation" that people experience comprises the duality of freedom and necessity. Freedom represents the possibilities for self-realization at the disposal of the Existenz, while necessity includes all the facts and constraints that restrict its ability to act (Ph1, 1).[17] Jaspers used the concept of "situation", which is significantly narrower than that of "world",[18] to express the fundamental insight that people never experience reality as a whole. Humans experience only very limited contexts in which they have freedom but at the same time are subject to restrictions that are not dependent upon them and that reduce reality. The concept of boundary is likewise typified by duality, portraying the limit of the possibilities of human experience and understanding, and at the same time the human desire to go beyond the boundaries of existence and consciousness. As Jaspers said: "every boundary immediately raises the question what lies beyond it" (Ph1, 45).

The duality typical of both the components of the concept "boundary situation" expresses the basic pattern of human experience that is split into the experience of enforced givenness and the wish to transcend it that represents human freedom. Against this background, Jaspers, following Kant, defined human reality as antonymous reality (Ph2, 249), meaning a reality trapped in an unknowable contradiction.[19] This is how Jaspers described the experience of this reality:

> [One] can never remain in the concrete finite, since everything concrete has at the same time both a finite and an infinite nature. No matter what the essential [thing] for him, he always encounters ways to the infinite or the whole. He can find in the face of the infinite in the evasive mystical experience a limited satisfaction in time and in quiet. However, if he remains alert, if he remains in the split between object and subject, any infinity leads him to the abysses of the contradictions that are called antonymous. (Psychology, 231).

---

[16] The "boundary situation" is an original concept of Jaspers'. Heidegger believed that this concept on its own could grant Jaspers his status as a philosopher, see: Heidegger, 1998, 10. For further discussion of Jaspers' concept of boundary situations, see: Latzel, 1957; Bollnow, 1964.
[17] An early version of the idea of "situation" appears in: Spiritual Situation, 23 ff.
[18] The concept of the world is discussed extensively in the first volume of *Philosophy* (*Philosophical World Orientation*); see especially: Ph1, 63; Truth, 85-107.
[19] Jaspers used the Kantian concept of antonym, referring to a logical contradiction between two premises, each of which can be proven by disproving the other. The secondary literature interprets Jaspers' philosophy as Kantian. In another article I have discussed this approach and proposed an alternative to it. See: Miron, 2006b.

So, the antonymous nature of reality is an expression of the undetermined duality which man encounters in existence in the world.[20] This means the simultaneous presence of good and evil, positive and negative, infinite and finite, whole and partial, day and night. The antonym, just like the element of "possibility", is entailed in any human experience as such. However, while these features are present on different levels in man's routine existence, in the boundary situations they appear in their full force and transparency. Jaspers described boundary situations as follows:

> These situations, like those I always exist within, that I cannot live without struggle and sorrow, that I accept upon myself inevitable guilt, that I must die, I call boundary situations. *They do not change*, but only their manifestations; **in their reference to our existence they are totally valid**. *We cannot see* beyond them; in our existence, we do not see [anything] behind them. They are like a wall that we push and walk into. **They cannot be changed through us**, but we can only bring them into clarity without being able to deduce them or explain them from something else. They exist with existence itself. (Ph2, 203).[21]

Guilt, like the other boundary situations (death, struggle, etc.), appears as an experience that people cannot avoid, just as they cannot change the antonymous nature of the reality revealed to them particularly in these situations. In guilt as a boundary situation, man is manifested both as a free Being (Ph2, 196), and at the same time as denied freedom, as subject to arbitrariness and impotence, as a "game ball" (Ph2, 216). Freedom and necessity appear as interconnected in the experience of guilt, or as Jaspers put it, "my guilt **inside** my freedom is each time something defined and thus something I experience **and not something I enable to approach me**" (Ph2, 197).

The lack of a connection between the experience of guilt and concrete behavior, revealed by the analysis of the two previous stages of the experience of guilt, becomes an explicit datum in the perception of guilt as a boundary situation. In Jaspers' words:

> Inaction [*Nichthandeln*] is in itself an action, meaning omission [*Unterlassen*]. Inaction would necessarily become a rapid sinking; it could have been a form of suicide. Non-entry into the world is a self-negation in the face of the demand of the reality turning to me... to dare to experience what has formed from it. (Ph2, 247).

Action and avoiding action thus express both freedom and necessity at the same time. Moreover, in terms of the manifestation of guilt there is no difference between the results of inaction and those of action, and thus one cannot attribute guilt to the difference between them. In other words, man is guilty whether he

---

[20] Jaspers discussed these contradictions in several contexts in his writings. See for example: Ph2, 248-249; Ph3, 102 ff.
[21] The term "boundary situations" is discussed in two contexts in Jaspers' writings: Ph2, 201-254; Psychology, 229-280.

acts or avoids acting. Finally, avoiding acting is a false choice as it distorts the person's manifestation, since human freedom is reduced by avoiding action. In fact, not only the absence of a connection between the experience of guilt and concrete actions but also its inevitability appears as an explicit datum in boundary situations. Now it transpires that boundary situations, delimiting the boundaries of human existence, do not leave another space for the existence of guilt, since beyond them the human Being ceases. The boundaries of existence are also the boundaries of guilt, and thus the ontology of guilt is also the ontology of reality.

However, the manifestation of guilt at the metaphysical stage is not limited to the absence of a link to concrete actions or to its inevitability. Another datum of human existence is also revealed in it. As Jaspers says: "every boundary immediately raises the question what lies beyond it" (Ph1, 45). This datum is transcendence.[22] Transcendence appears when man seems to himself to be "aiming at a different freedom", as "referring to a Being that is not himself but is his transcendence" (Ph3, 2). This discovery does not indicate that a person's entity is distorted in all the other experiences that are not included in the boundary situations. Just as the collective experience of guilt reveals the individual included in this collective more fully, so also the experience of guilt as a boundary situation indicates that turning towards transcendence constitutes part of human experience in general. In Jaspers' words: "we live in activity... I *must* want; because wanting must be my last [thing] if I finally want *to be*. However, the *way* I want to be can certainly be opened to transcendence" (Ph2, 197).

Transcendence grants meaning to the nature of human freedom as something existing in the face of an object existing beyond it, a reality exceeding the boundaries of the person's existence and consciousness. The boundary marking the end of the realm of freedom and necessity in human existence thus also marks the beginning of the realm of transcendence, spreading from that point onwards.

Furthermore, the meaning of transcendence for human existence is not exhausted by its sharing a common boundary with existence. It is portrayed as a source of meaning for the experiences within existence – especially since it exists beyond human existence: "Were there no existence, the question would have arisen why I need to want. I can actively want only when there is transcendence" (Ph2, 198). Wanting, one of the prominent expressions of human freedom, may now be seen to be lacking direction and meaning without transcendence. As Jaspers phrased it:

> Transcendence is not my freedom, but is present in it. Only in the freedom of my selfhood, where I think to surround all the necessariness of... necessity, am I aware that I did not create myself. It now occurs to me that where I am completely myself, I am not myself alone. Where I really was myself in wanting, I was at the same time subject to myself in my freedom. (Ph2, 199).

---

[22] The concept of transcendence is one of the most complex in Jaspers' thought. It was not defined anywhere, except indirectly. See for instance: Truth, 107-113; Ph3,1-35. On the problematic nature of this concept and on its philosophical implications, see: Collins 1952, 88-127.

Thus, the recognition of transcendence does not deny human freedom, nor does it change the range of restrictions in which it exists. However, through its function as the **object** of possibility and necessity, transcendence reveals the real dimensions of the two elements that constitute human existence: freedom and necessity. These are determined in light of, and perhaps even as a result of, another entity existing above and outside human existence, but sharing a common boundary with it. Becoming acquainted with transcendence complements the understanding accumulated so far regarding the elements of possibility or freedom and necessity, and thus it helps position more accurately the status of humans in Existence. In Jaspers' words: "It realizes that what is coming towards it fills it... It verifies its possibility only if it knows itself as based on transcendence" (Ph3, 4).

Transcendence, as the entity humans face, determines both their possibilities and their restrictions. These two elements, freedom and necessity, are thus clarified only by recognizing the existence of transcendence, a more encompassing and whole entity than them.

In the ontology of guilt, transcendence serves as an object for the experience of inevitable guilt, without which the experience would appear meaningless or arbitrary (Ph2, 198). Just as we think about something, want something, do not think about anything or want anything, so too does guilt require an object. We are guilty of something or about something. Since the explication of the experience of guilt reveals human ontology, we can state that all human activities including guilt manifest themselves in relation to an object. However, transcendence as an object has a more encompassing meaning than the other objects of human activity. Jaspers' perception of transcendence as an entity that exists independently of humans, even if this entity is revealed in human existence and has significance for it (Ph2, 22-23, see also Ph3, 164-165), enables a more accurate understanding of the human experience of guilt.

Guilt is not only being guilty of something, it is also being guilty in the face of something or towards something. We can clarify the significance of transcendence for human existence with the aid of Jaspers' statement: "the boundaries appear in their real function, to be immanent and already to indicate transcendence" (Ph2, 204). This statement confirms the obvious, that human actions take place in the world and are known there, but at the same time it indicates that human activity is not exhausted by this since a new ontology exists above and beyond its boundaries. To be precise: the ontology of guilt is not identical to the ontology of transcendence, but is tangential to it. This tangent is not a tangible point, but expresses a horizon of reference. Transcendence, like any otherness in relation to which human activity takes place, is now set in context:

> Against the tendency to self-sufficiency, against the satisfaction with the knowledge of general consciousness, against the individual's self-will, against the drive to self-closure in self-contained life... (Ph2, 60).

Transcendence as a permanent datum of human experience was posited by Jaspers against the distorting and harmful transience of human experiences. The fact that man stands alone in the face of transcendence reveals the basic connection between the first stage of experiencing guilt and its metaphysical stage where it appears explicitly as inevitable. The apparent immediacy of the inevitability of guilt restricts the horizons of human experience to a defined range from which there is no escape. However, the fact that the horizon that appears in the experience of guilt is that of transcendence, which in itself is not coextensive with the boundaries of human experience, and is not defined, may actually open new horizons for human experience directed at an entity rather than at itself or at the human at all.[23] Thus, the inevitability of guilt revealed explicitly in light of transcendence does not mark the boundary of the experience of guilt but the most appropriate starting point for clarifying human manifestation within guilt.

Conclusion

The three stages of the experience of guilt – individual, collective and metaphysical – have been shown from the proposed phenomenological-ontological explication of the concept of guilt in Jaspers' writings to belong to one reflexive and dynamic movement. Uncovering the constant process of boundary expansion of human experience has illuminated the complexity of the human experience of guilt, whose dimensions have wide-reaching implications for human experience, with the later stages elucidating the earlier stages. The link to guilt's starting point anchored in the individual's personal experience is constantly maintained. The basic feature of the entire phenomenological explication, arising from the first datum appearing in experience and returning to it at the end of the interpretative process, is clearly expressed in the merging of the metaphysical stage of experiencing guilt with the individual stage. This further supports the fruitfulness of the phenomenological perspective regarding Jaspers' concept of guilt. Once the first cycle of explication had been completed, it transpired that the three stages of experience did not denote different degrees of guilt, but were, instead, expressions of the basic patterns of human existence, themselves raised above any concrete context that might cause guilt.

Jaspers himself did not realize the potential for achieving an ontology of human existence from his perception of guilt, and he left it largely as a task for his interpreters. As we have seen, his approach contains a foundation on which the main stages of the experience of guilt can be formulated. However, Jaspers himself did not discuss the dynamic typical of the experience of guilt, nor did he usually connect other parts of his philosophy with his perceptions regarding guilt.

In this paper I have attempted to respond to these omissions by marking the three basic stages of the experience of guilt, explicating them and the relations between them, and linking them to other themes in Jaspers' thought that gave his statements regarding guilt a wider significance. In my opinion, the project of completing Jaspers' ontology of guilt should continue in this direction, examining the relevance of additional issues in his philosophy with a view to elucidating the basic stages of the experience of guilt, and perhaps even finding additional materials that could draw a more gradual progression in the transition between the various stages. This direction could both realize his original vision that the experience of guilt and the experience of existence are coextensive, but also

---

[23] See the demonstration in the diagram where transcendence appears as an open horizon. Truth, 142.

reveal his perception of guilt as a framework capable of containing the variety of subjects appearing in his philosophy and giving them an overall significance.

References

Jaspers' Writings and Their Abbreviations

Jaspers, K. *Allgemeine Psychopathologie. Ein Leitfaden für Studierende, Ärzte und Psychologen* (1st ed., Berlin, J. Springer, 1913) (Psychopathology1)
Jaspers, K. *Die geistige Situation der Zeit* (Berlin-Leipzig,1931) Walter de Gruyter (Spiritual Situation)
Jaspers, K. And Bultmann, R. *Die Frage der Entmythologisierung* (München, 1954) R. Piper & Co. (EM)
Jaspers, K. *Rechenschaft und Ausblick* (Reden und Aufsätze, Tübingen, 1958) R. Piper (Report)
Jaspers, K. *Der philosophische Glaube angesichts der Offenbarung* (München, R. Piper & Co., 1962) (Philosophical Faith in the Face of Revelation)
Jaspers, K. *Philosophie*. 1932. 3 vols. *Philosophische Weltorientirung* (Ph1); *Existenzerellung* (Ph2); *Metaphysik* (Ph3) (Heidelberg, Serie Piper 1994).
Jaspers, K. *Psychologie der Weltanschauungen* (Berlin, Serie Piper 1919), Heidelberg, 1985. (Psychology)

Secondary Literature:

Bollnow, O. F. *Existenzphilosophie* (Stuttgart, Kohlhammer, 1964).
Collins, J. *The Existentialists: A Critical Study* (Chicago, Henry Regnery Company, 1952).
Dilthey, W. *Weltanschauungslehre*, Abhandlung zur Philosophie der Philosophie, in *Gesammelte Schriften* (8, Stuttgart: B.G Teubner; Göttingen: Vandenhoek & Ruprecht 1962).
Fuchs, W. W. *Phenomenology and the Metaphysics of Presence: An Essay in the Philosophy of Edmund Husserl* (The Hague, Martinus Nijnoff 1976).
Fulda, H. F. "Über den spekulativen anfang," in Dieter Henrich and Hans Wagner (eds.), *Subjektivität und Metaphysik* (Festschrift für Wolfgang Cramer, Frankfurt a.M., V. Klostermann 1966).
Harries, K. "Shame, Guilt, Responsibility," in A. M. Olson (ed.) *Heidegger & Jaspers*, pp. 49-64 (Philadelphia, Tempel University Press 1994).
Hegel, G. W. F. *Vorlesungen über die Philosophie der Geschichte*, ed. G. Lasson (Leipzig, F. Meiner 1974).
Heidegger, M. *Sein und Zeit* (Tübingen, Max Niemeyer1927), 1993.
Heidegger, M. *Pathmarks* (Cambridge, Cambridge University Press 1998).
Husserl, E. *Ideen zu einer reinen Phänomenologie und Phänomenologischen Philosophie*, vol 1 (Tübingen, M. Niemeyer 1913), 1952.
Knauss, G. "The Concept of the 'Encompassing' in Jaspers' Philosophy," in P. A. Schilpp (ed.), *The Philosophy of Karl Jaspers*, pp. 141-175 (New York, Open Court 1957).
Kolle, K. "Jaspers as Psychopathologist" in P. A. Schilpp (ed.), *The Philosophy of Karl Jaspers*, pp. 437-466 (New York, Open Court 1957).

Latzel, E. "The Concept of 'Ultimate Situation' in Jaspers Philosophy," in P. A. Schilpp (ed.), *The Philosophy of Karl Jaspers*, pp. 177-208 (New York, Open Court 1957).

Miron, R. "From Opposition to Reciprocity- Karl Jaspers on science, philosophy and what lies between them", *International philosophical Quarterly*, 44/2: 147-163, Fordhum University Press, New York 2004 [Reprinted in this collection as Miron, 2004c].

Miron, R. "Transcendence and Dissatisfaction in Jaspers' Idea of the Self," *Phaenomenologische Forschungen*, NF.: 221-241, Felix Meiner, Hamburg 2005 [Reprinted in this collection as Miron, 2005].

Miron, R. "Towards Reality: The Development of the Philosophical Attitude to Reality in Karl Jaspers' Thought," *Journal of the British Society for Phenomenology* 37/2:152-172, Jackson Publishing 2006b [Reprinted in this collection as 2006a].

Miron, R. "Was Jaspers Really Kantian?" *Yearbook of the Austrian Karl Jaspers' Society* 19:73-106, Studen Verlag, Innsbruck 2006 [Reprinted in this collection as 2006b].

Miron, R. *Karl Jaspers: From Selfhood to Being* (Amsterdam, New York, Rodopi, Value Inquiry Book Series, 2012) [Miron, Monograph, 2012].

Plümacher, M. *Philosophie nach 1945 in der Bundesrepublik Deutschland* (Hamburg, Vowohlts enzyklopädie 1996).

Salamun, K. *Karl Jaspers* (München, C. H. Beck 1985).

Saner, Hans (ed.). *Karl Jaspers in der Diskussion* (München, R. Piper 1973).

Scheler, M. *Philosophische Weltanschauung* (Bern, Francke 1954).

Young-Bruehl, E. *Freedom and Karl Jaspers' Philosophy* (New Haven, Yale University Press 1981).

Original Publications

"The Covenant between Philosophy and Revelation: David Hartman's Thought in the View of Karl Jaspers' Philosophy", *Daat*, vol. 53 (winter, 2004), 161-192 (Hebrew) [Miron, 2004a].

"From Psychiatry to Philosophy: the Idea of the Self in Karl Jaspers' Philosophy", *Iyyun*, Vol. 53 (April, 2004), 123-150 (Hebrew) [Miron, 2004b].

"From Opposition to Reciprocity: Karl Jaspers on Science, Philosophy and what Lies Between Them", *International philosophical Quarterly*, 44/2, (2004), pp. 147-163 [Miron, 2004c].

"Transcendence and Dissatisfaction in Jaspers' Idea of the Self", in: *Phaenomenologische Forschungen*, NS. 10, 2005, 221-241 [Miron, 2005].

"Towards Reality: The Development of the Philosophical Attitude to Reality in Karl Jaspers' Thought", *Journal of the British Society for Phenomenology*, 37/2, 2006, 152-172 [Miron, 2006a].

"Was Jaspers really Kantian?", *Yearbook of the Austrian Karl Jaspers' Society*, 19, 2006, 73-106 [Miron, 2006b].

"Between Freedom and Necessity: The Conception of Guilt in Jaspers' Thought", *Iyyun*, 56/2 (April, 2007), 183-211 (Hebrew) [Miron, 2007].

"The Guilt Which We Are: An Ontological Approach to Karl Jaspers' Idea of Guilt", *Analecta Husserliana*, vol. CV, 2010, 229-251 [Miron, 2011].

Note:

The articles translated from Hebrew may differ slightly from their original versions, particularly where notes dealing with terminology in Hebrew were removed.

My monograph, *Karl Jaspers: From Selfhood to Being*, was written earlier than these articles. It was first published in Hebrew in 2006 (Bar-Ilan University Press) and then translated into English and published in 2012 (Value Inquiry Book Series, Rodopi). In some places in the articles I have added references to the English version, abbreviated as Miron, Monograph, 2012.

Jaspers' writings and their abbreviations:

The references to Jaspers' writings have been made consistent within this collection, using the abbreviations in parentheses listed below. References to other bibliography remain in the format used in the original article.

"Heimweh und Verbrechen" (Dissertation). In *Archiv für Kriminal–Anthropologie und Kriminalistik*, 35, (1909) (Doctoral Dissertation).

"Ein Beitrag zur Frage: 'Entwicklung einer Persönlichkeit' oder 'Prozess'?" *Zeitschrift für die gesamte Neurologie und Psychiatrie*, 1, (1910), 567–637 (Development).

"Die Methode der Intelligenzprüfung und der Begriff der Dimenz," *Zeitschrift für die gesamte Neurologie und Psychiatrie*, (referatential) (1910), 402–452 (Method).

"Zur Analyse der Trugwahrnehmungen" (Leibhaftigkeit und Realitätsurteil), *Zeitschrift für die gesamte Neurologie und Psychiatrie*, 6, (1911), 460–535 (Trauma Analysis).

"Die phänomenologische Forschungsrichtung in Psychopathologie," *Zeitschrift für die gesamte Neurologie und Psychiatrie*, 9, (1912), 391–408 (Phen.).

"Kausale und 'verständliche' Zusammenhange zwischen Schicksal und Psychose bei der Dementia praecox (Schizophrenie)," *Zeitschrift für die gesamte Neurologie und Psychiatrie*, 14, (1913), 158–263 (Causality).

Allgemeine Psychopathologie, Ein Leitfaden für Studierende, Ärzte und Psychologen. 1st Edition. Berlin: Springer, 1913 (Psychopathology1).

Die geistige Situation der Zeit. Berlin: Walter de Gruyter, 1931 (Spiritual Situation).

"Geleitwort," *Die Wandlung*, 1, (1945) (Introduction).

Die Idee der Universität. 1. Berlin: Springer, Schriften der Universität Heidelberg, 1946 (IdU).

Nietzsche, Einführung in das Verständnis seines Philosophierens. Berlin: Walter De Gruyter, 1950 (Nietzsche).

Vernunft und Widervernunft in unserer Zeit, Drei Gastvorlesungen. Munich: Piper, 1950 (VuW).

Einführung in die Philosophie, Zwölf Radiovorträge. Zurich: Artemis, 1950 (EdP).

Über Bedingungen und Möglichkeiten eines neuen Humanismus. Stuttgart: P. Reclamjun, 1951 (BuM).

Way to Wisdom: An Introduction to Philosophy. Trans. Ralph Manheim. New Haven: Yale University Press, 1951 (Way).

Die Frage der Entmythologisierung. Munich: Piper, 1954 (EM).

Schelling, Größe und Verhängnis. Munich: Piper, 1955 (Schelling).

"On my Philosophy", trans. F. Kaufmann, in: *Existentialism from Dostoevsky to Sartre*, ed. W. Kaufmann. Cleveland, 1956 (translation of "Über meine Philosophie") (OmP).

"Philosophical Autobiography." In *The Philosophy of Karl Jaspers*, Paul Arthur Schilpp (ed.). New York: Tudor, 1957, 3-94 (PA).

Philosophie und Welt, Reden und Aufsätze. Munich: Piper, 1958 (PW).

Rechenschaft und Ausblick, Reden und Aufsätze. Munich: Piper, 1958 (Report).

Max Weber, Politiker-Forscher-Philosoph. Munich: Piper, 1958 (Weber).

Vernunft und Freiheit, Ausgewählte Schriften. Stuttgart–Zurich–Salzburg: Europäischer Buchklub, 1959 (VuF).

Der philosophische Glaube angesichts der Offenbarung. Munich: Piper, 1962 (Philosophical Faith in the Face of Revelation).

The Great Philosophers, Ralf Manheim (trans.), Hannah Arendt (ed.), London, 1962 (GP).

Existenzphilosophie. 3rd edition. Berlin: Walter de Gruyter, [1937] 1964 (Philosophy of Existenz).

Allgemeine Psychopathologie. 8th edition. Berlin–Heidelberg: Springer, 1965 (Psychopathology4).

"Einsamkeit," *Revue Internationale de Philosophie*, 37, (1983), 390–409 (Loneliness).
Psychologie der Weltanschauungen. Berlin: Springer, [1919] 1985 (Psychology).
Vernunft und Existenz. Munich: Piper, [1935] 1987 (Wisdom and Existenz).
Von der Wahrheit. Munich: Piper, [1947] 1991 (Truth).
Philosophie (1–3). Berlin: Springer, [1932] 1994 (Ph1, Ph2, Ph3).
Die Schuldfarge, Von der politischen Haftung Deutschlands, Munich: Piper, 1996.
The Question of German Guilt. Trans. E.B. Ashton. New York: Fordham University Press, 2000 (Question of Guilt).

www.ingramcontent.com/pod-product-compliance
Lightning Source LLC
Chambersburg PA
CBHW070830300426
44111CB00014B/2504